ITEM NO: 2026847

before

the last date below

KU-214-710

-6 APR

1 2 JUN 2000

THE MERTHYR RISING

CROOM HELM SOCIAL HISTORY SERIES

General Editors:
Professor J.F.C. Harrison and Stephen Yeo
University of Sussex

CLASS AND RELIGION IN THE LATE VICTORIAN CITY
Hugh McLeod

THE INDUSTRIAL MUSE
Martha Vicinus

CHRISTIAN SOCIALISM AND CO-OPERATION IN VICTORIAN ENGLAND
Philip N. Backstrom

CONQUEST OF MIND
David de Giustino

THE ORIGINS OF BRITISH INDUSTRIAL RELATIONS
Keith Burgess

THE VOLUNTEER FORCE
Hugh Cunningham

RELIGION AND VOLUNTARY ORGANISATIONS IN CRISIS
Stephen Yeo

WORKING CLASS RADICALISM IN MID-VICTORIAN ENGLAND
Trygve Tholfsen

THE COLLIER'S RANT
Robert Colls

THE ORIGINS OF BRITISH BOLSHEVISM
Raymond Challinor

KEIR HARDIE: THE MAKING OF A SOCIALIST
Fred Reid

The Merthyr Rising

GWYN A. WILLIAMS

THE POLYTECHNIC OF WALES
LIBRARY
TREFOREST

CROOM HELM LONDON

942.975075
WIL

LC 323.269.3(429.724)
WIL

© 1978 Gwyn A. Williams
Croom Helm Ltd, 2-10 St John's Road, London SW11

British Library Cataloguing in Publication Data

Williams, Gwyn Alfred
  The Merthyr rising
  1. Merthyr Tydfil - Riots, 1831
  942.9'75   DA745.M47
ISBN 0-85664-493-5

T94528

Printed in Great Britain by
Biddles Ltd, Guildford, Surrey

10.9.90.

CONTENTS

For my son, Simon Alun
so that he remembers where he comes from

ACKNOWLEDGEMENTS

To the editors of the *Welsh History Review* and the *Bulletin of the Board of Celtic Studies* for permission to use material which originally appeared in the form of articles; to the Marquess of Normanby for permission to quote from papers in his possession; to Professor Harold Carter, Gregynog Professor of Human Geography at Aberystwyth for his help with the maps and to Dr T.E. Musson and Miss Ruth Evans of University College Cardiff for their assistance in the same enterprise; to Mr Tom Whitney and Mr Myrddin Harris of Merthyr Library and Cyfarthfa Museum for service well beyond the call of duty, Mr E.R. Baker of the Glamorgan Police Museum for a perspective new to me and to Merthyr Historical and Civic Societies and several score of Merthyr people for tolerating the innumerable lectures of inordinate length in which this book was worked out.

PREFACE

I have written a book about one year in the history of one Welsh town. I have written it because I think this one moment worth re-possessing, not only in its own right, but because of its possible meaning to historians who make it their business to rescue people from what Edward Thompson once memorably called 'the enormous condescension of posterity'. I would like it to displace and transcend everything else I have written on the theme.

Since it has certainly affected the tone and texture of the book, I should make it clear that it is written by one who is irredeemably a citizen of Merthyr Tydfil, mother town of iron and steel in south Wales and of much else beside. I am a typical citizen of my generation in that only one of my grandparents was actually born in the place and in that I can still remember the day when I encountered my first Conservative, a shock all the greater in that it coincided with the crisis of puberty.

Such traumas leave a mark on a man's work. Another is the fact that, within Merthyr Tydfil, I was born in Penywern, itself a community within Dowlais. The Valleys are as committed to the *patria chica* as any *pueblo* of those Spaniards who use the same word for a place and the people who live in it, a practice common in Welsh.[1] There were Spaniards in Dowlais, Irish too, but it was also one of those enclaves within Merthyr rooted in the chapel and the Welsh language. Furthermore, when I went down the hill to a justifiably celebrated secondary school, I found that the Welsh language, the history of Wales and even *the history of our own south Wales*, were actually *taught in it*! In retrospect, I realise that this ought to have been the most traumatic shock of all.

It has been my experience that non-Welsh readers, with such possible exceptions as Richard Cobb, the Oxford historian who moved from Paris to Aberystwyth, do not generally understand the significance of such a formation to a whole generation of Welsh people like myself. It has proved a much more painful business to be Welsh in my own capital than it ever was in the city of York. Unless people of my age and formation can achieve immersion of a Baptist totality in one closed world or another, being Welsh is not merely a predicament, it is as insufferable as it is inescapable.

11

Even in this book, which cannot wholly escape from contemporary idiocy, readers might encounter some difficulty on that score. I can only suggest that they read *The Dragon has Two Tongues*, an admirable and humane collection of essays by Glyn Jones, a fellow Merthyr citizen and one of the most distinguished of Welsh writers in English, whose grandparents actually lived in the world I try to describe in chapter 3.[2]

Of more immediate relevance to this book is the fact that I am unable to achieve the necessary immersion of Baptist totality in the great debate on Dissent, Methodism and popular life which engages many brother historians whose outlook I share, because I was trained in my early years in *Capel yr Annibynwyr*, Gwernllwyn. I cannot say that the essential purpose of this chapel of the Welsh Independents or its language, which to our generation of adolescents was only half-understood and sacerdotal, were particularly relevant to our primary concerns. It was, however, a place of warmth and fellowship and challenge, a centre of genuine intellectual liveliness, of drama societies, readings, eisteddfodau, above all a place dedicated to intellectual self-improvement as its members conceived it, devoted to the reading of books (in any language).

I have been unable to find quite such a chapel, and there were plenty like it in south Wales, in the voluminous literature of Dissent and Welsh nationality, in the hostile and parricidal writing which constitutes Wales's contribution to anti-clericalism, or in the work of historians who in other respects think like myself. I have found its like, in truth, only in F.R. Leavis's defence of D.H. Lawrence against T.S. Eliot. I therefore find myself virtually paralysed in one debate central to my craft. Perhaps this means there is a 'subject' here shambling towards some study to be born.

All I can say is that the fact that a group of us, after Gwernllwyn Sunday School, in which we were occasionally given to understand that Oliver Cromwell was a much maligned man, promptly adjourned to our own Young Communist reading class, now seems to me far less odd than it did when I knew far less about the history of south Wales.

Most central to the book is the fact that I was born in Lower Row, Penywern, in a house built by the Guests, attended a primary school which they had built and a secondary school in the Cyfarthfa Castle of the Crawshays. The first thing in the outside world I could have seen would have been the Ivor Works of the Guests. Since it blotted out the whole horizon, it would have been as difficult to miss as the crowd were outside the Castle Inn on 3 June 1831 when the Argyll and Sutherland Highlanders opened fire. A few yards away was Barracks Row, which commemorated the efforts of Captain Wharton of the 43rd, sent down later in 1831, after they had hanged Dic Penderyn, to keep us in our proper stations.

The first contact with 'history' I can recall is a story told by my mother about her grandmother: Sarah Herbert of Tredegar, whose schoolmaster brother in Nant-y-Glo was a Chartist and who herself worked for the return to Parliament from Merthyr of Henry Richard, the 'apostle of peace' and the first Nonconformist radical in Wales to be elected on working-class votes. Sarah Herbert once paid the princely sum of 4d to see what was alleged to be Dic Penderyn's ear on display in Dowlais market.

After I had withered into a professional historian, I learned that this no doubt profitable exercise in populist piety, oddly reminiscent of some aspects of popular Catholicism, in all probability stemmed from a false report which appeared in the workers' paper *Tarian y Gweithiwr* in July 1884. A correspondent claimed to have met the man who actually committed the crime for which Dic Penderyn was hanged. He met him in Pennsylvania in the USA, the man having fled through France. The writer, who was badly misinformed, said the man had lost an ear and recollected that a soldier who had seen a comrade 'killed' noted that the 'killer' had lost an ear![3]

Another rich source of 'history' were the periodical gatherings at the house of my paternal grandmother, which were a special treat every other Sunday evening. Preceded by the big evening service and the chapel 'monkey parade' along country roads in twilight, stags behind, does in front, with brilliantly witty badinage crackling between the two groups, of course, they opened with the scarcely less carnal delights of cold meat and pickles accompanied by Moscow Radio (a concession to Youth) and that lady who always sounded as though she had adenoids announcing the liberation of several thousand more inhabited localities from the Nazi invader, to the *Internationale* and cannonades like something out of *1812*. Then, as I dutifully chewed every mouthful 39 times according to the precept of William Ewart Gladstone, three old ladies would settle to a remembrance of things past.

It was astounding to me, or to be more accurate, it became astounding to me in retrospect, how often the talk curled back to 1831. One story lodged in my mind like a limpet intruder. They would shriek with laughter as they told of a young boy, Abednego Jones, who went about Merthyr during the Rising carrying a huge white banner as big as himself (by the end of the evening, it would be twice as big) and piping in a shrill, choir-boy treble: 'Death to kings and tyrants! The reign of justice for ever!'

I did in the end find one 'huge white banner'; it was carried by workers on the march to the Waun Fair which started the rebellion. The young boy I never found. But once, quite by accident, I came across a court case in the *Merthyr Guardian* for 1833. A miner sued two others for cheating him out of his stall, won, and was then exposed as a man who had 'carried a banner during the Merthyr Riots'. This phrase recurs constantly in obituary and other notices; it evidently marked a man out. The judge read the offender an appropriate sermon. His name was Abednego Jones.[4] In 1833, he was no boy. Perhaps he was short.

There is a wealth of oral tradition about 1831; there was even a ghost story.[5] Much of it, until relatively recently, was still alive in some parts of Merthyr. Quite young women talked to me about the Argylls coming through Cefn as if it had happened yesterday. Its relationship to recorded history makes a fascinating subject in itself.

On this occasion, however, having worked through all the material I can lay hands on, old and new, and having corrected earlier errors and mistimings, I have refrained from using any oral tradition which is not backed by written evidence. There are two exceptions. One is the story of the white bird settling on Dic's coffin at his burial in Aberavon. It could well have been a seagull, of course, but in the telling, it was charged with an even more transcendental significance than Chekhov's! The other is the remark which the women of Cefn are said to have addressed to the Argylls as they marched in. It sounds plausible and it would have been criminal negligence to omit it.

Principally, I have tried to 'tell a story' and I have tried to tell it through the words of the people who bore witness. Ordinary people, for most of the time simply anonymous crowds on the hills, here break briefly into the light; we can hear them talk. It has been a more difficult job than might be imagined, because witnesses often contradict themselves and get confused, particularly over the precise chronology of events. In such cases, I have this time forced myself *to make up my mind* and to 'tell the story' as I think it happened. I have done the same with the arresting stories of the feud between Dic Penderyn and Shoni Crydd. Only in such minor matters does my account of the Rising itself differ from that told by my friend and colleague David Jones of Swansea in an admirable essay in his *Before Rebecca*. The style and interpretation, of course, are my own. I have also been profoundly affected by his quite brilliant essay on the Scotch Cattle in the same volume.[6]

My former chief and the dean of Welsh historians, Professor David Williams of Aberystwyth, passed me his material on Dic Penderyn and put me in as desperate a debt to him as many workers were to the Court of Requests in 1831.

I have tried to set the Rising in context in the second chapter, which is structural and the third, which is conjunctural. It is not yet possible to construct a full, quantitative analysis of south Wales society in these years; there is an Apollyon's country to trudge through first. Such quantitative analyses as I have been able to make I have tried to incorporate, since they seem to correct the received wisdom sometimes, but the picture remains essentially impressionistic. I have been deeply influenced, though he may not recognise the influence since it has been indirect, by John Foster's remarkable book *Class Struggle and the Industrial Revolution*, particularly the core section on Oldham.[7] I begin my book in the first chapter with a kind of prologue which tries to locate this remarkable year in time, place and consciousness.

I have written at considerable length on Dic Penderyn and have tried to restrict myself to what is known. An attempt at interpretation, however, I thought proper. Men of greater talent and power than myself have written extensively on Dic Penderyn. Islwyn ap Nicolas's pamphlet became a minor popular classic in its day; unfortunately, he gave no sources for his stories and he sometimes confuses the martyr Dic Penderyn (Richard Lewis) with the hero Lewsyn yr Heliwr (Lewis Lewis).[8] Harri Webb's pamphlet is partisan, vivid, laced with black humour, constructed in deliberately mythic terms and catches the spirit of place. Harri Webb, of course, is a vivid and arresting poet, whose prose can sometimes be as pointed and memorable. Though an immigrant (as most Merthyr people are, at one remove or other) and a sophisticate, he seems to me to take his place very naturally at the end of that long line of radical Merthyr remembrancer poets, like some of Iolo Morganwg's revolutionary 'bards', stretching back through the eisteddfodau at the Lamb and the Patriot, back through Dic Dywyll, the blind ballad singer from Riverside who kept the Workhouse out of Merthyr for years with well-placed volleys of verse, to some of the *Jacobins* of Aberdare Mountain.[9] The intensely poetic novel *The Angry Vineyard* by Rhyden Williams I have not yet fully assimilated, but it is evidently going to prove a major achievement.[10]

Over this haunted field, of course, towers the giant figure of Alexander Cordell. He has succeeded where historians failed. He has actually found, or possibly even more remarkable, got the Public Record Office to find, most of the missing material which haunts every writer on this subject. A lot of it he published as an appendix to his powerful novel *The Fire People*.[11] While it was the Church in Wales, unexpectedly and to its lasting credit, which erected the first memorial to Dic, it was Mr Cordell, not any historian, who persuaded Merthyr itself to follow suit. I suggest elsewhere that historians of the Welsh people (as of any people) while mastering as many craft skills as they can, including the quantitative, should try to surmount the communication barrier which that very process may erect and serve as *people's remembrancers*. As far as south Wales in our times is concerned, it is evidently Alexander Cordell who is the people's remembrancer.

In all honesty, I cannot say that I relish the manners and modes of his writing. His fusion of fact and fiction (*faction* as the author of *Roots* called it, perhaps more aptly than he intended) is nothing to object to, on principle. It is not 'history' and cannot ever be so called, but in the service of particular moral, political or social purposes, such practices seem to me perfectly legitimate. Mr Cordell's particular blend of fact and fiction, while powerful and often done very skilfully, I am enough of a dry-as-dust, however, sometimes to find disconcerting. More important I think is the general conceptualisation and 'problematic' which informs his work and the style of discourse in which it is couched. I certainly mean no disrespect to his skills; I recognise his power and panache. He does seem to me, however, to be a grand master in a particular and established genre and the power and the popularity of that particular genre seem to me themselves symptoms of the painful historical predicament of industrial south Wales.

That said, Alexander Cordell remains and will remain a power in the land and historians of Wales owe him a great debt for what he has done as much as for what he has written. At one point in his book, he has his union preacher say: 'There can be no leaders in this fight — the people themselves are the leaders ... And when the history of our time is told, let the hero be the hungry man and his mistress, Merthyr Town'. That is well said, in the historian's terms no less than the novelist's.

On basic issues, I suspect, in all truth, that Mr Cordell and I are in fundamental agreement. It is precisely on this ground of leadership that I differ from him. I do not see Dic Penderyn as a leader, though I think he misreads me a little when he reads my 'innocuous' as 'insignificant'. To be one is not necessarily to be the other. I do not think, however, that we can take historical seisin of Dic Penderyn in terms of leadership.

The last word on Dic Penderyn has not been said. The last word may never be said.

Only one word needs to be said, his own, shouted from the scaffold: 'injustice.'

Gwyn A. Williams
Cardiff

Notes

1. Wales is full of valleys, but in Welsh practice, *The Valleys* refers exclusively to the industrialised valleys of Glamorgan and Monmouthshire and, by extension, to their spiritual kin in industrialised Breconshire and Carmarthenshire. Indiscriminate use of the term tends to give about equal offence on both sides of the shadow line.
2. Glyn Jones, *The Dragon has Two Tongues* (London, Dent, 1968).
3. *Tarian y Gweithiwr* (The Worker's Shield), 31 Gorffennaf, 1884: anon.
4. *Merthyr Guardian*, 21 December 1833, under Merthyr Police.
5. *Merthyr Guardian*, 20 February 1836: a young woman 'in an adjoining parish' had been troubled by nocturnal visits from 'a former lover who had died during the Merthyr Riots'. The week before (St Valentine's Day?), the lover had desired the girl to meet him at an appointed place; the girl, alarmed, took to her bed, but got up and went with her father and friends to the tryst. 'The Ghost was true to his time and carried her away over the mountain to Merthyr, from whence she returned home (a distance of about seven miles there and back) in a quarter of an hour.' The *Guardian* added that 'a great majority of the working people believe this absurd story'; the newspaper printed it presumably to demonstrate Olympian contempt.
6. David Jones, *Before Rebecca* (London, Allen Lane, 1973).
7. John Foster, *Class Struggle and the Industrial Revolution* (London, Methuen, 1974).
8. Islwyn ap Nicolas, *Dic Penderyn* (London, Foyle, 1944).
9. Harri Webb, *Dic Penderyn and the Merthyr Rising of 1831* (Swansea, Gwasg Penderyn, 1956).
10. Rhydwen Williams, *The Angry Vineyard* (Swansea, Christopher Davies, 1975). Writing in prose and verse on Dic Penderyn has now grown into a minor genre in its own right. I think, final accolade, that someone could now write a PhD thesis about it.
11. Alexander Cordell, *The Fire People* (London, Hodder and Stoughton, 1972).

1 SAMARIA

In June 1831, Mrs Arbuthnot, a highly political lady who greatly admired the Duke of Wellington, entered a resentful note in her diary: 'There has been a great riot in Wales and the soldiers have killed *24 people*. When two or three were killed at Manchester, it was called *the Peterloo massacre* and the newspapers for weeks wrote it up as the most outrageous and wicked proceeding ever heard of. But that was in Tory times; now, this Welsh riot is scarcely mentioned.'[1]

Mrs Arbuthnot's sense of political realities did not fail her. The 'great riot in Wales' was an armed insurrection at the iron town of Merthyr Tydfil. During the general election which followed the introduction of the first Reform Bill, thousands of working people in Merthyr, led by the ironstone miners and skilled puddlers of William Crawshay II, *King of the Iron Trade*, moved for the first time into independent political action. Public order in a distressed and excited community disintegrated. On 2 June, after a mass rally on the hills above the town, thousands of workers under a Red Flag broke into insurrection. They started a massive redistribution of property, destroyed a debtors' court, forced a general strike at the ironworks and called the men of Monmouthshire to rebellion, in the name of Reform. A detachment of the Argyll and Sutherland Highlanders marched from Brecon to restore order. Workers attacked them, in a direct, frontal assault. They lost at least two dozen killed and seventy wounded, but they forced the military to abandon the town. For four days, rebels held Merthyr and district, as around a core of 300 to 400 armed men, thousands rallied in what was virtually a communal insurrection. They defeated regular troops and yeomanry twice. They were beaten after 450 soldiers, across levelled muskets, faced down a huge crowd coming from Monmouthshire to join the insurrection and after some 800 troops had converged on the town, many coming in the new steam packets from Portsmouth and Plymouth.

Within two weeks of the Rising, the first trade union lodges which were branches of a national organisation were reported in south Wales. They grew in the shadow of the gallows. Lord Melbourne, Home Secretary in the Whig government, made the considered decision not to prosecute the rebel leaders for High Treason, in defiance of local magistrates. Twenty-eight scapegoats were tried for riot at the

18

Glamorgan Summer Assizes. A handful were imprisoned and four men were transported to Australia. One man was hanged as an example: Richard Lewis, a miner of twenty-three. People in Merthyr and south Wales believed, and were correct to believe, that he was innocent of the crime for which he was hanged. As *Dic Penderyn*, Richard Lewis has lived on in the memory of south Wales as an exemplary martyr.

Today, *Dic Penderyn* is more alive than Richard Lewis ever was. Poems are written to him. Pop groups sing songs to him. Eisteddfodau are held in his memory. A radical journal takes its title from his name. The Church in Wales, *yr hen fradwres* or the old traitress, as she was once familiarly known in the principality, has made generous historical amends by raising a memorial at his grave and in 1977, Mr Len Murray, Secretary of the TUC, unveiled a plaque to him at Merthyr Central Library.

After *Dic Penderyn*'s corpse had slipped into unconsecrated ground, Josiah John Guest, master of what was then already the greatest of ironworks at Dowlais, supported by Anthony Hill of the Plymouth works, ordered his men to renounce their union. When the men refused, the ironmasters locked them out. For two months, the men of Dowlais and Plymouth works, acting as a conscious vanguard for the working class of the whole south Wales coalfield, held out, in a struggle as bitter, unrelenting and dour as anything in the history of that coalfield, including the black year of 1926. They were beaten only when they were, quite literally, starved into surrender. Lord Melbourne, the Whig Home Secretary, lent his active support to masters and magistrates. He connived at a breach of the law to secure the men's defeat in what, in retrospect, looks like a dress rehearsal for the struggle of 1834, the breaking of the Owenite Grand National Consolidated Trades Union and the transportation of the Tolpuddle labourers. In the latter year, Merthyr Tydfil produced Wales's first working-class newspaper, a bilingual journal. The only number to survive is dated May Day, 1 May. Its Welsh-language section is a salute to the Tolpuddle Martyrs.

Mrs Arbuthnot was percipient in relating the Rising to Peterloo. In numbers killed and even in traumatic shock inflicted, it was as massive as Peterloo and equally as mythic. It certainly dwarfs the more familiar Chartist march on Newport eight years later. In 1839, at the time of that march, Lord Melbourne wrote to his successor at the Home Office: 'It is the worst and most formidable district in the kingdom. The affair we had there in 1831 was the most like a fight of anything that took place.'[2]

Merthyr Tydfil, in terms of numbers, at least, the first 'town' in Welsh history and for three generations the strongest single concentration of Welsh people on earth, had been the first and proved to be the most persistent stronghold of *Jacobinism* in Wales at the time of the French Revolution. It produced Wales's first working-class martyr and its first working-class press. In 1836, it became the first Welsh town to be captured by radical Dissent. It was a heartland of Chartism and the home of the Welsh Chartist press in both languages. In 1868, it became the first Welsh constituency to elect a Nonconformist radical MP on working-class votes. Even in 1900, in the days of its relative decline when iron and steel had given way to coal, it elected, though as a second member and on a minority vote, the first Labour MP in Wales, in the highly appropriate person of James Keir Hardie.[3]

When Merthyr became a county borough in 1906-8, during that Liberal high noon in which not a single Tory MP was returned from Wales, it took as its motto a slogan invented by Iolo Morganwg (Edward Williams) a *Jacobin* Bard of Liberty who had been the puckish eighteenth-century genius of Welsh renaissance, reviver of the eisteddfod, inventor of a *Gorsedd* (order) of revolutionary *Bards*, fabricator-in-chief to a new and radical Welsh 'nation': *nid cadarn ond brodyrdde*, no strength but brotherhood. Iolo's son, Taliesin, a schoolmaster in Merthyr and a shaper of its rich Welsh and bilingual cultural life, translated 'brotherhood' as 'combination'; he used the word in the sense of the Combination Acts, to signify that brotherhood which was exemplified by the early and embattled trade unions. The inhabitants of Merthyr cheerfully mistranslated the motto into something more euphonious and oecumenical, but it seems historically appropriate that Wales's first working-class martyr should have been provided by *The Town of Tydfil the Martyr*, as its inhabitants equally cheerfully mistranslated the very name of their community.[4] Throughout much of the nineteenth century, working people in Merthyr Tydfil were more accustomed to making history than to studying it.

Yet for generations, the Merthyr Rising of 1831, in marked contrast to its infinitely adjustable Martyr, was banished to a wasteland on the margin of limbo, as magical but as barren as the high, tawny *twynau* (moorland hills) which roof and rim the Valleys of south Wales. One of the many reasons for its historical invisibility was the nature of a 'Welshness' which formed in response to industrial capitalism in the nineteenth century and which developed into a singularly articulate Welsh tradition. To this way of thinking and feeling, the industrial

Valleys which it perceived as 'disappearing' into godlessness and west Britain, were increasingly alien. Their people were at best prodigal sons, at worst changelings and bastards.

In the 1830s, Dafydd Rolant, minister with the Calvinistic Methodists, a powerful denomination whose influence on Welsh history however has been systematically exaggerated, was preaching on Samaria. 'Samaria? What was Samaria?' he thundered (I translate into the less sacerdotal of Wales's two languages), 'Samaria was their ashtip. An ashtip where they threw all their stecks and rubbish. A hotbed of paganism and heresy and everything. Yes, my friends, Samaria was the Merthyr Tydfil of the land of Canaan.'[5]

It is not necessary to take Calvinistic Methodist ministers too literally in their moral accountancy: that way madness lies. Edward Bishop, 'the great Birmingham thief', took rather a different view. He was captured in Merthyr as he was stealing a bundle of combs in the summer of 1831 and was transported for seven years. He was unmanned by the disgrace of being caught in 'so unknown a country'. To think that he, the great Birmingham thief Edward Bishop, he bellowed at the jury, should have been taken by 'such a bloody set of Nanny Goats'![6]

What the speeches of Dafydd Rolant and many others like him reflect is the fact that, in the perspective proper to a small and hitherto marginal country, Merthyr and its neighbouring communities were as much a 'shock city' as Manchester was to England and the world at large. The new society evidently came upon south Wales like a thief in the night. The Glamorgan magistrates of that old Wales which could still write verses to the beauty of the Vale of Taff and embrace within beauty the occasional *Forge of Vulcan* belching and blazing away in a wooded nook, were clearly taken by surprise. It was only after the first census of 1801 that they learned that Merthyr township, in its long straggling parish perched up in the foothills of the Beacons, at the far end of the even longer Hundred of Caerphilly which stretched down to the environs of that village which was the Borough of Cardiff, had suddenly emerged as the most heavily populated parish in Wales. Their response was brisk if not brilliant: they divided the Hundred, so that petty sessions could be held at *Vulcan's Forge*.[7] As people poured in, the first effective legal action, characteristically, was taken by a growing regiment of shopkeepers worried over small debts. In 1809 they secured a Court of Requests to handle them.[8] In 1822, the shopocracy of Merthyr, in alliance with ironmasters, created a select vestry and colonised it.[9] The new communities in the hills began to acquire a juridical personality with the appointment of a stipendiary magistrate in 1829, to control Merthyr and four neighbouring parishes.[10] The Whigs had intended in their Reform Bill to make the new Merthyr simply a contributory borough to Cardiff, but the Rising forced them to give it an MP in 1832.[11] It was the new Poor Law of 1834 which shaped a 'province' for Merthyr by assembling seven parishes around it into a Union. By 1831, in the territory covered by that Union, some 40,000 people were grouped around 44 iron furnaces.[12]

Clearly the Almighty had never intended 200,000 human beings to live at those valley heads. The ironmasters corrected Him on the point. The borders of what was later called the Black Domain are most immediately visible to travellers from the north and east.[13] South of the vale of Usk, the triple peaks of the Brecknock Beacons, Cribyn, Corn Ddu, Pen-y-Fan rising to nearly 3,000 feet, tower over a mountain wall which marches west into the Black Mountains of Carmarthenshire. Eastwards, the wall is lower and abuts on the northern outcrop of the coalfield. To walk from the Usk up to the summit of Llangynidr Mountain is to cross from one world to another. Further east, above the Usk as it runs through to the market town of Abergavenny and cuts off the Black Mountains of Monmouthshire-Herefordshire, forming one of the traditional entrances into Wales, Llangattock Mountain noses into a ridge corner bewildering in its richly industrial chaos, as the high country forms an angle and, sloping down into an escarpment, marches south across the face of Monmouthshire to taper away a little short of Newport.

From valley heads opening on to the northern plateau under the Beacons, where settlements cluster at 500 to 900 feet, deep parallel trench valleys run south between high but sloping spurs and a complexity of saddles and cwms, thrusting for the ports of Newport and Cardiff. The highlands, the *Blaenau*, sweep west in a great and often breathtaking curve around the vale of Glamorgan; the coalfield, 10 to 20 miles across, runs with them, southerning a little. At the western end of the curve in the Glamorgan coast, where the hills nearly touch the sea at Port Talbot, the vale of Neath cuts to the north-east and defines a human community, but an outlying spur of the *Blaenau* curls on west behind Swansea and into the anthracite belt of the coalfield as it swerves a little to the north-west. Here the rivers Tawe and Gwendraeth mark off a distinct region. Around the older centres of Neath and Swansea was the older industry of copper, with more variety, slower and more balanced growth until the development of tinplate and the anthracite. Swansea in 1831, while half Merthyr's size, was a fully articulated and well equipped little social capital; the more open anthracite valleys of its hinterland nurtured a mixed and very Welsh economy. To move eastwards across the vale of Neath into the bituminous coals was to encounter different dialects and, further east and south, a different language. The steam coal basin, ribbed by the Rhondda rivers, was to create the almost legendary 'south Wales' of a falsely familiar history, but the original nucleus of industrial society lay beyond, to the north-east, across the Cynon and the Taff. The ironworks ran in a thick, clamorous belt along the northern rim of the valley heads from Hirwaun, north of Aberdare and just within the Breconshire parish of Penderyn, through the Merthyr complex and across the valley tops of Monmouthshire, encroaching upon Breconshire at Llanelly and Clydach, on around the curve of the coalfield to Blaenavon, within hailing distance of Abergavenny, and thrusting southwards towards the river confluences at Pontypridd and Pontypool. Here were the great names of British iron: Dowlais and Cyfarthfa, Rhymney and Bute, Tredegar and Ebbw Vale, Brynmawr and the rest, with a small host of ancillary services and industries, while exemptions granted to the port of Newport nurtured a native sale-coal industry under a shoestring Welsh plutocracy in the more southerly stretches of the valleys of Monmouthshire.

There had been patchy development earlier, sometimes much earlier. There were some charcoal furnaces, some coal levels, quarries, but most of the uplands and their valley heads (where people still die in heavy snow) were virtually empty, except for sheep and drovers. Abergavenny was the market centre to the east and was to become the Mecca of the Domain's eisteddfodau; to the west the focus was the Waun Fair above Merthyr. Merthyr was the only human settlement of consequence in the pre-industrial *Blaenau*, in its less exposed and more open valley head, on its river Taff which ran more swiftly to the sea at Cardiff. Roads ran from it to Brecon and Abergavenny, Neath, Cardiff. There were 93 farms in the parish and a distinctly commercial population of farmer-dealers, auctioneers, artisans, innkeepers, strong in an old Cromwellian tradition of Dissent (it had been one of Vavasor Powell's fiefs) which in the eighteenth century was softening and liberalising into an Arminian Presbyterianism, soon to become Unitarianism and to breed a surprising number of back country intellectuals, amateur mathematicians and astronomers, builders and gadget-makers vividly reminiscent of Tom Paine.[14]

At Merthyr, the rich resources in iron ore, limestone, coal, which outcropped on the northern rim were even more easy of access, particularly around Dowlais and the Taf Fechan (Little Taff) to the north.[15] Merthyr became the matrix of the iron industry as industrial capitalism stretched out from England in the late eighteenth century. Bristol and London capital, the technology of Staffordshire and Shropshire which made coal usable, started the first experimental furnaces within Merthyr parish in the late 1750s and early 1760s: Dowlais, launched by a partly local consortium and soon managed by the remarkable Guest family from the hub at Broseley in Shropshire; Cyfarthfa, sited down on the Taff by Merthyr village, in the vast 'mineral kingdom' of the London and Cumberland merchant Anthony Bacon who, like the Dowlais company, leased lavishly endowed land at an incredibly cheap rate from great and often noble landowners who lacked the gift of prophecy. Richard Crawshay, a shirt-sleeves Yorkshire entrepreneur, by reputation at least straight out of classical capitalist mythology, built Cyfarthfa with its London merchant house into the first giant of the iron trade as, from the Bacon-Crawshay empire, dynasties of managers turned owners budded out: Homfrays, Hills at Plymouth, Formans at Penydarren, Baileys and Halls who moved to Monmouthshire among the Harfords, Kenricks, Hunts. The extended partnership to tap local capital persisted at Dowlais, but within a generation or so, most of the firms, despite a fringe network of associated share-holders, had become, if they had not always been, family concerns.

The invention of the vital puddling process in the late 1780s, 'the Welsh method', was the point of breakthrough. It enabled coal to be employed to make malleable iron and in the context of massive demand generated by wars and the growth of British industry, large, technically-advanced firms mushroomed. The region became a pace-maker, at least in the basic processes of production. The 1790s saw a canal mania in both counties, as much to take food up to the workers as iron down to the ports. Tramways ribbed the valleys; in 1804, Trevithick's steam locomotive, the first in the world, made its run from Penydarren. In an area with virtually no industrial tradition, skill and managerial talent had at first to be imported and the practice persisted, but there had always been some locally and from the 1800s, when there was breakneck growth around puddling, south Wales rapidly became a reservoir of talent and skill, which was to fertilise such remote regions as Pennsylvania and the Donetz basin in Russia. After 1810 there was a troubled period, through the crisis of 1811-13 into the post-war depression, but the 1820s were years of interrupted

Table 1.1: Estimated Pig Iron Production (tons)[16]

	Britain	South Wales
1788	68,000	12,500
1796	125,000	34,000
1806	244,000	71,000
1823	455,000	182,000
1830	677,000	277,000

but strong and significant expansion.

Outstripping Staffordshire and Shropshire by 1796, south Wales in 1830 was producing as much as 40 per cent of British pig iron. In historical terms, advanced capitalist industry in the Valleys sprang virtually full-grown from Croesus's head.

Merthyr remained the matrix. Military men organising the defence of south Wales against revolutionary outbreaks early in 1832 listed 21 works operated by 14 companies. Ten of them, operated by six companies, were within the jurisdiction of Merthyr's stipendiary magistrate; five of them and four of the companies were within Merthyr parish.[17] In 1829 the works contributing to the salary of the Merthyr stipendiary were Dowlais with 12 furnaces, Cyfarthfa with 9, Plymouth with 7, Penydarren with 5, Aberdare 7, Bute 3 and Gadlys 1.[18] In that same year and in 1830, years of deep depression, the four works within the parish, Dowlais, Cyfarthfa, Plymouth and Penydarren, together with the Crawshays' Hirwaun, sent 74,000 tons of mixed iron down to Cardiff and production within the parish was put at 65,000 tons a year; in a good year, it could be much higher, nearing 100,000 tons. In 1830, with its heavy unemployment, Dowlais was reported to be employing 3,500 men, Cyfarthfa 3,000, Plymouth 1,500 and Penydarren 1,000. Had 1830 been a reasonable year, the four works would probably have been using 13,000 to 14,000 men.[19]

Those men were mostly Welsh. Skilled English workers had moved in from the beginning; others followed, from most neighbouring English counties and some over long distances. Their numbers were small. Nor were the Irish very numerous at first, though there were several thousands of them in Monmouthshire by 1831; it was their religion and their tribal cohesiveness which set them apart. As late as the 1840s, a survey which overstated the extent of English immigration registered

61 per cent of the males of Blaenavon as Welsh, at the easternmost limit of the region. Proportions fell sharply valley by valley to the west. In Merthyr, non-Welsh immigrants were less than 9 per cent of the population and at Aberdare, just over the hill, their numbers were negligible. Monmouthshire was peopled largely from Breconshire and Glamorgan in these years. In Merthyr, there were immigrants from north Wales and other long-range newcomers, but most people, when they were not from neighbouring parishes in Glamorgan and Breconshire, came from west Wales, turbulent and troubled Cardiganshire and the kindred communities in north Pembrokeshire and upland Carmarthenshire.[20]

At Merthyr there was an overlay of English masters, managers, newspapers, an official world which was English in speech, but the language of house, pub, chapel and street, and probably much of the works, was largely Welsh. One of those who knew no Welsh at all, whose numbers cannot be determined, was the witness whose testimony hanged the martyr Dic Penderyn. Another who said he knew none, however, understood quickly enough when he heard two miners talk about killing him! Advertisements for official jobs and shop assistants almost invariably required Welsh. The ironmasters William Crawshay and Josiah John Guest certainly understood it and may even have used an everyday version of it. The magistrate Anthony Hill could not speak it, but the stipendiary J.B. Bruce was fluent. On the other hand, the leading personality of the Rising, *Lewsyn yr Heliwr*, Lewis the Huntsman, whose oratory was Welsh, used English freely enough to insult an army captain, and the crowd leaders during justice raids on shops and houses wrote out 'receipts' for their victims to sign which, as documents intended to be in some sense 'legal', would have been in English. Orators speaking English regularly conducted a dialogue with Welsh-speaking crowds and no-one seems to have experienced any difficulty (nor should they have; this was precisely how I used to converse with my grandmother). The community was as effectively bilingual as its Owenite and Chartist press.[21]

It grew at astonishing speed. During the early decades of the nineteenth century, the population of Monmouthshire was growing more quickly than that of any other county in England and Wales; Glamorgan came third on the list. Monmouthshire's numbers doubled in the first decade of the century, increased by over 70 per cent in each of the succeeding two. Some of its mining villages witnessed ten-fold increases in population between 1801 and 1831. Merthyr parish, with nearly 8,000 people in 1801, increased by over 50 per cent in every decade to reach around 27,000 in 1831, easily the most heavily populated community in Wales, twice the size of Swansea and four times that of Cardiff.[22]

The conditions in which these people lived and worked have grown into a Black Legend. Hours of work were long, the work itself was dangerous. Sanitation and drainage, like public services, official religion, orthodox social control, were virtually absent. The truck system, universal in Monmouthshire and strong in Glamorgan, enmeshed thousands of families in a form of debt slavery. Housing, some built by ironmasters, most by middle-class speculators, sprouted in every corner without plan, in and around works, in between tramways and canals, among tips and mines; near the Taff in Merthyr there were shanty towns and people lived under the arches of canal bridges.

In fact that popular housing, however mean it might seem to those numerous visitors who cried aloud at the very sight of these implausible townships lurid with furnaces and black with smoke, was no worse than that of rural communities and small towns and better than much of the housing in west Wales. It is necessary to exercise caution. The death rate was certainly high and south Wales became notorious as a black spot, riddled with the diseases of poverty. A great deal of this evidence, however, comes from a later period. Merthyr evidently suffered an ecological disaster in the 1830s and 1840s, but some of the most harrowing evidence is very late. It was not until 1953 that south Wales, in public health, climbed up to the average British level, but perhaps the worst period of all had been the Depression of the twentieth century itself. Such demographic evidence as we have for the earliest period does not support the more catastrophic interpretations. Merthyr parish registers between 1813 and 1830, admittedly an inadequate source, nevertheless suggest very strongly that it was the appalling child death rate which was the real killer; this was an exaggeration of the characteristic predicament of the old regime, which could not keep its children alive. Beyond the age of five, however, the vigorous immigrant community of Merthyr suffered death rates markedly lower than those prevalent in Swansea, Cardiff and rural districts of Glamorgan. Tentative calculations of life-expectancy at birth for the 1820s and after suggest that Merthyr people would generally outlive their country cousins, though a shopkeeper's child could expect to live twice as long as a collier's.[23] Women and young children worked in pits, but their experiences in the iron industry, even in its coal sector, appear to have been less harrowing. In fact, I am slowly being driven to the tentative conclusion (which took me by surprise) that, while there were no doubt genuine gains in some respects, the increasing predominance of coal in later years and the great shift from iron and steel to coal probably resulted in a deterioration in the quality of living.

Moreover, among people long accustomed to the high birth and death rates of pre-industrial society, *community* is not to be measured by the number of privies per square mile. Government commissioners and ministers of religion provide the bulk of the evidence and they were men with a mission. Observers with no axe, or a different one to grind, present a very different picture. What struck the English *Jacobin* John Thelwall, for example, was the sheer *pride* of ironworkers,[24] the overweening pride of skilled men, the secretive pride of those thousands of men and women who nursed their craft lore in an industry which counted about 40 separate 'trades'. The inordinate caste pride of the miner, whether in coal or ironstone, becomes visible very early. On country cousins constantly confronted by the backsides of sheep, they often looked with a tolerant and easy scorn. Visitors equally early noted that characteristic phenomenon of working-class south Wales, the open door; traditional community and conviviality, of course, but it was also open to show off the new mahogany inside. Wages could fluctuate wildly from year to year, but in reasonable times they were several times those of farm workers in the west and many workers must have lived better than the small hill farmers out there. If the picture presented by official investigations were the whole truth, the influx of those thirsty thousands would become incomprehensible. They were coming for the money, of course, and at first many came by season, but they were also coming for a fuller if chronically insecure life; they were coming for what many of them called 'freedom'.

Popular life was rich, vigorous and turbulent.[25] These communities were certainly rowdy, but the rowdiness was that of the villages they came from, intensified by sheer number. Their sports were generally rural. It is too often forgotten that, even in Merthyr itself, no-one was more than fifteen minutes' walk away from some of the most striking, varied, sometimes dangerous country in Wales, as rich in sport as it was in muscular local tradition. They developed a peculiar passion for foot-racing, probably a local tradition since the legendary exploits of Guto Nyth Bran of Llanwonno to the south.[26] Foot-races, usually accompanied by all the accoutrements of a fairground, were held everywhere and anywhere, even along the tramways. In 1814, there was a famous race between Howell Richard of Vaynor and Thomas Llewellyn of

Penderyn which ran the length of the vale of Taff. Thousands would tramp down to the coast at Ogmore Down, if need be, to watch *Flower of the Forest*, Robert Williams or John Rees, *Pannwr* (The Fuller). The great fist-fighters would be there, challenging all comers, for pugilism was virtually a way of life. The red-haired giant Shoni Sgubor Fawr, who could draw vast crowds and claimed to be the champion of all Wales, served briefly as *Emperor* of a celebrated outlaw district around the Taff bridges at Merthyr, notorious as *China*.[27] Hard by was the Glebeland, teeming with travelling hucksters and shysters, with 'nymphs of the pave', circus performers, 'boys doing tricks for beer' one jump ahead of the police, the ballad singers, the harpists, the singers of traditional *pennillion* (a form of contrapuntal singing as complex and demanding as the *cante jondo* of the Andalusians). On the hills and *twynau* just over the way, there was hunting and poaching, collective and individual, dog and horse racing, mass gambling, ritual sexual relaxations. These people brought with them the *cwrw bach*: the little beer, bid-ales, communal festivals, marriages, celebrations, really collective exercises in self-help and mutual petty loans wreathed in fellowship and liquor. When the new free beer shops were created by the Beer Act of 1830, scores of working-class families moved into a form to trade and their beer shops took the name of *cwrw bachs*. The eisteddfodau in the Merthyr pubs, over a score of which are on record in the 1820s, for the town was a leader in the Welsh revival, were as vigorous as the races and the boxing matches. So was the burgeoning world of music and poetry in the chapels with their fiercely competitive choirs and even more combative working-class conductors.[28] ~pugnacious~ ~aggressive~

Public order was certainly precarious, but that situation had long been familiar. Numbers were the problem. Any crowd drinking beer alarmed magistrates and maddened ministers, whether they had met to bet on a race, draw up a wage claim or prepare a petition to parliament. This was, without doubt, a frontier town, but any frontier has to be a frontier of *something*. It was the practices of rural solidarity that these people brought to confront an unstable industrial society. The *ceffyl pren,* the wooden horse, the cock-horse instrument of an extra-legal communal discipline with its mock trial and 'rough music', stalked streets more crowded than those of the villages it had come from. This was certainly one root of that remarkable, quasi-Luddite secret society of the Scotch Cattle in Monmouthshire.[29]

These 'primitive rebels' were hardly primitive in their bargaining skills. (Many of them after all were *Cardis!*[30]) Craft combination to resist a wage cut was a frequent ad hoc practice; indeed, ironmasters' correspondence during depressions suggests that it might have been virtually an annual phenomenon. Skilled men took the lead in forming more coherent organisations, which become visible from 1810, but by the early 1820s, particularly in Monmouthshire, colliers and miners were assuming initiative. There were some spectacular outbreaks, the great food revolt in Merthyr during the terrible dearth of 1800-1, the troubles during the *Luddite* crisis which brought a permanent military garrison to Brecon, the mammoth south Wales strike of 1816. Colourful and violent though these often were, they were essentially traditional, defensive, a rally around a customary standard of living; they belong to the world of what Edward Thompson has called the 'moral economy'. It is during the 1820s in both Merthyr and Monmouthshire, that there is evidence of a qualitative change.[31]

The French historian Edouard Dolleans once argued that a 'working-class movement' in both Britain and France emerged over the years 1829-34; he could cite powerful evidence. There is no call to subscribe to any linear concept of progress, evolution, the growth of 'consciousness' to recognise that there *are* moments in the history of the 'secret people' when there seems to be a sudden qualitative change, a kind of Döppler shift, when in terms of one kind of 'time', people seem to move, quite abruptly, out of one 'century' and into another. The European revolutionary crisis of 1792-3 was one such moment, in the emergence of 'sans-culottes' in France, and, in a different way, of popular corresponding societies in England.

In south Wales, working people in the new and raw communities of the Valleys seem to have approached such a conjuncture as the 1820s drew to a close. As far as a 'working class' in south Wales is concerned, it seems to me possible to locate a 'point of emergence' with some precision. It was Merthyr Tydfil, *Samaria*, sprawling across its lacerated hills in the hot and bitter summer of 1831.

Notes

1.   F. Bamford and the Duke of Wellington (eds.), *Journal of Mrs Arbuthnot* (1950), ii, p. 424. Fifteen were killed and about 400 wounded at Peterloo.
2.   Melbourne to Normanby, 5 November 1839, Marquess of Normanby archives, Mulgrave Papers, Mulgrave MM/242; I am grateful to Roger Custance for the reference and to the Marquess of Normanby for permission to reproduce.
3.   For a general survey of the town's history and its tradition, Glanmor Williams (ed.), *Merthyr Politics: the making of a working-class tradition* (University of Wales, Cardiff, 1966).

4.   The matter is trenchantly argued by D. Andrew Davies, then Director of
       Education for Merthyr in 'Merthyr Tydfil: the motto, the name and the
       saint', *Merthyr Express*, 27 April 1963; I thank Mr Davies for a photocopy.
       The mistranslations are in fact reasonable. *Merthyr* in conversational
       Welsh means 'martyr', derived from the Latin *martyrem*, but in place-
       names, it means burial place of a saint or church dedicated to his/her
       bones (*martyrium*). There was an old Welsh proverb *nid cadarn ond brodyr*
       (nothing is as strong as brothers) but Iolo Morganwg wished 41 'proverbs'
       ending with *brodyrdde* on Saint Cadog, prominent in the early history of
       south-east Wales. The word *brodyrdde* first appeared in a dictionary in
       1793, produced by one of the leading 'Jacobins' of the Welsh revival,
       William Owen, and the motto in the classic production of that generation,
       the *Myvyrian Archaiology* of 1807. Taliesin translated it as: 'There is
       nothing so strong as combination.' The current, popular translation is:
       'Not force but fellowship.' On the remarkable Iolo Morganwg, Prys
       Morgan, *Iolo Morganwg*, Welsh Arts Council Writers of Wales series
       (University of Wales, Cardiff, 1975). I deal with his role as a Gramscian
       'organic intellectual' in *Frontier of Illusion: America and the Welsh people
       in the Age of Revolution*, text to be published, and in a forthcoming study
       of the *Jacobins* in Welsh history.
5.   Free translation (though all too accurate) of the quotation in R.T. Jenkins,
       Hanes Cymru yn y Bedwaredd Ganrif ar Bymtheg (University of Wales,
       Cardiff, reprint, 1972), p. 64.
6.   *Cambrian* (Swansea), 2 July 1831.
7.   Merthyr Tydfil Parish Minute-Book (Merthyr Central Library, henceforth
       MT Minutes), April, May 1801; I am grateful to Mr Tom Whitney and his
       staff at the Library and Cyfarthfa Museum, particularly Mr Myrddin
       Harris, for their invaluable assistance.
8.   Parliamentary Papers, Return of Courts of Requests, 17 February 1836,
       Accounts and Papers, 1836, xliii; *Merthyr Guardian*, 29 December 1832,
       quoting *Gorton's Topographical Dictionary*; Samuel Lewis, *A Topographi-
       cal Dictionary of Wales* (1833 and 1843).
9.   MT Minutes, 11 and 15 January 1822; chapter 2, tables.
10.   *Acts of Parliament concerning Wales 1714–1901*, T.I. Jeffreys Jones (ed.)
       (Cardiff, 1959), nos. 1639, 1641; MT Minutes, 15 October 1829.
11.   *Cambrian*, 12, 19 March, 23 April 1831; W. Thompson to W. Crawshay II,
       19 April 1831, Crawshay Papers, Box 2 (569) (National Library of Wales,
       henceforth NLW); chs. 3 and 10 below.
12.   Samuel Lewis, op. cit. (1843); *Census 1831: Enumeration Abstract*.
13.   'Black Domain' was a term used by government commissioners about
       Monmouthshire; the iron complex in 1831 was this area plus Merthyr
       'province'; David Jones, *Before Rebecca*, ch. 4.
14.   A. Strahan, *The Geology of the South Wales Coalfield* (HMSO, 1927);
       Charles Wilkins, *The History of Merthyr Tydfil* (Merthyr, 1867); ch. 3
       below.
15.   Most useful on the process of industrialisation are A.H. John, *The Industrial
       Development of South Wales* (University of Wales, Cardiff, 1950);
       John P. Addis, *The Crawshay Dynasty* (University of Wales, Cardiff,
       1957); M.J. Daunton, 'The Dowlais Iron Company in the Iron Industry',
       Welsh History Review, vi (1972), pp. 16-48.
16.   B.R. Mitchell and P. Deane, *Abstract of British Historical Statistics*
       (Cambridge, 1962), p. 131; totals rounded off.
17.   Colonel Love to Home Office, 20 April 1832, Home Office Papers 40/30
       (Public Record Office, Home Office: henceforth HO).

18. MT Minutes, 15 October 1829.
19. Record of Iron and Coal delivered at Cardiff, 1829 and 1820, Marquess of Bute Papers XIV/54 (Cardiff Public Library; henceforth CPL); Samuel Lewis, *Topographical Dictionary of Wales* (1843); my estimate of full employment based on isolated figures given for the slump and lock-out of 1829-31 set against company records and newspaper comment.
20. A.H. John, op. cit., pp. 58-68, citing the articles by G.S. Kenrick in *Journal of the Royal Statistical Society*, iii (1840) and ix (1846); B.H. Malkin, *Scenery and Antiquities of South Wales*, i, 272, speaking of Merthyr, wrote: 'The workmen of all descriptions at these immense works are Welsh men. Their language is entirely Welsh. The number of English amongst them is very inconsiderable.'
21. The evidence for this paragraph appears in the narrative chapters below. *The Cambrian* and the *Merthyr Guardian* yield an abundance of advertisement material.
22. *Census 1801-31, Enumeration Abstracts;* and David Jones, *Before Rebecca*, pp. 86-7.
23. For this demographic material, such as it is, see ch. 2 below and my 'Some demographic indicators in Merthyr Tydfil 1813-30', to be published shortly in *Welsh History Review*; as an example of the governmental approach, Henry de la Beche, *Report on the Sanitary Conditions of Merthyr Tydfil* (1845). An excellent ecological analysis is Harold Carter, 'Phases of Town Growth in Wales', in H.J. Dyos (ed.), *The Study of Urban History* (1968), especially map and text, pp. 244-51, and his *The Towns of Wales: a study in urban geography* (1965).
24. Quotations from Thelwall's journal in C. Cestre, *John Thelwall* (1906); his diaries unfortunately were lost during the Nazi occupation of France (they were in Cestre's possession); we have lost a Defoe or a Cobbett; there are some suggestions also in Thelwall's own *Poems written chiefly in retirement* (1801), some of which were composed in Merthyr and Breconshire during his enforced 'exile'.
25. What follows is drawn from a vast variety of sources. Perhaps most convenient are the scrapbooks compiled by Mr E.R. Baker, former Deputy Chief Constable of Glamorgan and now custodian of the Police Museum at Glamorgan Constabulary Headquarters, Bridgend. They have been built out of county records, police records and newspapers and are hypnotic documents. The *Cambrian* has some similar material from an earlier date. I thank Mr Baker for the loan of Scrapbook 1, covering the first years of the Glamorgan Constabulary, 1841-50.
26. Reported on his gravestone in Llanwonno church, a typical mountain-parish and isolated church of the *Blaenau*.
27. There is a portrait of Shoni, who became a 'tarnished hero' of Rebecca, in David Williams's classic *The Rebecca Riots* (University of Wales, Cardiff, 1955), pp. 247-58, 286-7; for the 1814 race, Tom Lewis, *History of the Hen Dŷ Cwrdd Cefn* (Llandysul, 1947), p. 210.
28. Ch. 3 below.
29. See David Jones, *Before Rebecca* (particularly on the Scotch Cattle); and David Williams, *The Rebecca Riots*.
30. *Cardis*: justly or unjustly, the people of Cardiganshire enjoy the same reputation in Wales as Aberdonians in Scotland and Scots the world over. I think there are historical reasons for the modern superstition and will argue the case in the forthcoming study of the *Jacobin* period of Welsh history; Cardiganshire was hit harder by the population explosion than any county in Wales and was probably the most disturbed Welsh county during the early nineteenth century. In many ways, it was the Galicia

of Wales.

31. Chs. 2 and 3 below; David Jones, *Before Rebecca*, cites plenty of material.

2 MERTHYR IN 1831

In the parish of Merthyr Tydfil in 1831 at least 9,000 persons of a population of about 27,000 worked for four great iron companies. Some 4,000 families of workers lived by selling their labour to four families of capitalists.[1]

The parish is an unreal measure. Merthyr's Court of Requests, created in 1809, was the tribunal for the recovery of small debts. It embraced the parish of Gelligaer, which curved around Merthyr to the east and south along the border of Monmouthshire, as well as the Breconshire parishes of Vaynor and Penderyn and Llangynidr to the north in the folds of the Beacons.[2] So did the jurisdiction of Merthyr's stipendiary magistrate, appointed in 1829, who covered Aberdare as well and drew half his £600 salary from a levy on the ironworks. The new parliamentary borough of Merthyr, invented by the Reform Act of 1832, included Aberdare and Cefn, the big industrial village which was the core of Vaynor parish. The Poor Law Union of 1836 centred on Merthyr a 'province' which incorporated Aberdare, Vaynor, Penderyn, Gelligaer, the hill parish of Ystrad Dyfodwg west of Aberdare which looked on Hirwaun works and two more southerly and compact parishes opening on the confluence of the rivers Taff (Merthyr) and Cynon (Aberdare) just above Pontypridd (Newbridge) the gateway into the vale of Glamorgan; these were Llanwonno, a Cynon-side extension of Aberdare, and Llanfabon, a colliery cluster serving Gelligaer.[3]

In neighbouring Monmouthshire, there was a difference in character between the northern ironworks settlements and the bare and functional colliery villages to the south.[4] Within Merthyr's province, too, even within Merthyr parish itself, stretching 15 miles from the foothills of the Beacons to the Taff-Cynon confluence, people concentrated to the northwards. By 1831, in Merthyr and Vaynor (in practice Cefn township) 96 per cent and 82 per cent respectively of all families worked at non-agricultural jobs; the next highest concentration (serving the Bute works) was the 70-75 per cent of Gelligaer-Llanfabon. In Merthyr, where iron companies owned or occupied about a third of the acreage of the parish, population density, according to the 1831 census which would have underestimated it, was almost 800 per square mile, nearly twice as heavy as that of any other industrial parish in either Glamorgan or Monmouthshire; within its own hinterland, only Vaynor could remotely approach it, thanks to Cefn, which served Cyfarthfa works and was virtually a suburb of Merthyr. In the more mixed northerly parishes of Aberdare and Penderyn straddling the Brecon-Glamorgan line, 60-65 per cent of all families were non-agricultural, while in Ystrad Dyfodwg and Llanwonno to west and south, over 50 per cent of families were still counted agricultural.

In fact, the industrial families of Ystrad Dyfodwg, the southerly parishes and the southern villages within Gelligaer were families of labourers and the unskilled; in Gelligaer and Llanfabon they accounted for over 50 per cent of the adult males. Rural craftsmen, including traditional weavers, were relatively numerous and a much higher proportion of the women and girls went into service. To the north, far fewer women and girls worked as servants and there was a heavy concentration of skilled men. The census of 1831 for Merthyr itself is totally inadequate because of the Rising of the summer and the autumn lockout which threw out at least 4,000 men, but it is clear from company records that skilled men formed at least 35 per cent of the working population.[5] They were fewer in Aberdare, but the really startling parishes were Vaynor and Penderyn. They were in the foothills of the Beacons; they looked rural, in many important respects their life *was* rural. But no fewer than 42 per cent of the adult males of Penderyn, nearly 50 per cent of those of Vaynor, were skilled workers at the furnaces and forges. These two 'rural' parishes were in fact dormitories of skilled industrial workers.

Outside the concentration of Merthyr-Cefn itself, its province retained a strongly rural ambience in which Merthyr workers spent half their lives; functionally, however, it was strictly industrial. In October 1831, William Williams who had gone bankrupt (a fairly common and repetitive experience for middle-class speculators who made small fortunes in the intervals) offered for sale his estate at Perth-y-Gleision, five miles from Merthyr town. Its attractions were multiple: 275 acres stretching from the Taff to the ridge and covering the whole valley side, two farms and three tenants. The Glamorgan canal ran through it, the Cardiff road nearby. A vein of coal was working and there were iron mines, but it also held 16,000 larch trees, was well stocked with game and was 'picturesque'.[6] Some of the fiercest battles the ironmaster William Crawshay ever fought were over his 'rural' estates around Cefn and Gurnos. They centred essentially on hunting, shooting, fishing and poaching. He had to fight on two fronts, against the Gwynnes and other local squireens and against the hundreds of his own workmen who periodically invaded his privacy.[7] This aspect of living in Merthyr was central.

Nevertheless, practically everything that stood or moved which could be pressed into the service of iron was commandeered. These mountain parishes by 1831 were ribbed by tramways, canal and feeders, turnpikes, quarries, coal levels, reservoirs, tips, clusters of isolated cottages, *tai unnos* (one-night houses thrown up by squatters who believed, sometimes citing the medieval Laws of Hywel Dda, that this action conferred freehold) Klondike settlements of considerable variety, often simultaneously tribal and mobile. Separate communities could differ radically within a short distance, but there was a uniform tonality to the district. Thanks in part to the early concentration in Merthyr, in part to the commercial, artisan, *Jacobin*-Unitarian character of its pre-industrial population, the whole region seems more integrated than comparable districts in Monmouthshire. Within the province of Merthyr, its 40,000 people clustered around 44 furnaces, seven thousand families in fact lived under the control of seven. Two of those ruling dynasties were of critical importance.

The peculiar character of Vaynor and Penderyn derived from the precocious development of the Crawshay enterprises at Cyfarthfa, later at Ynysfach and Hirwaun; not until the late 1820s did the rival giant at Dowlais under Josiah John Guest catch up and surpass the *Kings of the Iron Trade*.[8] One striking consequence was the emergence of two working-class communities at opposite poles of Merthyr parish which also came to constitute two polarities of Merthyr politics, specifically of its popular politics.[9]

At Dowlais, on Gwernllwyn hill, the highest and most exposed northerly slope of the parish, abundant in easily accessible raw materials and empty of people except for a handful of craggy and Independent farmer-dealers, there emerged a strongly paternalist society. From it, a distinctive working-class community was to struggle into a kind of independence, rich in a Welsh and Welsh-language culture, but wrestling endlessly within itself with deference and respectability. The Crawshay settlements were near the heart of the town and the old village, down by the Taff and largely on its western side, clustering around traditionally busy, populous and picaresque bridge-side communities which looked towards Cefn, Aberdare, Penderyn. This was to be the locale of a radical tradition transmitted direct, face-to-face, from pre-industrial days; it was also to become the heartland of the most characteristic 'dangerous district' to emerge in south Wales, the 'no-go area' outside the law

radical, fundamental
holding extreme views.

which became celebrated as *China*, with its own Emperor and Empress. While the 'nymphs' of Pont-y-Storehouse by the canal bridge were as 'well-known', to use the current expression, as the 'cellars' to which even Londoners on the run fled by homing instinct, up in Dowlais attempts to establish nests of nymphs were frustrated by crowds of up to 400 workmen at a time, cheerfully demolishing houses and sometimes going on to attack the soldiers' barracks which would have provided many of the customers. Down by the Taff bridges, alongside the cellars and the rabbit-warren lodging houses and brothels, were the Dynevor Arms, the Miners' Arms, the Three Horseshoes, strongholds of the persistent *Jacobin*, Owenite, Chartist, and indeed eisteddfodic traditions; up in Dowlais, towering over the cottages to be built by the Guests in Penywern, were the barracks, constructed by Captain Wharton of the 43rd in 1831, after the Merthyr Rising of that year, to keep 'these cyclopes' in their proper stations.[10]

Both communities in time became 'radical'; for all their differences, they were both variations upon recognisably Welsh themes. The distinction between them, however, was to prove important, not least for that 'working-class tradition' of Merthyr, which is virtually unique in Wales. It is difficult to avoid the inference that certainly one major, if not the only, cause was the fact that two ironmasters differed in personality and policy.

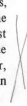

Whatever William Crawshay II was, he was no gentleman; 'volcanic' Lady Charlotte Guest called him, builder of that stupendous mock-medieval folly of Cyfarthfa Castle in 1825, which cost £30,000 and which caused such pain to his irascible London-based father. In 1820 the Crawshay London agent was afraid of William's commitment to Queen Caroline; his radicalism would 'spoil his iron'. Splenetically hostile to the secular claims of the Church, he once threatened a cleric that he would pay his tithes in kind and never plant anything again. His most memorable comment on the French Revolution of 1830 was an expression of keen regret that he had not been there with his fowling-piece, to pepper the backside of the fleeing King.[11] His radicalism, however idiosyncratic, was without doubt a contributory factor to the Rising of 1831.

Josiah John Guest, however, was an Anglican, though the family tradition had been Wesleyan (one of them had been rejected for the Volunteers for that reason) and his brother, the rather inaptly named Thomas Revel, a minister manqué.[12] Guest served as sheriff of Glamorgan and Tory MP for Honiton before taking the new Merthyr seat in 1832. During the 1820s, he was apparently enmeshed, tenurially and socially, with the Lord Lieutenant the Marquess of Bute and the Tory landed oligarchy of Glamorgan, partly in dependence for supply, partly in rivalry (Bute dreamed of creating a rival works to Dowlais on a Rhymney site; Crawshay vainly offered to do it for him in 1831). Guest was, in consequence, sometimes suspected by the other iron-masters; they combined against him at the election of 1835 and there had been an attempt to deny him the seat in 1832.[13]

More significantly, Dowlais was one of the strongest centres of the truck system in Wales and possibly in Britain; it was taken as a model during the parliamentary debates over Littleton's anti-truck bill in 1830. Originally a human necessity in an isolated district and still supported by many workmen, truck was the root from which a whole paternalist world grew at Dowlais: a Guest school, a church, housing, support for chapels, Sunday schools, friendly societies and a savings bank, joint efforts against drink. There was a mechanics' institute at Dowlais by 1829.[14] The ironmaster enjoyed great respect and a detached, deferential popularity, noticeably warmed after 1833 by his cultivated wife, Lady Charlotte.

The Crawshays were significantly different. During these years, no Crawshay served in a public capacity except under some compulsion. They prided themselves on not being truck-masters, though the son veered dangerously near it during depressions at the fragile settlement of Hirwaun. Crawshay men elected their own doctors.[15] William Crawshay I took infinite pains with his skilled men and even the 'poor devils' of miners and went to great lengths to avoid labour trouble.[16] He was original enough to see no harm in trade unions, in fact thought they would help trade by raising costs, reducing the make and putting his neighbours (whom he regarded as crooks) out of business.[17] The son was a trifle less insouciant over this matter, but basically, he had the same contractual, individualist, 'man-to-man', almost American instincts. On the eve of the Merthyr Rising, Cyfarthfa was the only works in the town to which workers were still moving; no less characteristically, however, it was among Crawshay men that the Rising started. Tocqueville, no doubt, could have found an appropriate comment.

The Crawshays' strength was their great and, by now, matured capital and their London merchant house.[18] During depressions, despite family quarrels, they generally tried to avoid price and wage cutting wars, resorting to price maintenance, stockpiling and the toleration of 'over-manning' for as long as they could. In 1826 the London House came close to recommending this policy as a weapon against the other works.[19] At first, no other firm in the Merthyr region could afford fully to follow suit, but from the 1820s, the growing power of Dowlais ranked it with Cyfarthfa. By 1831, this Crawshay reaction to depressions had become something of a regular practice. The consequent influx to their works, particularly of ironstone miners, coupled with the yet more unhinging shock when even the Crawshays had finally to cut wages, was another critical factor in the Rising of 1831.

The power of the ironmasters was determinant. They lived their lives, public and private, in a permanent dialectical tension between co-operation and conflict. The Crawshays at Cyfarthfa, the Guests at Dowlais, Hills at Plymouth, Formans sharing with Alderman Thompson at Penydarren, were closely intermeshed with the Hills, Harfords, Baileys and Kenricks of Monmouthshire. When William Forman died, beady-eyed investigations by the Marquess of Bute in 1831 revealed that he had held a three-eighths share of Penydarren works, which carried an annuity of £1,200 to the descendants of a previous owner Jeremiah Homfray. Forman had contributed towards a Penydarren-inspired investment of £170,000 in the Bute and Rhymney works. In Tredegar, he held four and a half 1/24th shares, totalling £22,000 and in Aberdare, a 1/16th share at over £7,800. He held 50 shares in the Sirhowy tramroad in Monmouthshire, on which were charged three annuities, two in favour of his late brother's widow and one in favour of himself, for £1,000 a year until the age of 72, with a lump sum of £5,000 on death. His income from Penydarren had fallen from £10,000 a year to £1,600 between 1825 and 1830, that from Tredegar from £5,600 to £2,200. In a good year he got over £15,000 from the two works, in a bad year some £4,000. Bute's agent calculated that his average annual income over five years from these sources, annuities excluded, had been some £9,000.[20]

Such relationships, and such incomes, were common and extended into the field of land-holding. Early leases had been ridiculously cheap, but there soon grew up a Byzantine complexity of leases, sub-leases, royalties, shares and charges on tramways, water rights, rights of way, which embraced every landowner from Bute to local farmers. When the leasing of Caedraw at the southern tip of Merthyr village and itself growing into a second *China*, came up for discussion in 1828, so many interlocking interests were involved that the Crawshay solicitor Meyrick confessed himself baffled.[21]

There were sustained efforts to achieve joint action, to eliminate competition among themselves and to form a bloc against the

Staffordshire ironmasters.[22] The south Wales quarterly meeting was active between 1802 and 1826 and there were other ad hoc combinations. These instincts rarely survived the onset of a boom, when the demand for labour drove ironmasters into a distracted competition among themselves. During depressions, joint action was usually disrupted by the Crawshays who generally refused to lower their prices and tried to stockpile in preference to reducing the make. Smaller firms like Penydarren and Plymouth, the Crawshays claimed, could not go a week without payment and were forever undercutting the large. The Crawshays had their own London House, which tried, often vainly, to channel all sales. As Dowlais grew during the 1820s, it opened its own London house and started a bank. These two giants could normally hold aloof from price wars, unless a depression were prolonged.

The fairly prosperous 1820s saw some qualitative changes. Firms had often been dependent upon each other, even for different grades of pig iron. At one point, purchases from other Merthyr works amounted to a third of Dowlais's total production. The puddling process induced some to so over-develop their forges that they became dependent on their neighbours for basic pig iron. During the 1820s, however, interdependence was much less pronounced, except for joint contracts. Repeated attempts to co-ordinate policy over prices, wages, skilled labour, stockpiling, repeatedly broke down. Competition was particularly severe over the recruitment of skilled labour and over the supply of iron ore, which proved peculiarly difficult.[23]

Ironmasters, therefore, while sharing basic interests and generally managing to act in concert on fundamental issues, rarely formed a bloc. Even during the critical struggle over trade unions in 1831, they failed to act together.[24] Relationships were often intensely personal. 'That paltry fellow', William Crawshay II called Josiah John Guest and very often Merthyr was a cockpit for the Gog and Magog of Dowlais and Cyfarthfa.[25] His relations with Richard Fothergill of Aberdare were no less steeped in *machismo*. 'Fothergill was quite well yesterday,' his brother George informed him one bright May morning in the 1820s, 'but certainly greater than ever. He told us he drank 2 bottles of port the night before and then finished with grog. We told him we hoped he had not broke any body's head which he might do if he ever got fighting. I do not think he knows you hit him, he was too infernally drunk.'[26]

While these quarrelsome titans formed an *interest* within south Wales, they often seemed as external in, but not of, county society, as the hill communities they had created. The Commission of the Peace of Glamorgan in October 1831 listed, under the Marquess of Bute, 4 baronets, 3 knights, 55 esquires, 25 clergymen and 3 heads of chartered corporations. Only four JPs were ironmasters, though two of the others were Homfrays turned gentlemen.[27] It would be unreal to draw too hard a line; one of their number had entered the Commons, while industrial and commercial interests were absorbing many of the landed gentry. The Marquess of Bute was as much of a 'capitalist' as any Crawshay. Ironmasters took part in the rituals of county society, paraded with the other peacocks at Cardiff and Cowbridge, patronised good works and eisteddfodau, played the same game in county elections, hunted, fished, shot, staged elegantly competitive balls and dinners. The 'landed interest', however, held firm to the distinction between Trade and Gentility which was as invisible but as impenetrable as an electronic force-field. Ironmasters' wives suffered the traditional agonies, even the remorselessly civilised Lady Charlotte Guest.[28] Their husbands, in turn, nursed a deep suspicion of the 'Cardiff Castle Set'; hence their uneasiness over Josiah John Guest, hence the complementary anger and sense of betrayal among Glamorgan Tories when the Dowlais master came out for Reform during the 1830 crisis. One central argument in the Commons debates over the Reform Bill against the 'demotion' of Merthyr into a contributory borough of Cardiff (as ironmasters saw it), the 'subjection' of Cardiff to the plutocracy of the hills (as the Bute interest saw it) was that there never had been and never would be any organic connection between Merthyr and Cardiff![29]

In some respects, the ironmasters were hardly less external to the communities they had created. In sharp contrast to many of the landed oligarchs, they were resident. Alderman Thompson was MP for the City of London and his visits to Merthyr were seasonal, but the others were physically present, in their 'sooty mansions': Dowlais House, plain, classical and straitlaced though porticoed, fulcrum for the hunchback huddle of houses and chapels which was its dependent fief; Plymouth Lodge, as plain and more modest at the southern end of town; Penydarren House, rather more spacious in its own comfortable grounds near the heart of Merthyr and, towering over the whole northwestern corner of the parish, as visible and much more eye-catching than Dowlais on its windy hill, the turrets and towers of Cyfarthfa Castle in its vast parkland, fixing Georgetown, Cefn and Aberdare Mountain with its imperious eye. Around these palaces, a 'society' developed, with its imported managers and dancing-masters, newspapers and theatrical companies. But, while the Homfrays had always been active in local affairs and were followed by Josiah John Guest and Anthony Hill, to a large extent the parish of Merthyr was at first left to run itself.[30]

The rectory, worth £675 a year in the 1830s, was in the gift of the Marquess of Bute, but the incumbent, the marquess's former tutor, G.M. Maber, a 'capital trencherman who could even dispose of a goose', left the cure to a succession of curates named Jones, of varying degrees of zeal, who presided over a largely empty church. Two church-wardens, one a rector's nominee, the other selected by vestry meeting, supervised four overseers of the poor and five administrative hamlets. Chief constables were appointed in practice by county magistrates and were served by the usual gang of ruffianly, ill-paid and corrupt parish constables. There was a vestry clerk and a shadowy parish clerk and in 1804 the parish was ordering law-books. Administration before the 1820s was amateur. Records were kept clumsily and infrequently, attendance at parish meetings averaged between five and nine; a third of the attesting signatures were by mark. In the first decade of the century, more substantial figures appeared: William Milburne Davies, chief tradesman of the village and David Williams, its first post officer; Joseph Coffin, tanner and Unitarian, was zealous in his attendance. The major connection with the ironworks was effected through the industrialists' Agents, who became the backbone of the vestry, if it is not anomalous to apply the term to so amorphous a body.

Early records were simply a series of relief payments: in the good year of 1805 the parish was paying out nearly £14 a week to 49 people. A jail, the Black Hole, was built in 1809 to serve the debtors' court; during the depressions of 1811 and 1814-15, poor houses were leased and a lace manufactory created for pauper girls. The most important enterprise in these early years was the rebuilding of the church, authorised in 1806 after a series of heavily attended and controversial meetings in a parish full of Dissenters.

It was at those meetings that Josiah John Guest first put in an appearance in vestry. The canal, the Cardiff road, much of the very fabric of the town itself were the ironmasters' creation. Every important decision required their presence. What brought the iron-masters into parish affairs, above all, were the periodic crises of slump, unemployment and poor relief which ravaged this people. This pressure that had created the debtors' court was to create the stipendiary magistrate. Ironmasters' commitment to parish affairs followed the graph of the poor rate like a Pavlov reflex. For what was the human fabric of the settlements which were becoming the town of Merthyr but their own workers?

A striking feature of that working population was its sheer complexity and the strongly corporate spirit which this often engendered among groups of workers who were self-recruiting or organised by dozens of sub-contractors.[31]

One perennial problem was skilled labour: the 'firemen' at the complex of furnaces with their attendant balling, refining, nailing and other processes and the aristocrats of the labour world at the puddling forges and rolling mills, with their multiplying specialisms of boring, slitting, stamping mills, their trains of service workers. But the supply of raw materials by those thousands in what are often considered 'mass, unskilled . . .' occupations also posed problems. In 1824 at Penydarren works, 15,800 tons of pig iron had swallowed up over 87,000 tons of coal, 47,000 tons of mine and 5,000 tons of cinders; by 1831 most Merthyr plants seem to have been working to the rule-of-thumb Dowlais calculation that a foundry pig required four tons of coal and three and a half tons of mine; a ton of bar iron needed seven tons of coal.[32] While coal levels were more expensive to open up than ironstone (£25,000 against £15,000 for the supply of ten furnaces, according to Bute's mineral agent[33]), ironstone miners and their auxiliary workers cost more than colliers. In the one month of August 1829, some 3,800 tons of coal cost the Bute works, in the necessary 'dead work', timber, bricks, castings, engine feed, stores, as well as the hewing, stacking and hauling, over £573, while some 1,500 tons of mine cost over £565; miners getting well over twice the tonnage rate for colliers.[34] In fact, despite the rich resources of the area, many of them commandeered by Dowlais, there was a substantial import of iron ore, at a price a third higher, even by Cyfarthfa; Plymouth works brought ore estates in Cumberland.[35] And these 'mass, unskilled' occupations were not only themselves honeycombed with carefully-defined and defended areas of 'craft mystery'; they operated in a bewildering web of trades, each of which tried to sustain its own lore.

A rather small and simple plant of five furnaces with one puddling forge and a rolling mill classified its workers a few years later:[36]

	Men	*Women*	*Boys*
Collieries	280	0	27
Mines	396	40	73
Furnaces	257	39	36
Forge, Mill	145	0	0

The women were generally stackers of some kind. At Cyfarthfa, the women were all surface workers, supervised by the Unitarian minister of Cefn, who was unhappy at his work.[37] Boys did the usual subordinate jobs, though some at least would have been in fact if not in name, 'apprentices' to a 'craft'. It is surprising to find no boys listed among the skilled puddlers. In the Plymouth works model settlement which was growing into a celebrated housing estate called The Triangle, the boys were trainee puddlers, the men in their prime puddlers, in their old age labourers.[38] A familiar hierarchy, however, emerges, with skilled men occupying a substantial (and underestimated) position: collieries and mines taking 23 per cent and 39 per cent of workers, ironstone miners the largest single category, furnaces and forge-mill 26 per cent and 11 per cent.

Something of this hierarchy is also visible in a detailed report of four weeks' working during August 1829 at the Bute works. The cash cost per ton of coal was 2s 2½d, though miscellaneous dead work added 7d; mine cost 5s 6¼d a ton with dead work adding 1s 5d. Furnace labour cost 9s 9½d a ton cash, with haulage taking 2s ½d more; refining cost 2s 6¾d, rolling 7s 4¼d, puddling 11s 9½d. In fact, every operation was complex, with relays of different workers, skilled and unskilled, performing a variety of jobs within each process.[39]

When the Hills advertised the Plymouth works for sale a few years later, at an assessed value of over £400,000 and an estimated annual profit of 10 per cent, Plymouth, with its satellite plants at Pentrebach and Duffryn, embraced eight furnaces and twelve refineries worked by a powerful steam engine and four overshot water wheels, two rolling mills worked by two overshot wheels, puddling and balling furnaces, air furnaces, stoves, cupolas, turning machines, brick kilns, carpenters' and smiths' shops, tramways and their maintenance services. It also included casting shops for odd jobs, canal wharves, basin and plant, not to mention stabling for 160 horses, 154 workmen's houses, farm buildings and other subsidiary enterprises, each of which called for a multiplicity of skills and practices, not least from an amorphous army of 'engineers', who ran and maintained a variety of machines.[40]

The giant plant, of course, was a world of labour in itself. Cyfarthfa had 55 subsidiary furnaces, 3 forges, a foundry and 8 rolling mills, 8 steam engines, 8 water wheels, several thousand trams on 120 miles of internal tramway. Its annual wages bill totalled £300,000. It had built Georgetown to house its most valuable workers. Towering over Dowlais, a third of which had been built by the Guests, were the elegant stables raised by the ironmaster, hard by his church and the site he had chosen for the town market; the upper floor served as a school and a ballroom. Indeed the servicing of the ironworks' 500 horses was a minor industry in itself. At Dowlais, which had no fewer than 50 forges, 7 steam engines and from 1832 several steam locomotives, it was said that the tramways within the works and running to collieries and mines, if re-aligned in a straight line, would stretch for 2,000 miles.[41]

Between 1831 and 1834, the Marquess of Bute was thinking seriously of launching a ten-furnace plant on a Rhymney site as a rival to Dowlais. He feared that Guest would break free from his dependence on Bute estates. Crawshay warned that Guest might even transfer Dowlais itself, monstrous engines and all, to Rhymney (as the Cyfarthfa master planned to do with Hirwaun). The reports and surveys prepared by Bute's mineral agent in consequence offer a brief but valuable insight into the realities of ironworks management, from the entrepreneur's viewpoint, about the time of the Merthyr Rising. The complexity, even of the 'mass occupations', is painfully visible.[42]

To supply 6,000 tons of mine a month for the ten furnaces, for example, Bute's agent calculated that the marquess would need 750 miners. These were to be deployed by the opening of 375 stalls 80 yards apart; each stall would need 10 yards of 'rise heading' and 8 yards of 'level heading'. There would have to be major road-making above and below ground, tramways and their services, which included casting shops and a variety of engineering plant, 6 balance pits and 500 trams. The coal levels would cost substantially more and these large bodies of miners and colliers, operating in teams stiff with their own internal grading patterns, would need a small army of supporting workers of many different ranges of experience and practice, hauliers and stackers, road makers, tram operators, horse handlers, experts at driving levels, at balance pits and inclines.[43]

The small plant, which divided its 1,292 workers into four broad categories, tried to define them more closely. 'Firemen' it split into at least 16 'trades', skilled and unskilled: keepers, fillers, refiners, cokers, pig weighers, engineers, fitters, moulders, smiths, carpenters, sawyers, brick-makers, masons, machine-men, carriers, stable-men, followed by an ubiquitous 'etc'. Puddlers and rollers worked with shinglers, catchers, straighteners, ballers, engineers, smiths, bar weighers, clerks, and 'etc'. Colliers and miners included road men, stackers, loaders, timbermen, horse-tenders, hauliers and 'labourers' (a humanised version of 'etc').[44]

At present, it is not possible to get at the human realities of living and working in Merthyr through this web of information, which conceals as much as it reveals. Despite the strength of corporate feeling, there was a deal of mobility between several categories of work, a common hinterland of labour which had become 'semi-skilled' through a couple of generations of 'craft-lore' transmission by work-group, from which both the skilled men and 'labourers' were differentiated. Two truths need to register limpet-like in the mind. As is clear from their correspondence, ironmasters and their agents relied heavily on the *known personal* skills and capacities of workers at *every* level, down to the hewer. On the other hand, when the new colliers' union struck root from the summer of 1831, and in fact tried to enrol all grades, including 'firemen', the central plank of its platform, cemented by a fearful Biblical oath, was the strict preservation of 'craft secrets' from management.[45] There was evidently a wide range of workplace autonomy and group corporatism, a great deal of informal 'workers' control', in natural if dialectically tense co-existence with well-nigh universal piece-work and sub-contracting.

Works were a mosaic of sub-contractors. In the early days, in an area without an industrial tradition, management and skilled labour had been imported, generally from Staffordshire, Cornwall, the Midlands, Yorkshire and Scotland; the practice persisted but from the 1800s, after the vital puddling process had become 'the Welsh method', south Wales became a reservoir of talent. From the native Watkin George who built 'the greatest wheel the world has seen' for Crawshay to Adrian Stephens of Dowlais who conferred on mankind the inestimable blessing of the steam-whistle, the Merthyr complex was rich in technical talent and, given the limits imposed by the family basis of companies, in managerial skill; Unitarian miners of the Cyfarthfa Philosophical Society became positively notorious for inventiveness.[46] Such skill inevitably became the object of ruthless poaching between companies. For several ironworks, the handling of the endless fluctuation in the price paid to colliers and miners on the one hand, the bribery of skilled labour at the other works on the other, was virtually the sum total of their 'industrial relations'.

In September 1832, George Crawshay, William's brother, denounced the quality of Cyfarthfa bar iron No. 2. At the same time William Jeffreys, a furnace manager and successor to the celebrated Unitarian engineer Mathew Wayne, reported that Ruabon works in north Wales and Abersychan in Monmouthshire were trying to bribe him away. The response of both William Crawshays, father and son, was identical; first of all, a vigorous defence of 'old Will' Williams, who made the best

No. 2 iron in Britain. His son 'young Will' *had* to be kept; if his pay were reduced, he was going to America. As for Jeffreys, he did *not* receive double the wages of a London House labourer; he was paid £130 a year for a thirteen-month year, with a £26 a year cut, in the interests of the company. Ruabon and Abersychan had offered him 15 guineas a month, with a house, firing and 'the keep of a cow for five years certain'. William Crawshay II calculated that, with the cow counting at 2s 6d a week, this would be £170 a year, but Jeffreys had made a sworn statement: born and bred in Cyfarthfa, he would finish there. 'Such feelings towards us', the senior Crawshays agreed, 'are not to be valued at nothing or considered as worth the price of a common labourer.'[47]

Puddlers and rollers, of course, were in a less independent position, but every ironmaster everywhere was hungry for them and the strategically placed puddlers were the first working men in south Wales known to have created effective organisations.[48] Visible from 1810 onwards, particularly during the *Luddite* crisis, the puddlers' organisations were for a generation leaders of the working class in south Wales. Only in 1822 in Monmouthshire, at this time growing around coal at an even more break-neck pace, did colliers and miners take the initiative. It took longer in Merthyr. Puddlers' agreements, often concerned more with conditions and workers' control than wages alone, were *contracts*. The action which probably ignited the Merthyr Rising of 1831 was Crawshay's desperately reluctant dismissal of 84 puddlers. William Thomas Williams, the 32-year-old man who carried the Red Flag during the Rising, possibly the first time it was so used in Britain, was a Crawshay puddler.[49]

Sub-contracting extended deeply into the 'mass occupations' of miners and colliers. A folklore of craft had built up around the 'master miners' and 'undertakers of job work', who were the fulcrum of the whole process of finding, running and keeping work. They contracted for a stint, controlled their team, exercised the vital command over tools (the Bute agent thought that, for the new mines and levels, tools to the value of £400 would have to be advanced).[50] For many workers, perception of the reality of their predicament was refracted through the filter of these 'butties', who often ran the friendly societies which were sometimes a cover for craft organisation, as they presided in chapel and as sleeping partners in those pubs where they sometimes paid their monthly-contract wages. The 'butties' occupied a critical and essentially ambivalent position in the economic and social structure, in some ways parallel to that which Independent and Baptist chapels occupied in the spiritual.[51] One of them served on Merthyr Select Vestry in the 1820s; some sent their children to the school for the middle class run by Taliesin Williams, son of Iolo Morganwg; during the crisis of 1831, several of them petitioned to be enrolled as Special Constables to protect property. On the other hand, they were often the channel for 'responsible protest' and workers' petitions (the Dowlais miners of Ffos-y-Fran were peculiarly articulate); they could also serve as the fulcrum of political radicalism.[52]

Some occupations were paid by the day, notably hauliers. Technically an unskilled trade, it called for ability to handle horses, sometimes for a command *of* horses; several of the leading figures in this trade came from marginal areas like Penderyn. Both *Lewsyn yr Heliwr* and *Dic Penderyn*, folk-heroes of the Merthyr Rising, had been hauliers in Penderyn; the former, certainly, would have been recognised as a folk-hero anywhere from Mexico to the Water Margin of China.[53]

Most workers were paid by the piece, in the 'long pay' of the monthly contract. There was an at present impenetrable network of perks, from concessionary coal and ritual ale to 'the shilling' or even 'the guinea' on special and arduous occasions. The employers used the long pay and many other devices in the customary battle against drink and the irregular rhythms of Saint Monday and Frantic Friday (or at least frantic end-of-the-month Friday).[54] It is not possible at present to construct adequate wage scales though it is clear that, in good times, south Wales was a high wage area.

In times of prosperity and full employment on a normal 12-hour day, miners and colliers could earn 22 to 24 shillings a week, furnace-men from 25 to 30 shillings, puddlers over 35 shillings and the most skilled men as much as 50 to 60 shillings. Men were taking this kind of money home during the dramatic Chartist year of 1839.[55] Earnings had reached something like this level in 1810, but at that time prices had risen equally sharply. Prices fluctuated as wildly as wages and it was precisely this fluctuation which was the human reality.[56] Workers in Merthyr could often earn anything from three to six times the wages of rural workers in west Wales and many of them may well have been distinctly better off than the small farmers of that oppressed country. In 1831 in Merthyr, colliers and even labourers owned *watches*; one watch-maker who was robbed had nearly a hundred watches under repair at the time. During the justice raids on shops and houses which were a feature of the Merthyr Rising, poor widows were recovering furniture which would have seemed positively palatial to any cottager in Cardiganshire.[57] But people could literally plunge from plenty to destitution in a matter of months. During 1816, colliers' wages fell in two stages over nine months from 21 to 15 shillings, labourers' from 17 to 12 shillings, at a time when food prices were rising sharply, while puddlers, who had kept themselves over 25 shillings, were suddenly confronted with a wage cut of no less than 40 per cent.[58] *General* unemployment was usually less common than in England or in the sale-coal districts of Monmouthshire, but *full* employment was equally rare. What *was* common was frequent short-time, serious unbalance in employment between trades and a permanent uncertainty. It was the instability of the iron trade which made rational budgeting on the long pay so difficult.

Technical advances seem to have unhinged masters and management; accurate forecasting of market conditions seems to have been extraordinarily difficult. Shortly after the puddling process had been introduced, works found themselves seizing up from a shortage of pig iron to service it and similar bottlenecks seem to have followed every innovation.[59] In Merthyr town, of all places, there were periodical coal famines![60] The most sensitive area seems to have been ironstone. Ironstone miners often lived on a roller-coaster. In 1824, when the market price of iron was £9 10s a ton, Rhymney works were sold for £72,000; the very next year, when the price of iron was up to £15 10s a ton, they were resold — for £147,000.[61] This *rate* of change was typical, in all fields, from unemployment to the marriage rate. Population was constantly shifting as people moved from works to works, out of a depression and after a rumour of higher wages. Between the censuses of 1821 and 1831, the population of Aberdare was said to have increased by 1,900 thanks to the ironworks, but the census-taker added a note that it had fallen by over 1,000, because of a slump, since 1828.[62] Many of the workers in unskilled and semi-skilled trades were seasonal; the trek home to Cardiganshire and south-west Wales for the harvest was a recognised phenomenon; in the 1830s, it was estimated that as many as 10,000 people might circulate through Merthyr in a year.[63] When work was available, wages were often high, but short-time working and sectional unemployment were chronic.

Ironmasters resorted to all sorts of devices to hold the labour force together.[64] Truck was one such: while strong at Dowlais and Penydarren, it was never the omnipresent phenomenon it was in Monmouthshire. The strength of the local shopkeepers, local supplies of money, at least after the Napoleonic Wars, and the pull of 'penny capitalism' among workers themselves saw to that; in fact Merthyr was attractive to many Monmouthshire families because of its markets and money. The Court of Requests, however, could also advance credit; technically, it handled debts worth less than £5. In practice it, too, could act as a holding force and during depressions could exercise an influence not unlike that of truck, as virtually every working-class family, even among the 'aristocrats', shuddered into debt servitude. In truth, debt, in the high and millenarian political tension of 1831, was the forcing-house of a *working-class* consciousness.[65]

Even the appointment of a stipendiary magistrate in 1829 was, at least in part, governed by the need to hold the labour force together, to handle the epidemic crises of debt and relief. The choice of J.B. Bruce, a non-industrialist landowner in Aberdare, by removing suspicions of jobbery, made it easier to press claims for maintenance on the home parishes of distressed immigrants, to lubricate removals and appeals against removals. The local newspaper claimed that the parish had saved £500 a year by the appointment.[66]

The very structure and dynamics of the population intensified the instability and class incoherence. In its experience of death Merthyr differed dramatically from the small county capital of Cardiff and the commercial-industrial town of Swansea, which, at half Merthyr's size, was growing at a more aldermanic pace.[67]

Towering over Merthyr people higher than Pen-y-Fan in the Beacons was a child mortality rate which halved the life-chances of every generation. In 1813 67 per cent of all recorded burials were of children under five; in the crisis year of 1819, the figure was 64 per cent; in the best year on record between 1813 and 1830, it was 46 per cent.[68] Burials of children under the age of one expressed as a proportion of every thousand baptisms ranged from 145 to 250 a year between 1821 and 1830, at an annual mean of 190 (the averages for England and Wales between 1838 and 1847 were 142 to 164).[69] There was a marked worsening in the second year of life: burials of children under the age of two per thousand baptisms ranged from 274 to no fewer than 573 in the awful year of 1823, when there was clearly an epidemic of some kind. The annual mean was 398, as against 264 for Swansea and 200 for Cardiff. In 1823 in fact burials of children of five and under reached the colossal total of 713 per thousand baptisms; the annual mean over 1821 to 1830 was 497, by three-year averages, no less than 549, again a good deal higher than the rates for either Swansea or Cardiff.[70] Given the inadequacy of the sources, these figures can only be approximations, indications of trend, but the trend is unmistakable and terrible. In Merthyr in these years, you had to fight to get through your first five years.

The dreadful year of 1823 was in fact a year of prosperity and, apart from the peaks in 1813 and 1819, there is little clear correlation between years of depression and years of severe child mortality. Nor were women of child-bearing age, 15 to 44, particularly vulnerable, by these figures. On the contrary, from about the age of five onwards, the population of Merthyr seems to have been a good deal *more* resilient than that of Swansea and Cardiff. The threats to life posed by the mushroom and uncontrolled growth of Merthyr are painfully familiar, though it was during the 1830s and 1840s that the town experienced its real ecological disaster. Drainage and sanitation were conspicuous by their virtual absence; overcrowded housing sprouted like killer weed; the very nature of the work was heavy, taxing and dangerous. Drink, a necessary social lubricant, was also an anaesthetic, though that school of interpretation which sees it as the quickest way out of Merthyr as well as Manchester, seems to forget that the Waun and its sports, the Glyn and its blackberries, Pontsarn and its girls were only a walk away.

The cholera of 1849 was murderous; that of 1831-2 frightening but not in fact particularly bad. In the present state of the evidence one can do little beyond surmise; but at a guess, it was the environmental conditions which bred disease which raised Merthyr's child death rate so far above the Glamorgan threshold. In the more primitive industrial conditions of 1813 and 1819, the death rate seems to have responded in a fairly direct fashion to dearth and low wages (Merthyr suffered classic subsistence crises in 1800-1 and 1816-17).[71] The evidence suggests some qualitative change during the prosperous 1820s, probably an improvement in the regularity of supply. On the main supply route, the Glamorgan canal, carriage rates fell by 50 per cent.[72] At every economic crisis, however, working-class families would be plunged into debt and unemployment tended to coincide with an inflation of food prices.[73] From 1828 onwards, the advancing slump finds reflection in the mortality figures. The marriage rate reached a peak in 1825 and then tailed off sharply; so did the baptism rate, while the burial rate climbed. Once again it was among children under five, and particularly under two, that it began to climb towards the desperate levels of 1823; in 1829, burials of children under five were 613 per thousand baptisms; in 1830, they were 624.

What is very striking, however, and in some senses surprising, is that in the age-structure of burials, there is a break so sharp at the age of five that it virtually amounts to a rupture. From the age of five onwards, the burial rate per thousand estimated population in Merthyr *improves* very visibly indeed. Between the ages of three and twenty-nine, as also from thirty to fifty-nine, the rate falls well *below* those of Swansea and Cardiff. The difference is quite remarkable. Old people, however, from these figures, Merthyr would seem to have lacked. Burials over sixty are proportionally a half those of Cardiff and Swansea (which, of course, did not prevent some people, even in the hardest jobs, living to their eighties). This may not be quite as stark as it looks; there is some evidence that men and women who could work no longer were taken over by families who might well have stayed put in south-west Wales or elsewhere. Nevertheless, it seems ominous.

Overall, then, the picture derived from the parish returns, blurred though it is, confirms the impressionistic portrait which may be built up from qualitative evidence: a vigorous *immigrant* community, over-charged with young men and women. Certainly the local *Merthyr Guardian* a couple of years later was full of complaints about the hordes of children who infested the streets, as ill-bred as the packs of mongrel dogs who romped with them (Merthyr had few 'genteel' weddings, it grumbled, though this was because it lacked bells not belles).[74] Merthyr slaughtered those children wholesale, but if you could get through your first five years, you might well live longer than your country cousin (in fact the same sets of figures suggest that you certainly *would*) and you would surely enjoy a fuller, if insecure, unpredictable life, though Merthyr was no country for old men. The blank and often bleak rows of figures on crabbed sheets confirm the folk-lore: in Merthyr it was a short life but a full one, or a good life if you didn't weaken.

Through this world passed thousands of young stags in the mating season, taking a break from the bracing rigours of life in the west, circulating endlessly around the Black Domain, drawn endlessly back to its flaring, noisy, exciting, distressing, 'free' and reassuringly *peopled* Samaria. Those who did settle often glossed an older, near-tribal commitment with a quite ferocious craft or corporate, *butty* loyalty and a commitment to 'Dowlais' or 'Cyfarthfa' which was scarcely less tribal. The prospect of 'organising' this lot would have made a Bolshevik blanch. It was a world capable of responding to a hero, to 'the man who makes himself respected', rarely to a rationality, or an impersonal doctrine; both, after all, were so conspicuously absent among their 'betters'! Into this world went the earnest young men with their holy books, the Bible (Old Testament often *against* New — Damn your mere morality! shouted the *Cardis* as they split chapel after chapel), Tom Paine, Voltaire, Volney (they were teaching *The*

Ruins of Empires as a set book in Nant-y-Glo a few years later), John Wade's *Black Book, The United Trades Co-operative Journal*.[75] And a dusty time they often had of it.

Their world was for two generations essentially *external* to that of the townsmen (whose life expectancy at birth was *double* their own), to the world of Thomas Darker, for example, who after a sketchy start, became one of the town's leading radical traders, with a grocery and drapery opposite the Castle Inn and a house stocked with very superior mahogany, a superior piano and an elegant organ, 'big enough for a chapel'. Darker served as church-warden, overseer of the poor and select vestryman from 1822 and was the first man to use gas in the town. He also slept with two large pistols loaded with swanshot at his pillow, 'Merthyr fashion'.[76]

As late as 1831, the parish minute-books still distinguished between *Inhabitants of the Village* and *Inhabitants of the Ironworks*. Even the registers of chapels with working-class members, the big congregations of Baptist Zion and Independent Zoar, designated members either by a place-name or a craft-name, which suggests a similar distinction.[77] The first crisis in Merthyr, the massive subsistence actions of 1800-1, had taken the form of an onslaught by the workers on the town middle class. When, in 1803, Glamorgan called for a tripling of the Merthyr militia, the *Inhabitants* protested that the men in the works were not to be trusted and offered to raise the quota themselves. Characteristically, they found an ally in the Dowlais works, which did not want to lose any workers and offered to subsidise the town enterprise![78]

Yet relations between workers and townspeople were bound to be intimate. Housing was one nexus. Most of the housing for ordinary workers was supplied by middle-class investors either as adjuncts to small industrial enterprises, as the celebrated Thomas family of Waunwyllt (whose widow Lucy shipped the first Merthyr coal to London and became the 'mother' of the steam-coal trade) raised cottages at Abercanaid, or as speculations in their own right. Seven cottages at Pontmorlais in the middle of the town, for example, brought in annual rents of £7 12s 6d and a ground rent of £4 10s to a grocer who had leased the property for £3 a year, while W.D. Jenkins, a prominent druggist, let out six of nine cottages in Bridge Street at £28 a year.[79] The bulk of the workers' houses were £6 cottages; it was difficult to get either rent or rates out of them. Walter Morgan, a Georgetown solicitor who ran beerhouses, reckoned he could not get 2 per cent a year on his money and the town middle class as a bloc resisted to the end every effort by the ironmasters to rate the owners rather than the occupiers of such cottages, which by 1833 accounted for £13,900 of a total housing valuation of £25,000.[80]

Townsmen and workers also met, however, in chapel, in friendly society, in local eisteddfod and, at least from 1830, in political unions. There was a range of 'respectable' working-class families which could inter-marry with those village-type shopkeepers, as the Census called them, who formed the rank and file of the Merthyr Trade.[81]

It was the local strength of this Trade which inhibited truck in Merthyr, attracted people from Monmouthshire. Many shopkeepers were more dependent on workers than they were on the quality. Exclusive dealing by workers proved a potent political weapon when the town finally won its MP. Given the instability of the iron trade and the opportunities offered by a booming community, a whole hinterland of floaters and 'penny capitalists' sprang up, alongside the butties and between workers and shopocracy. The Beer Act of 1830 released scores of working-class families into a form of trade; the anti-truck act of the following year had the same effect on 'any one who could raise the price of a tea and tobacco licence'.[82] The bankruptcy records of the county are full of such people.[83] From those of 1831-2 alone, how is one to categorise John Rees, 'miner, grocer, general shopkeeper, haulier and retail butcher' or Evan Evans of Dowlais, 'carpenter, beer-dealer, grocer and miner', John Bannister who came from Hereford to set up in Merthyr as a 'strawbonnet maker, currier and general shopkeeper' or Morgan Williams of Ystrad Dyfodwg, who moved from Ty Isha to Bedwellty to Llanelly (Breconshire) back to Bedwellty and then on to Merthyr as 'farmer, butcher, retail brewer, miner, horse-dealer and inn-keeper'? John Garnons, a coroner's witness after the Rising, who called himself a 'gardener and journeyman bookseller' was clearly a cultivated man, even if he began work at the uncultivated hour of six in the morning![84]

It was drives like this, coupled with the shopocracy-worker nexus in housing which created the rationale of *China* itself. As ironmasters moved out into their mansions and workers settled into the housing of Georgetown and the indescribable tangle of Caepantywyll east of the Taff, a rising tide of squatters flooded after them, camping in shacks and shanty towns, living between the arches of the canal bridges, overflowing into the cheap lodging houses around the bridges, as even the hastily thrown up cottages of the middle-class speculators failed to cope with rising demand. This was the natural home for marginal people, receivers, sharpers of infinite variety, with the recreation centre of the Glebeland nearby, quick get-away routes over Aberdare Mountain and the Beacons to hand and two county borders within reach. Such pockets developed in every settled area, Dowlais included, but nowhere else did they grow into no-go areas such as those on the Taff. The Pont-y-Storehouse district and Caedraw further south on the east side became notorious. *China* in particular grew up through and around Georgetown, hitherto a settled area of established radical tradition; it washed the very foundation stones of Ynysgau chapel, mother church of Merthyr Dissent. And as Georgetown slithered into a Beggar's Opera ambience, Heolgerrig, a little farther up Aberdare Mountain drew itself in with pursed lips.[85] Similar dichotomies formed all over the parish. For out of that same half-world between middle and working classes came the men of the friendly societies and the 'Firemen's Benefits', marching hundreds strong behind their banners, in sashes and watch-chains, the chapel men, the men who raised money to found building societies, who attended the Dowlais Mechanics' Institute, who won prizes at the eisteddfodau at the Patriot Inn (hard by *China*), the men with window-sashes.[86] In Merthyr Tydfil, the distance between notoriety and respectability was often measured in feet.

In the fragmentation of Merthyr society, every serious outbreak of class war almost invariably took the form of a head-on clash between workers and shopocracy. Yet in the almost automatic process, centred on poor relief, which was fusing village and ironworks settlements into a new urban community of highly distinctive personality and in the far from automatic process in which working people built an awareness of themselves as *a working class*, the crucial role was played by that social group which has largely been an absentee from our social history, the town middle class.

At first glance, that middle class was the weak and undeveloped force one might expect in such a settlement. The clear contrast was with the mercantile and developed community of Swansea, a small but fully articulated social capital. The quality of Swansea's housing and its rateable value were markedly superior to Merthyr's.[87] The structure of its shopocracy was equally revealing. (See Table 2.1.)

Merthyr's 111 publicans and brewers, 39 butchers, 23 carters, 18 tea dealers, 13 tanners, 11 curriers, 5 chandlers, 11 glaziers, 10 clothiers, 9 saddlers, 7 coopers and 5 chemists do little to redress the balance, though the town clearly had a strong complement of artisans. Eight clockmakers were listed, and the place was already famous for the craft. The overall picture is the one convention would dictate. It is, however, deceptive. Equally characteristic of Merthyr were the London

Table 2.1: Shopocracy

Census of 1831	Merthyr	Swansea
Total population	22,083	13,694
'Capitalists, bankers, professional and other educated men'	143	221
Men over twenty engaged in trade and handicrafts	1,270	1,419
Number of crafts represented	64	81
Village-type shopkeepers	82	18
Hucksters	15	8
Cobblers	222	191
Blacksmiths	182	58
Booksellers	2	9
Printers	4	8
Builders	151	185
Carpenters	162	231
Tailors	68	94
Linen-drapers	16	30
Hatters	6	10
Grocers	2	29
Fancy bakers	10	18
Pastrycooks-confectioners	0	6
Gunmakers	0	1
Coachmakers	0	7
Cutlers	0	1
Engravers	0	5
Opticians	0	1
Pipemakers	0	1

and Bristol Houses which opened seasonally; the china traders from the Potteries who were visitors more regular than the theatre companies.[88] No less a characteristic sight in Merthyr was Adolphe Scherman of the Depot du Palais Royale, Paris, French Bazaar and Dutch Fancy Fair suppliers By Appointment to the Royal Family, who offered displays in the Ball Room of the Castle Inn of fancy goods from Paris, Geneva, Vienna, Frankfurt and Berlin, musical clocks and boxes, gold and silver watches, Dresden china, Flemish paintings and jewellery, Berlin jewellery, Venetian shell combs, Paris perfumes (he doubled as an agent for Farina's Eau de Cologne).[89]

'It was a time when money was absolute trash', one contemporary recollected.[90] In the records of Merthyr through the late 1820s and early 1830s, some eighty to ninety men regularly re-appear as a directive force in the town.[91] These were in no sense a mere gaggle of shopkeepers. Wide-ranging in their interests and connections, they were men of power and substance.[92]

Very striking is the survival within this group of many of the older pre-industrial families of the district. The 'squire' of Merthyr, for example, William Thomas of the Court estate, prided himself upon being 'an aborigine of the place'. His father had been a maltster, but the son was trained as a surgeon by the Cyfarthfa works' doctors Davies and Russell and continued to practise even after his fortunate marriage. For his wife was Jane, daughter of Samuel Rees of Y Werfa estate in the Aberdare valley. The Rees family and the vicar ran Merthyr parish in the mid-eighteenth century; the father had acquired the celebrated Court estate there from the Lewises of the Van. Jane Rees had first married another Aberdare landowner Rees Davies. One of their daughters married William Milburne Davies, another local *coq de village*. Originally from Abercanaid, where he opened coal works, Davies had become 'draper of the village' in the early days of its growth and established himself in Gwaelod-y-Garth House, before he moved to Monmouthshire and left it to William Crawshay II. Another of the daughters of Jane's first marriage herself eloped with the son of William Meyrick, immigrant and lawyer to the Crawshays and the parish and after his death, married Edward Lewis Richards, geologist son of the keeper of the Greyhound Inn, Merthyr, who became a barrister and was to end his days as Chairman of Flintshire Quarter Sessions.

After Rees Davies's death, Jane married William Thomas and took the Court estate with her. Notorious for his after-dinner anecdotes, William Thomas *the Court* served as a bluff and racy Tory magistrate and, immensely popular in Merthyr, was virtually a permanent member of the Select Vestry.[93]

Richard Jenkins of Aberfan, on the other hand, came of yeoman farmers who had been the backbone of the old Dissenting conventicle at Cwm-Glo on Aberdare Mountain. Celebrated throughout Glamorgan and Monmouthshire as an auctioneer, he was a member of Cefn Unitarian cause, linear descendant of Cwm-Glo and rivalled Thomas in his vestry service. There were many others, as family after family quit farm and market for the furnaces. William Milburne Davies's father-in-law, David Williams, tried to start a bank in rivalry to the branch of

Brecon Old Bank which monopolised Merthyr and himself took the lion's share of the wholesale trade of the town. The Thomases of Wernlaes went into Plymouth works agency as those of Waunwyllt went into coal. The Josephs of Breconshire, long half-citizens of Merthyr, tried their hands at furnaces and haulage before making it at Cyfarthfa and branching out as coal suppliers to Plymouth. The pattern is repeated at every level. The Lewis family of freeholders at Gwernllwyn supplied magistrates' clerks. Ann Nicholas, who married William Williams, a respected Unitarian of Heolgerrig and became the mother of the future Chartist leader Morgan Williams, came of local stock so rooted that her father, a blacksmith at Pant, on the Brecon side of the parish, claimed descent from Dafydd Gam, 'cross-eyed Davey Gam' who had fought at Agincourt and against Owain Glyn Dŵr![94]

It was, however, the immigrants who predominated, even if they married into this network of 'old standards'. The redoubtable William Meyrick, for example, was the son of a Neath publican. Articled as a boy to Merthyr's solitary attorney, he was parish solicitor by 1805 and made his fortune as attorney to the Crawshays. The Glamorgan Canal Company was his milch cow, particularly in its quarrels with the Melingriffith works near Cardiff. He presented a bill for £20,000 on one occasion: 'Damn it, Meyrick, you're coming it a bit steep this time.' With the ironmaster he was on Christian name terms. He made a mess of the Caedraw lease in 1828 — 'He knows nothing of his business or anything else,' William informed his father, 'since the Lady fell in love with his corduroys at the picture shop window . . .' When the ironmaster moved into Cyfarthfa Castle, Meyrick bought Gwaelod-y-Garth house from him for £2,500. He was powerful. Portly and commanding, he ranged the shadowy hinterland of Glamorgan politics with 'a cold, grey eye', helped to secure the return of Guest as a Tory for Honiton, for he had connections in the London clubs. William Thomas the Court was a friend, but the generality hated the sight of him.[95]

No-one hated him more than the James family.[96] Young Charles Herbert James, formerly articled to Meyrick's rival William Perkins, fought pitched battles with the Tory in Glamorgan courts which became a local epic and punctuated James's advance to the parliamentary seat. For the Jameses were Merthyr's radical dynasty par excellence. Christopher James, from the Whitchurch area, moved into supply via the Canal; he became the spokesman for the carriers, who from 1806 to the 1820s were able to charge 16 to 18 shillings a ton; not until the 1820s did the rates fall to 8 to 10 shillings.[97] He married a daughter of David Williams the banker, built the Bush Hotel, opened a business in draperies, groceries and wine and scored 'a fortunate hit' in leasing turnpikes which made him. His estate at Treforest supplied flour to Merthyr and timber to Crawshay; he leased a £500 stretch there to the ironmaster in 1833. 'His very servants became gentlemen' and when he retired to Swansea, the burgesses elected him mayor.[98]

With him came his brother William who owned the Globe and the Merthyr Swan and much property and married into the Herberts of Abergavenny, saddlers and ironmongers. Another brother was Job James, former naval surgeon and a bookseller admirer of William Cobbett. Around this thrusting family grew a whole connection. William Jones, a draper who owned the town meat market and could offer loans of £800 at a time at an interest of 4 per cent, was a cousin;[99] so was another landowning draper Henry Jones, 'gentleman', who had a gift for verse (of a sort) and was a pillar of Taliesin Williams's Eisteddfod Society. William Howell, influential keeper of the radical and eisteddfodic inn, The Patriot, was linked by marriage and business, as were Richard Jenkins the auctioneer, William Williams of Heolgerrig, the managerial families of Joseph and Kirkhouse, the solicitor Perkins and a whole cluster of associates, kinsmen and friends.[100]

The memoirs of Christopher Herbert James, William's son, who divided his youth between Merthyr and the family branch in Bristol, have left an entertaining but quite striking portrait of this circle, which by the late 1820s was in fact growing into Merthyr's first political élite.[101] These were the men who sent their sons to Taliesin Williams's school on the Glebeland, where many of them spent their time copying out the Iolo Manuscripts; the boys attended the eisteddfodau, waited outside Job James's shop for the mail with its load of magazines and papers, publications of the Society for the Diffusion of Useful Knowledge, Cobbett, and the radical press. They went on, some to the 'gentry school' in Swansea, Shaw and Griffiths, most to Unitarian establishments or Goulstone's at Bedminster near Bristol, en route for Glasgow University or the Inns of Court. Christopher James's second son, William Milburne, became a QC, a Justice, and married the daughter of the bishop of Chichester. Walter Morgan, the Georgetown solicitor, brewer and land speculator, produced a barrister son who moved to Calcutta and was made Secretary to the Legislative Council of India by Dalhousie. The son of John Petherick the Peny-darren agent became Consul to the Sudan and the son of W.D. Jenkins, a highly successful grocer and druggist, became an ecclesiastical historian at Jesus College, Oxford and 'apostle to the railwaymen'.[102]

The James political dynasty stemmed essentially from Christopher's eldest son, David William James, who dominated Merthyr politics and opened coalmines in the Rhondda and from Job James the follower of Cobbett.[103] It was characteristic that Christopher Herbert James was articled to William Perkins. Over six feet and lazy, very fond of hunting, Perkins knew little law but plenty of workmen, since his practice was mainly in small debts. A deadly rival to Meyrick, he had an entry into the working-class world denied his fellows and often acted as a spokesman and defender of the 'responsible working man'. Only a few of the James connection could equal him in this respect: David John the Unitarian minister and his sons and Morgan Williams, son of William of Heolgerrig, known as the Young Mountain Solomon for his mathematics. They were to become first-generation leaders of Merthyr Chartism.[104]

For one of the outstanding features of the Reform crisis of the 1830s was the entry of these men into local political power.

The process which carried them there, however, was simply the latest pulse in a series of almost automatic reflex actions which were hammering Village and Ironworks into a town.[105] The key was the poor rate. At every economic crisis, whenever the poor rate rose to the threshold of alarm, the ironmasters stepped in to take over the town and impose administrative reform. In 1830, when depression coincided with national and local political crises, intervention became continuous and permanent, reform virtually total. The pattern was set by the *Luddite* crisis of 1811 and the brutal post-war depression of 1816. On each occasion, the poor rate rose to an unprecedented level, committees of townsmen failed to cope, the ironmasters led by Crawshay, Guest and Anthony Hill intervened. In these interventions, a small but influential group of merchants, solicitors and shopkeepers of the town appeared and re-appeared, as executants of the schemes which the masters' initiative had produced. It was during the crises of 1811 and 1816, for example, that Joseph Coffin, a Unitarian tanner, first figured as a parish 'strong man', ruthless in his zeal for retrenchment. Every reform drive entailed a new valuation of the town and every new valuation meant a crisis. In 1817, for example, Guest and Meyrick proposed to bring the owners of small cottages worth £6 a year or less under the rates; the town middle class, rallied by Walter Morgan and Taliesin Williams, vetoed the proposal and demanded instead a heavier rate on the ironworks. Every crisis therefore also marked a stage in the evolution of the Merthyr shopocracy and its self-consciousness.[106]

One climax was reached after the post-war depression. From 1820 there was an abrupt improvement in the quality of the parish records. In January 1822, 47 men, six of whom signed by mark, met under the chairmanship of William Thomas the Court and declared, evidently in response to an agitation, that it was not expedient to appoint a Select Vestry. Two weeks later, 'a most numerously attended meeting' resolved to the contrary that it was highly expedient to appoint one and promptly did so. Only one signature was appended, that of the chairman William Crawshay, who had copied out the minutes in his own hand.[107]

From this moment to its virtual supersession by the Board of Guardians in 1836, the Select Vestry, with its double vote for property, was to serve as the government of the town.[108] Every April, the parish elected two churchwardens, four overseers and twenty select vestrymen. The first vestry made automatic provision for the representation of the ironmasters, but after 1823 they ceased to attend and many of their agents sat as townsmen rather than works representatives. The creation of the Select Vestry marked the coming of age of the mercantile middle class of the district. A Dowlais miner served in 1825 but he was almost certainly a 'master of levels'. From 1823 to the crisis years after 1831, the Select Vestry was in the pocket of the town Trade. (See Table 2.2.)

It was from 1828, when the curate's name was dropped from the lists, that the James family and their associates began to appear with increasing regularity on the Select Vestry, but it was the simultaneous onset of economic and political crisis which installed them in local power. On this occasion, the ironmasters' response was more considered and sustained. In June 1829, their bill for a stipendiary magistrate passed into law. The crisis deepened. By 1831, the poor rate had rocketed to the unprecedented figure of eight shillings. There was widespread distress. By the spring of 1830 the parish was £660 in the red and behind the terse formulae of parish minutes there is a mounting desperation. In January 1830 William Crawshay entered angrily upon the scene, calling meeting after meeting, writing out minutes in his own hand. Throughout 1830, a year of multiple tensions, there were testy and fruitless assemblies. The climax came in March 1831 when, in an obviously co-ordinated series of resolutions moved by Anthony Hill and supported by D.W. James and his cousin Henry Jones, a parish meeting demanded a total reform of parish administration.[109]

Table 2.2: Composition of the Merthyr Select Vestry, 1822-36

	1822 (Jan)	1822 (Apr)	1823	1824	1825	1827	1828	1829	1830	1831	1832	1833	1834	1835	1836
Masters	4	2	2	0	0	0	0	0	0	3	4	4	5	5	5
Agents	1	3	7	5	4	3	3	7	5	6	7	5	5	2	2
Professional men	2	1	2	1	2	1	1	1	1	1	1	1	2	2	1
Merchants	0	0	0	0	0	0	1	1	1	0	1	0	0	0	0
Shopkeepers	3	3	0	2	2	2	4	0	2	0	2	3	2	5	5
Grocers	1	1	1	3	3	6	4	3	2	5	0	1	1	2	3
Drapers	1	2	1	2	2	0	2	0	2	2	0	0	0	0	1
Ironmongers	2	1	1	2	2	0	0	1	0	0	0	2	0	0	0
Tanners	0	0	0	0	0	1	2	1	1	2	2	2	2	2	0
Chandlers	0	1	1	1	1	1	0	1	2	0	0	0	0	0	0
Nailers	1	1	1	0	1	1	1	1	1	1	1	0	1	1	1
Innkeepers	1	0	0	0	0	0	1	0	1	0	1	0	2	0	2
Curriers	1	2	1	0	0	0	0	1	0	0	0	0	0	1	0
Saddlers	0	0	0	0	0	1	0	1	0	0	0	0	0	0	0
Carpenters	0	0	1	1	0	0	0	0	0	0	0	0	0	0	0
Shoemakers	0	0	0	0	1	0	0	0	0	0	0	0	0	0	0
Miners	0	0	0	0	1	0	0	0	0	0	0	0	0	0	0
Farmers	2	2	2	2	1	3	1	2	2	0	2	1	0	0	0
Unknown	1	1	0	1	0	1	0	0	0	0	0	0	0	0	0

Column totals indicate the number of select vestrymen elected at every election, viz. in January 1822, April 1822, and in March or April 1823, 1824, 1825, 1827, 1828, 1829, 1830, 1831, 1832, 1833, 1834, 1835, 1836.

Sources: MT Minutes, under March or April of the appropriate year. No vestry was elected in 1826. Individuals may be identified from other entries in MT Minutes and from the *Merthyr Guardian* and the *Cambrian*, advertisements, marriage notices, and obituaries in particular.

A standing reform committee was set up, consisting of the iron-masters, the overseers, William Thomas the Court, D.W. James and Henry Jones. Its first report, presented on 25 March, called for the appointment of an examining accountant and the creation of new offices; it set out in detail the duties of officials and the procedure they were to follow. It was an attempt to write a new parish constitution, sponsored primarily by William Crawshay and the group led by the James family. At the same meeting, the ironmasters re-entered the Select Vestry, where they were to remain until its end and works representation on the Vestry increased sharply. There was a parallel increase in the strength of the James connection. The new overseers, who were to serve on the reform committee, were Christopher James, Richard Jenkins and two men closely associated with them, Henry Charles, a grocer and William Teague, radical keeper of the Dowlais

Table 2.3: Select Vestrymen: Frequency of Service

1822-36: Total number of vestries: 15

Elected to:	12	William Thomas, Court
		Abraham Jones, nailer*
	9	Henry Jones, draper*
	8	Joseph Coffin, tanner*
		Richard Jenkins, farmer*
		William Jones, grocer and draper*
		Benjamin Martin, agent, Penydarren
	7	D.W. James, tanner*
		Thomas Burnell, chandler
		Abraham Davies, farmer
		John Petherick, agent, Penydarren
		John Lewis, agent, Cyfarthfa
	6	Henry Charles, grocer*
		Joseph Oakey, half-pay naval captain*

1828-35: Total number of vestries: 8

Elected to:	8	Benjamin Martin, agent, Penydarren
	7	Joseph Coffin, tanner*
		D.W. James, tanner*
		Abraham Jones, nailer*
	6	William Thomas, Court
		Joseph Oakey, captain*
	5	William Crawshay, ironmaster
		Anthony Hill, ironmaster
		John Lewis, agent, Cyfarthfa
	4	Christopher James, merchant*
		W.D. Jenkins, grocer
		E.J. Hutchins, ironmaster
		George Kirkhouse, agent, Dowlais*
	3	Richard Jenkins, farmer*
		Henry Jones, draper*

---

* Indicates *Unitarian* or *kinsman/close associate of Unitarian.*

Swan. The net effect of the crisis was to install in local power the ironmasters and their men, Crawshay in particular, and a group of leading townsmen who shared a distinctive ideology. (See Table 2.3.)

For, of the effective governors of Merthyr chosen in March 1831, from a third to a half were either Unitarians themselves or close associates and kinsmen of Unitarians. Among village representatives, the proportion was nearly two-thirds. On the standing committee, the real force in parish life, every man, apart from the ironmasters and William Thomas, was a Unitarian or a Unitarian's kinsman. Three were members of the James family.

What made this conjuncture peculiarly significant was the fact that, by this time, whoever pronounced himself Unitarian pronounced himself radical. The majority were in fact doctrinaire political democrats. A handful of their young men were Chartists in the making. Their alliance with William Crawshay, himself at this time a fire-eating radical, was in no sense restricted to parish affairs. And their own local crisis had broken at the first climax of the national crisis over the Reform Bill. The conjuncture was decisive. Within two months of their radical triumph in March 1831, working people in Merthyr rose in insurrection.

Notes

1.   This estimate and those which follow on the 'province' of Merthyr are my own calculations from *Census 1831: Enumeration Abstract*.
2.   In fact, it also covered Ystrad Dyfodwg (like the Poor Law Union) and even the parish of Bedwellty in Monmouthshire. See Parliamentary Papers, Return of Courts of Requests, 17 February 1836, Accounts and Papers, 1836, xliii; I have been unable as yet to trace the records of this Court; they must be a gold-mine.
3.   Samuel Lewis, *Topographical Dictionary of Wales,* 1843.
4.   David Jones, *Before Rebecca,* ch. 4.
5.   The Census, which had to be postponed, put Merthyr's population at 22,083. In the spring, a citizen census of the town, undertaken by ten sworn and respectable men, credited Merthyr parish, within its narrowest limits, with 26,700 people and added another 2,000 from Cefn. *Cambrian,* 19 March 1831.
6.   *Cambrian,* 17 September 1831, advertisement for auction on 22 October.
7.   Crawshay Papers (NLW), many scattered references.
8.   M.J. Daunton, 'The Dowlais Iron Company in the Iron Industry 1800–1850', *Welsh History Review,* vi (1972), p. 46.
9.   On Dowlais, the voluminous Dowlais Company records in Glamorgan Record Office (henceforth GRO); and M. Elsas (ed.), *Iron in the Making: Dowlais Iron Company Letters 1782–1860* (Cardiff, 1960); K.S. Weetch, 'The Dowlais Ironworks and its Industrial Community 1760–1850', University of London M.Sc. (Econ.) thesis, 1963; for Cyfarthfa, the

Crawshay Papers, NLW, and Cyfarthfa Castle Museum and Scrapbook 1, Bridgend Police Museum.

10.   On Wharton, *Cambrian*, 30 September 1831; on the radical taverns, chs. 3 and 9 below.

11.   Robert Thompson to William Crawshay II, 19 September 1820, Box 1 (41); William Crawshay II to Morgan Walters, 10 February 1831, Letter-book 3 (79); William Crawshay II to William Crawshay I, 26 February 1828, Box 2 (404); William Crawshay II to Walter Coffin, 9 August 1830, Letter-book 3 (33); (NLW) Crawshay Papers.

12.   Charles Wilkins, *History of Merthyr Tydfil*, pp. 184-5 and passim; Dowlais Letter Books (GRO), pp. 1798 ff; *Iron in the Making*, pp. 207 ff; ch. 9 below.

13.   See below and my 'The Making of Radical Merthyr 1800–1836', *Welsh History Review*, i (1961), pp. 161-91.

14.   Samuel Lewis, *Topographical Dictionary* (1843); *Iron in the Making*, passim; Charles Wilkins, op. cit., passim; Earl of Bessborough (ed.), *Lady Charlotte Guest, extracts from her journal 1833-52* (1950); memories of Lady Charlotte (who presided over a celebrated translation of the *Mabinogion*) at least were still vivid in the Dowlais of my youth; on truck see ch. 3 below.

15.   W. Crawshay I to W. Crawshay II, 7 September, 6 December, 1831; 13, 23 May 1832; W. Routh to W. Crawshay II, 13 December 1830; Crawshay Papers (NLW), Box 2 (587, 588, 620, 622, 539).

16.   For example, W. Crawshay I to W. Crawshay II, 16 June 1825, 22 September 1832, 28 September 1832 (through Robert Moser), Crawshay Papers (NLW), Box 1 (320), Box 2 (665, 668).

17.   W. Crawshay I to W. Crawshay II, 27 August, 7 September 1831; Crawshay Papers (NLW), Box 2 (585a, 587a and b).

18.   J.P. Addis, *The Crawshay Dynasty* and J.D. Evans, 'The uncrowned iron king – the first William Crawshay', *National Library of Wales Journal* (*NLWJ*), vii (1951).

19.   W. Crawshay I to W. Crawshay II, 12 April 1826, Crawshay Papers (NLW), Box 1 (364).

20.   Account of Mr Forman's Interest, Bute Papers (CPL), XIV/8, 51.

21.   W. Crawshay II to W. Crawshay I, 26 February 1828, Crawshay Papers (NLW), Box 2 (404).

22.   Particularly useful on these subjects is M.J. Daunton, 'The Dowlais Iron Company in the Iron Industry 1800–1850', *Welsh History Review*, vi (1972).

23.   The last sentence reports a strong impression I have derived from the Dowlais and Cyfarthfa papers and the crisis of 1830-1.

24.   Ch. 9 below.

25.   W. Crawshay II to W. Crawshay I, 12 December 1822, Crawshay Papers (NLW), Box 1 (190).

26.   George Crawshay, postscript to W. Crawshay I to W. Crawshay II, 31 May 1823, Crawshay Papers (NLW), Box 1 (221 b).

27.   Return of JPs, 4 October 1831. Glamorgan Quarter Sessions (GRO), Clerk of the Peace, correspondence 1831; Bute was reluctant to make ironmasters JPs.

28.   Earl of Bessborough (ed.), *Lady Charlotte Guest, extracts from her journal 1933-52*, pp. 131-3, under 7 May 1842, conversation with Mrs Waddington, mother of the future Lady Llanover.

29.   *Hansard's Parliamentary Debates*, 3rd series, v, pp. 828-9, 840-72 (August 1831).

30.   The account of the parish which follows derives from my 'The Making

of Radical Merthyr 1800–1836', *Welsh History Review*, i (1961) based
essentially on MT Minutes; Charles Wilkins, op. cit., is rich in biography.

31.   A.H. John, *The Industrial Development of South Wales*, chs. 3 and 5,
on the labour force and technology, opens up the field.

32.   Bute Papers (CPL), VI/33, XIV/76.

33.   Robert Beaumont to Bute, estimate of cost of erecting works on
Rhymney estates, 17 May 1834, Bute Papers (CPL), XIV/85.

34.   Making Iron, report to Bute, 29 August 1829, Bute Papers (CPL), XIV/12.

35.   Cyfarthfa ledgers, Cyfarthfa Castle Museum; in 1826-7, local ore cost
13s 4d a ton, Lancashire ore (Furness) £1; ores also came from
Cumberland, Somerset and the Forest of Dean; see also Bute Papers (CPL),
XIV/21.

36.   NLW Ms. 7885c.

37.   Tom Lewis (Mab y Mynydd), *History of the Hen Dŷ Cwrdd Cefn*
(Llandysul, 1947), p. 81.

38.   Information kindly supplied me by Mrs Frances Beechey of the University
of York who, with Professor Eric Sigsworth of that university, is
attempting a family reconstitution study of The Triangle from the 1841-61
Census returns.

39.   Making Iron, 29 August 1829, Bute Papers (CPL), XIV/12.

40.   Prospectus of the proposed Plymouth, Pentrebach and Duffryn Iron
Company, London, November 1839, in my possession; copy in Bute Papers
(CPL), XIV/55.

41.   Descriptions quoted in E.J. Jones, *Some Contributions to the Economic
History of Wales* (1928), pp. 56-7.

42.   Many reports, surveys, etc., in Bute Papers (CPL), XIV; Crawshay's
memorandum of 24 December 1831 (the Santa Claus touch?) is in XIV/
56.

43.   Robert Beaumont, Calculated Expence Opening Mines on Bute (Rumney),
16 May 1834, Bute Papers (CPL), XIV/86.

44.   NLW Ms. 7885c.

45.   On the union programme, see ch. 9 below; the remainder represents a very
strong impression derived from ironmasters' correspondence; see, for
example, *Iron in the Making*.

46.   For the Philosophical Society, see ch. 3 below; Watkin George's wheel
(cast-iron, 50 feet in diameter and costing £4,000 in 1800) was remembered
and specially noted as late as 1843 in Samuel Lewis's *Topographical
Dictionary of Wales* (ii, p. 217); the engineers and inventors are duly listed
in Charles Wilkins, op. cit., and in a NUT school history of Merthyr.

47.   W. Crawshay III (reporting George Crawshay) to W. Crawshay II, 4 September 1832; W. Crawshay II to W. Crawshay I, 6 September 1832
(enclosing sworn affidavit from W. Jeffreys), Crawshays Papers (NLW),
Box 2 (655, 658); Wayne apparently got £500 a year, but he owned his
own coal levels and was virtually an entrepreneur.

48.   A.H. John, op. cit., ch. 4 and David Jones, *Before Rebecca*, chs. 3 and 4.

49.   Chs. 3 and 4 below.

50.   Robert Beaumont, Calculated Expence Opening Mines on Bute (Rumney),
16 May 1834, Bute Papers (CPL), XIV/86.

51.   It may be significant that in south Wales English in my youth, 'butty'
meant 'friend . . . mate', very much in the sense of Australian 'mateship'.

52.   MT Minutes, April 1825; C.H. James, *What I remember about Myself and
Old Merthyr* (Merthyr, 1892), pp. 8-13; E.L. Richards to Josiah John
Guest, 12 November 1831 (at the crisis of the great anti-union lockout)
. . . he called for the enrolment as Specials (as a result of an appeal from

some of them) of 100 of the 'upper class of workmen' from each works . . . 'swear they never so stoutly in their Union Lodge, will always fear the loss of the little properties they have built . . .', *Iron in the Making*, p. 218; the Ffos-y-Fran miners' petitions may also be found in the same volume, p. 42. The most celebrated political leader among the butties was, of course, Zephaniah Williams of Nant-y-Glo, Deist and a leader of the Chartist march on Newport, see David Williams, *John Frost* (reprint, 1969) and ch. 3 below.

53. Chs. 4 and 8 below.
54. W.P. Lambert, 'Drink and Work-Discipline in Industrial South Wales 1800–1870', *Welsh History Review*, vii (1975), pp. 289-306.
55. Report of Samuel Homfray of Tredegar to the *Times*, 15 November 1839, quoted in David Williams, *John Frost*, p. 118.
56. On wage rates, see A.H. John, op. cit., ch. 4, and David Jones, *Before Rebecca*, chs. 3 and 4.
57. Based on the records of the Rising; see below; comparisons with west Wales from David Williams, *The Rebecca Riots*.
58. David Jones, *Before Rebecca*, pp. 71-2.
59. A.H. John, op. cit., p. 101; M.J. Daunton, op. cit., p. 20.
60. *Merthyr Guardian*, 3 December 1836; letter dated 28 November from A Merthyr Tradesman, comparing Merthyr with Tantalus.
61. Bute Papers (CPL), XIV/43. The price was admittedly boosted by a Crawshay intervention.
62. *Census 1831: Enumeration Abstract*, Aberdare and note.
63. A.H. John, op. cit., p. 72, quoting the *Westminster Review* for 1849.
64. W.R. Lambert, op. cit.; A.H. John, op. cit., ch. 4.
65. Ch. 3 below.
66. *Merthyr Guardian*, 13 February 1836, letters to paper against the radical campaign to unseat the stipendiary; they were given editorial support. It may be noted that the payment of 'large sums' from their home parishes to immigrants in Merthyr who were sick or in distress, through the stipendiary, was normal practice.
67. The calculations which follow are based on Census of 1831: Clergymen's Returns, annual parish register lists of burials by age and sex, 1813-30 and totals of burials, baptisms and marriages 1821-30; the Welsh counties are in HO 71/120, 121; summary totals for Wales in HO 71/130 (Monmouth-shire excluded).

    These figures cannot be used to establish firm totals, of course; they are beset by the usual problems which cluster around parish registers, notably under-registration, peculiarly acute in areas where Dissent was strong. The Merthyr curate, for example, estimated unregistered baptisms at an annual 150 and burials at 100 for 1821-30; Cardiff put the figures at 50 and 25 respectively; Swansea considered its records perfect! It is impossible to be certain about such matters as consistency in variation. Nevertheless, these figures are virtually all we have for this period and, while they cannot be accorded any aldermanic weight, they do seem to me to indicate, in broad terms, some unmistakable trends. I have tried to use them, therefore, as tentative indicators, concentrating on Merthyr, and making some comparison with Swansea, Cardiff, Glamorgan generally; I have also taken some samples in Brecon and its county and in north Wales. I publish the evidence in 'Some demographic indicators in Merthyr Tydfil 1813-30', to appear in *Welsh History Review*.

68. The Merthyr figures are in HO 71/120; I see no compelling reason why the unregistered totals should have been radically different, so far as

children are concerned, in terms of 'internal' distribution; it is possible that unregistered burials of adults might increase the adult proportion and diminish the child proportion, but the omission would have to be *colossal* seriously to modify the picture.

69.   B.R. Mitchell and P. Deane, *Abstract of British Historical Statistics*, p. 36; again, obviously, no serious 'comparison' is intended, simply some tentative indication.

70.   For three year averages, I have copied the method used by John Foster in *Class Struggle and the Industrial Revolution*, pp. 93 and 301-2 (n. 52), i.e. for focus on 1823, all burials for 1822, 1823 and 1824 against all baptisms for 1822 and 1823 plus three-tenths of the 1821 baptisms and seven-tenths of the 1824 baptisms; the only serious difference from the ordinary annual averages in the five-and-under age group is a statistical quirk, but confirms the distinction between Merthyr on the one hand, Cardiff-Swansea on the other. Before civil registration and the censuses of 1841 and 1851, these 'methods' are simply threads to hang guesses on, but I think the *trends* revealed, which are very strongly scored into the record, reflect realities.

71.   David Jones, *Before Rebecca*, pp. 206-20 (1800-1), 69-85 (1816-17).

72.   *Merthyr Guardian*, 8 March 1834: letter from Christopher James on behalf of the Canal carriers, in response to complaints from a Merthyr tradesman. Freight charges, which had been 18 shillings a ton in 1806 and 16 shillings in 1812, had by the early thirties fallen to 8 shillings on flour, potatoes and other necessities (indeed to 6s 8d a ton on potatoes) and to 10 shillings on groceries and 'other valuable articles'.

73.   Empirical observation of evidence from 1800-1, 1816-17, 1829-31; David Jones, op. cit.; chs. 3, 4 and 9 below.

74.   *Merthyr Guardian*, 21 May 1836; the dogs were 'curs . . . not only of the low but of the very lowest degree of underbreeding . . .', as such, one with the inhabitants, clearly in the *Guardian*'s opinion. There were evidently some 'young ladies' in the place, however, since they were starting a subscription to pay for six musical bells for the parish church. They faced even worse hazards than the Sunday evening drunks. Thomas James, perhaps appropriately nicknamed Tom Hussey, was sent to Swansea prison on 4 August 1831 as a streaker, having run naked through Merthyr streets for a sixpenny bet. *Cambrian*, 13 August 1831.

75.   Early comments in the chapel histories mentioned in ch. 3 and in David Morgans, *Music and Musicians of Merthyr and District* (Merthyr, 1922) for immigrant-inspired chapel splits and see Charles Wilkins, op. cit., passim; for the *Jacobin* writers, see ch. 3; Wade's book was advertised in the *Cambrian*, February 1831 and evidently used during the Rising (ch. 3); the United Trades' Journal of the NAPL inferred from a speech at the Waun Fair, May 1831 and from union practice in the autumn (chs. 4 and 9); Volney's *Ruins* was taught by my great-uncle Roger Herbert, a Chartist in Nant-y-Glo (oral testimony, members of my mother's family, one of whom said, however, that she had burned 'all those old Chartist books and things'). It is possible that the journals of Richard Carlile, the *Republican* or, more likely, the *Lion* were also in circulation, as Cobbett's journals certainly were (ch. 3). Benjamin Flower's 'Jacobin' *Cambridge Intelligencer* had been present from an early date (ch. 3).

76.   For Darker, MT Minutes, 10 April 1882, 4 April, 30 October 1823, 15 April 1824, 1 April 1825, 23 November, 22 December 1826, 5 April 1827, 27 March 1828, 8 December 1830, 2 May, 23 November 1831, 23 March 1837; for the mahogany, *Merthyr Guardian*, 5 March 1834:

auction on his removal to Dowlais; for the pistols, *Merthyr Guardian*, 3 August 1833: attempted robbery by 'some of the admirers of a more equal distribution of property'. Darker was a witness at the trial of Dic Penderyn (chs. 7 and 8). He was also involved in a rather remarkable trial at the Glamorgan Assizes, spring 1836, when Esther Price, née Treharne, once an ironstacker at Dowlais, was accused of robbery at Thomas Purnell's. She, who had two children by different men, in turn accused Purnell of 'taking liberties with her'. Darker was one of the respectables (she had been in his service) who said they would not believe her on oath. Counter-oaths in her support came from Mrs Mary Williams of the Angel pub 'and others' and the judge summed up in her favour! *Merthyr Guardian*, 12 March 1836. This Purnell may have been the chandler Burnell who was also involved in the case of Dic Penderyn (ch. 8).

77.   Membership lists of Zion Baptist chapel, 1796 and 1812 in CPL Ms. 4593 and 4851; membership list of Zoar Independent chapel, July 1842 and register of baptisms 1810-39, at Zoar chapel, High Street, Merthyr (I thank the secretary and deacons of the chapel for permission to inspect).

78.   W. Taitt to T. Guest, 24 August 1803, *Iron in the Making*, p. 208.

79.   *Cambrian*, 30 July 1831, 6 August 1831: advertisements of sales and auctions.

80.   This assertion is based on the fact that these £6 cottages were the subject of endless dispute between ironmasters and the town middle class from at least 1817 onwards; the cottages were regarded as peculiarly a middle-class preserve: MT Minutes, 20 December 1816, 7 January, 30 October, 2 December 1817; for Walter Morgan's comment, *Merthyr Guardian*, 23 November 1833 and C.H. James, op. cit., pp. 8-13; for the new valuation and the near-physical struggle to which it gave rise in 1833, MT Minutes, 21 November 1833 and the vivid account in *Merthyr Guardian*, 23 November 1833. See my 'The Making of Radical Merthyr 1800–1836', *Welsh History Review*, i (1961), which prints the parish budget for 1833.

81.   Impressionistic evidence from *Merthyr Guardian* in the 1830s; for a later period, it should be possible to construct 'neighbourhood' analyses in the style of John Foster, op. cit.

82.   On the beershops, the violent controversy in the *Merthyr Guardian* during the election of December 1834/January 1835, especially the report of and comment on a political meeting of the beershop keepers, 13 December 1834, when the 'kiddlewinks' or *cwrw bachs* were specifically linked to 'the poor and our labouring brethren'. On the anti-truck act, the moaning letter from A Grocer of Blaenavon in *Merthyr Guardian*, 14 February 1835, when he complained about the hordes of people who had moved into tea, tobacco and groceries, 'of all sorts and sizes and sexes', opening shops, taverns, even Tom and Jerries (yet another name for the beershops).

83.   Examples which follow taken from releases of imprisoned debtors, Glamorgan Quarter Sessions (GRO) Minute Books, Midsummer 1831 to Epiphany 1833.

84.   Testimony of John Garnons, Inquest on Rowland Thomas, 22 June 1831, Merthyr Tydfil, in T. Thomas, coroner to Melbourne, 26 June 1831, HO 52/16.

85.   E.R. Baker, Scrapbook No. 1, Glamorgan Police Museum, Bridgend; Harold Carter, 'Phases of town growth in Wales', *The Study of Urban*

History (1968), H.J. Dyos (ed.), pp. 244 ff.

86.   For friendly societies, my 'Friendly societies in Glamorgan 1793–1832', *Bulletin of the Board of Celtic Studies* (BBCS), xviii (1959), based on a return from the Glamorgan Clerk of the Peace, October 1831, supplemented by material in the Quarter Sessions Minute Books.

87.   *Cambrian*, 17 September 1831; e.g. Merthyr had 259 houses worth over £10; Swansea, at half Merthyr's size, had 599; even Cardiff had 277; in assessed taxes, Merthyr paid £1,588 in 1830, Swansea £3,012.

88.   The Turner family, for example were Merthyr based, even if endlessly travelling to and from the Potteries; the head of the family died in Bristol in 1836, en route for Staffordshire: *Merthyr Guardian*, 24 December 1836; the *Guardian* is full of advertisements for these seasonal Bristol, London, Manchester, Staffordshire 'houses'.

89.   *Merthyr Guardian*, 19 October 1833; one of several similar advertisements during the decade, which might give some of us (including myself) pause when we talk too glibly about frontier towns and working-class camps. Fortunes could be, and were, made in Merthyr by other people than ironmasters. It is no accident that several good poets, *pennillion* singers and ballad mongers came down from north Wales; they went where the audience, *and the money,* was.

90.   Quoted by Charles Wilkins, op. cit., precisely when he was talking of the emergence of a middle class in Merthyr; see especially, pp. 112-15, 117-18, 130 ff, 250 ff.

91.   MT Minutes and correspondence over the 1831 crisis in HO 52/16.

92.   The basic biographical evidence comes from MT Minutes and Charles Wilkins, op. cit., supplemented by material in the *Merthyr Guardian* and in Tom Lewis, *History of the Hen Dŷ Cwrdd, Cefn*; some people figure in *Dictionary of Welsh Biography* and *Bywgraffiadur Cymreig*, even the *DNB*. This section of the book is an elaboration of the core section of my 'The Making of Radical Merthyr 1800–1836', *Welsh History Review*, i (1961).

93.   Charles Wilkins, op. cit., pp. 112-15, 117-18, 332, and chs. 3, 5 and 7 below.

94.   Charles Wilkins, op. cit., pp. 101 ff, 130-3, 142-3 and passim; Tom Lewis, op. cit., pp. 26-8, 148.

95.   On Meyrick, W. Crawshay I to W. Crawshay II, 10 December 1824, 3 March, 22 August, 18 September 1825, W. Crawshay II to W. Crawshay I, 26 February 1828, W. Crawshay II to T. Pierce, 29 June 1832, W. Crawshay II to Jane Tyler, 26 July 1833, in Crawshay Papers (NLW), Box 1 (278, 302, 324, 330), Box 2 (404), Letter-book 3 (218, 298); Charles Wilkins, op. cit., pp. 163, 333-6; see chs. 3, 7, 8 and 10 below and my 'The Making of Radical Merthyr'.

96.   On the James family in general, see *Dictionary of Welsh Biography*, under Charles Herbert and Sir William Milburne James and *DNB* for the latter; C.H. James, op. cit., Charles Wilkins, op. cit., pp. 251-2.

97.   *Merthyr Guardian*, 8 March 1834: letter from C. James.

98.   Christopher James to W. Crawshay II, 19 July, Job James to W. Crawshay II, 30 December 1830, W. Crawshay II to George Thomas, 2 April, W. Crawshay II to D. James, 15, 16 July 1831, W. Crawshay II to Christopher James, 1 November, W. Crawshay II to W.M. James, 15 November 1833, in Crawshay Papers (NLW), Box 2 (521, 544), Letter-book 3 (97, 116, 123, 321, 324 — where the calendar reference reads Jones for James); Charles Wilkins, op. cit., pp. 215-52.

99.   *Merthyr Guardian*, 7 September 1833; advertisement; C.H. James, op.

cit., p. 20.

100. For these relationships, a rich and richly sulphurous source is the *Merthyr Guardian* during 1833 and 1834, when the Tory newspaper whipped itself into a fury over the looming threat of a Jamesian Corporation, reaching a climax during the election of December 1834—January 1835; Tom Lewis, op. cit., pp. 26-8, 43, 60-1, 143-5, 231; MT Minutes, Charles Wilkins, op. cit., C.H. James, op. cit., passim.

101. Charles Herbert James, *What I remember about Myself and Old Merthyr* (Merthyr, 1892: the text was actually written in 1881).

102. Petherick's son claimed to be the discoverer of the source of the White Nile; Jenkins's son ended as vicar of Aberdare; *Bywgraffiadur* and *DWB* under John David Jenkins; Charles Wilkins, op. cit., pp. 252, 253, 260-5, 294.

103. See David Williams James writing as a professional liberal politician to Lady Charlotte Guest in 1852 in *Iron in the Making*, pp. 229-30, and my 'The Making of Radical Merthyr 1800—1836'; chs. 3, 8 and 10 below.

104. On Perkins, C.H. James, op. cit., pp. 36-9; for Morgan Williams's nickname, *Merthyr Guardian*, 13 and 20 December 1834; Charles Wilkins, op. cit., pp. 288, 307-9; *Bywgraffiadur* and *DWB* under David John and Morgan Williams and see David Williams, 'Chartism in Wales' in Asa Briggs (ed.), *Chartist Studies* (1959); David Jones, 'Chartism in Welsh communities', *Welsh History Review*, vi (1973); Angela V. John, 'The Chartist endurance: Industrial South Wales 1840-68', *Morgannwg*, xv (1971).

105. The process is described in some detail in my 'The Making of Radical Merthyr 1800—1836'; MT Minutes are the prime source; indeed only their 'discovery' made such a study at all possible.

106. MT Minutes, 1811-12, 1815-17, 20 December 1816, 7 January, 30 October, 2 December 1817.

107. The parish minutes assume what became standard form on 17 April 1820, with copy of notice of meeting, systematic lay-out of minutes, chairman's signature. For the rather amusing creation of the select vestry, see MT Minutes 11 and 25 January 1822.

108. By an act of 1818, voters even in open vestry who were in arrears with their rates lost the right to vote, while persons rated at more than £50 gained an additional vote for every additional £25 up to a maximum of six. An act of 1819 made the alternative to a select vestry the surrender of the management of poor relief to magistrates. For an interesting study of the effect or non-effect of all this on a town dominated by a working class, see John Foster, op. cit., pp. 57 ff. In terms of vestry control there is not the remotest parallel in Merthyr, but in other aspects of working-class life and an increase in effectiveness, one can detect similar 'rhythms', despite the great differences; see below.

109. MT Minutes 1829-31 and those for 25 March 1831 in particular.

3 CRISIS

'Proclamation Extraordinary! REFORM!! At Last Obtained!!!

For the WORKING CLASSES!!!!

ran an announcement in the *Merthyr Guardian* in April 1836. A.M. Hughes, of the Plymouth, Duffryn and Pentrebach shops announced his return from tour with an extensive stock of linens and woollens, teas from 2s 2d a pound, Turkey coffee at 2s 11d. 'Setting competition aside,' he offered them 'for the benefit of the working classes.' A little earlier, the *Guardian* itself had commented on the new public gas light in the Merthyr streets: 'It fizzed and bounced and frothed like as many tailors at a political meeting.'[1]

If a shopkeeper could build Robert Owen and the National Union of the Working Classes into an advertisement and a Tory editor's scorn for petty-bourgeois radicalism into a casual metaphor, then clearly, *political* lightning had penetrated Merthyr soil.

The years from 1829 were years of an unprecedentedly high and sustained political temper among working people.[2] When the crumbling of the English *Ancien Regime*, announced by Catholic Emancipation and the repeal of the Test Act, coincided with the first recognisable cyclical crisis of an industrial order, it was perhaps to be expected that the *Reform* crisis of 1829-34 should acquire a near-European intensity, with its first mass syndicalist movement inspired by Owenite socialism, its popular and virulent anti-clericalism, its conflict between populist democrats who were self-consciously 'working class' and populist democrats, marshalled by Francis Place and the Birmingham Political Union, who were supporters of 'an alliance of the industrious against a parasite aristocracy', its explosion of popular journalism and cultivation of novel techniques of mass propaganda: Chartism was a natural projection. That national crisis assumed divergent forms in localities of differing historical experience. In Merthyr Tydfil, the impact of a complex national crisis on local tensions produced a revolutionary insurrection of the working class and brought a pre-history to an end.

'All our parishioners are Presbyterians professing themselves Arminian', reported the gloomy curate of Merthyr in 1771; he was echoed by his colleague in Aberdare.[3] The Unitarian caucus which took local power in Merthyr in the 1830s represented the third generation of a tradition; the only village tradition which survived the transition to industrial society. It had its roots in that rich and literate Glamorgan of the late eighteenth century, one of the nurseries of the democratic ideology in the Atlantic world; the Glamorgan of Dr Richard Price of Bridgend, defender of the new American republic (invited over to be its financial adviser by Congress) and sacrificial scapegoat of Edmund Burke; of David Williams of Caerphilly, friend of the Girondins and author of a Deist liturgy which won praise from Voltaire and Rousseau; of Morgan John Rhys of Llanfabon, publisher of the first political periodical in the Welsh language (in 1793) and founder of a free Cambria in the New World; of Iolo Morganwg, Edward Williams of Llancarfan, reviver of the eisteddfod, inventor of a Gorsedd of druidical, *Jacobin* and masonic Bards, co-founder of the Welsh Unitarian Association at Cefn in 1803.[4]

Merthyr village in the 1790s was a stronghold of *Jacobinism*. In the early days of its growth, only two men took an English newspaper, Guest the new manager of Dowlais and Rhys Howell Rhys the cele-brated stone-mason astronomer of Vaynor, whom bishops used to consult; the paper was Benjamin Flower's 'Jacobinical' *Cambridge Intelligencer*.[5] 'Sturdy old Republicans', the men of Merthyr welcomed John Thelwall; driven into 'exile' at Llys-Wen in Breconshire, the most celebrated English *Jacobin* lecturer wrote poems in the *Vale of Vulcan* and was present when Merthyr's workers rose in a classic grain action during the terrible subsistence crises of 1800-1.[6] Merthyr's Independent minister had written a poem denouncing the defector Dumouriez as a traitor to the French Revolution to Morgan John Rhys's journal and in 1807, sixty of its Inhabitants, artisans and workers formed the Cyfarthfa Philosophical Society at the Dynevor Arms in the George-town which a Crawshay had built. They subscribed a guinea each to buy instruments and they used to read Tom Paine, Voltaire, Volney, d'Holbach in secret on Aberdare Mountain, even as the Merthyr devout had their boot-nails stamped in a TP to trample Infidel Paine under foot.[7] Iolo Morganwg spent much of his old age in the town; when his son Taliesin moved in to open his school, he found most of his kindred spirits passionate supporters of Napoleon.[8] They tried to launch a petition for parliamentary reform in 1815, but Crawshay quashed it; they made the village a stronghold of Queen Caroline.[9] They created a climate of opinion and turned Georgetown and the district facing Aberdare and Cefn and Penderyn into a miniature *Faubourg St Antoine* of the spirit. This was the geographical heartland of *Jacobinism*, of the

Freemasons, of the eisteddfod, revived at the Patriot Inn (the very name a political programme) during the 1820s; this was Morgan Williams's country, the headquarters of Chartism.[10]

The root, as in so many localities, was the minority and liberal Dissent (often a shield for Freethought) of that vital third quarter of the eighteenth century which witnessed the birth of the democratic ideology, in struggle against the oncoming tide of 'vital religion' in Methodism and the 'methodised' majority of Dissent.[11] The original Dissenting nucleus at Cwm-Glo on Aberdare Mountain which dated from the days of Cromwell and Vavasor Powell and which in longevity could rival Llanfaches, mother church of Welsh Dissent, broke up under the liberal Arminian tide in the middle of the eighteenth century; the Arminians, moving swiftly through Presbyterianism towards Unitarianism, set up causes at Cefn and at Aberdare.[12] By 1749 the Calvinist rump had moved to Ynysgau in the heart of the village by the Taff. Troubled by further 'Arminian' dispute there and riveted into orthodoxy by the influx from west Wales, Ynysgau, the mother-chapel of Merthyr, witnessed a further secession in 1812 when the immigrant Christopher James licensed a meeting place for the dissidents. By 1821 they had a chapel in the heart of the town in Twyn-yr-odyn, the settlement clustered around the original road east.

The three Unitarian congregations were small, not more than 50 members each. They were, however, distinctive. Mathematics, astronomy, applied science and music of quality were a passion. Benjamin Saunders, master-moulder at Cyfarthfa, built his own planetarium and made a quadrant, a thermometer and a water-gauge; Morgan Davies, a self-educated collier, expounded Priestley's chemistry to his apprentices. While Jones of Baptist Ebenezer was being hooted in the streets for trying to introduce hymns into chapel, Cefn had its own string orchestra.[13]

There were two great schoolmasters in the Unitarian tradition, Owen Evans at Cefn and Dr David Rees, the first pastor at Twyn; the latter's successor, David John a blacksmith mathematician, was a father of Chartists. And at Aberdare during the critical years from 1811 to 1833 and a frequent preacher in Merthyr, was the celebrated *Old Jack* Thomas Evans, *Tomos Glyn Cothi*, jailed once in Carmarthen for singing *Jacobin* songs, a republican who stuck to his guns throughout the repression — *Priestley Bach*, succeeded by John Jones who was a social democrat before the term had been invented.

Moreover, it was precisely along this Unitarian network stretching into the fat and comfortable congregations of that Vale of Glamorgan which had supported the brief and radical General Baptists as they had done minority radicals among Methodists and minority Deists, overt and covert, that came a major flow of significant immigrants, headed by the James family. The roll-call of Merthyr Unitarians is a register of men who shaped the town: the Jameses, William Williams the famous clockmaker, William Williams of Heolgerrig, father of Chartist Morgan, Joseph Oakey, half-pay master in the Navy, Mathew Wayne, Richard Jenkins, Joseph Coffin the tanner, descended from the family of Richard Price; even Josiah John Guest's nurse, Mary Aberteifi, was a member at Cefn; so were the Thomases of Waunwyllt. Nor were they by any means exclusively middle or lower-middle class; the trustees of Cefn numbered two miners, a coker, a mason, a machine-weigher and three weavers from Vaynor.[14]

By the 1830s most of them were fairly orthodox petty-bourgeois democrats like David William James, believers in universal suffrage and the ballot, Free Trade opponents of the Corn Laws and the 'taxes on knowledge', stout spokesmen for the shopocracy and chilly towards parish expenditure and trade unions. On their right hovered Iolo's son, Taliesin Williams, a pained but candid friend of the Anglican church, admirer of Josiah John Guest and advocate of the abolition of primogeniture and the restoration of the *cyfran* (gavelkind) of Hywel Dda.[15] Their attitude was not uniform. How could it be? 'They do love to be dissenters' as one curate keened.[16] On their left a newer breed was emerging, Morgan Williams, the Johns, friends and tutors to workers not half as respectable as Taliesin's masters of levels. Taliesin himself, for that matter, translated the 'brotherhood' of the slogan: 'no strength but brotherhood', which his father had wished on an ancient sage, as the 'combination' of the trade unions.

What was in effect trade unionism had appeared in Monmouthshire by 1830. Trade union lodges which were branches of a national organisation and were organised in sophisticated style appeared in both Merthyr and Monmouthshire only in the aftermath of the Merthyr Rising of 1831. In the peculiar form which the historical conjuncture of that year took in Merthyr, the Unitarian democracy of the town, stemming from the *Jacobin* tradition, served as the crucial *area of translation*.

It is difficult to trace direct connections between that tradition and the forms of working-class activism to which the region had become accustomed.[17] There is no evidence of any forms of organisation approximating to trade union practices before 1810, though this does not mean that they did not exist. In the massive grain actions of 1800-1, there certainly was organisation of some kind. Generally speaking, combinations were formed as a period of expansion gave way to depression and attempts to lower wages. Their effectiveness was limited but should not be under-estimated. Puddlers are known to have taken the lead, at least from 1810. The monthly contract, with its long notice, gave workers opportunity to organise. Outside the pub meeting of a trade, the mass meeting on the hills was the usual method by which puddlers, say, could rope in mass support from colliers and miners; the marching gang tried to spread any strike action which might be taken. It was these massive and visible public actions which caught the eye of observers, but in fact there is evidence of quite frequent, if sporadic, organisation to confront shifts in wages and conditions. Some practices grew into something of a 'tradition': mass meetings at some such place as the Waun Fair above Dowlais to mobilise Monmouthshire men; Cefn figured as a natural rally point quite early. Delegates and deputations moving from works to works were common. The striking feature of these movements, however, was that they were all *defensive* and short-lived. It is difficult to trace any continuity of men or ideas beyond the obvious practices that experience had taught.

There were some spectacular outbreaks which earned the region its exaggerated reputation for violence. It is immediately obvious that there was a qualitative change around 1820.[18] Nearly all the troubles before that date, although wage struggles were involved, were in the classic pre-industrial tradition of 'the moral economy', the price-fixing grain or food action or the 'collective bargaining by riot' which characterised the eighteenth century in Britain and France. In 1800 the *Inhabitants of the Ironworks* imposed price control by force on Merthyr village, attacking truck shops, levying money from the inhabitants and demanding the traditional beer. Repressed by dragoons, the movement threatened a renewal in the spring of 1801, this time with political overtones. Two hitherto respectable ironworkers were hanged.

There was a spate of troubles, both through organisation and through riot, over the whole tense period after 1810, when the garrison was established at Brecon, but the most spectacular movement of all and possibly the most widespread and massive single action to convulse south Wales in the nineteenth century, was the great strike of 1816. Once again, the origin was 'classic', rising food prices coinciding with a heavy reduction in wages. Beginning in Merthyr, the strike, spread by marching gangs throughout Monmouthshire, proved persistent, well organised and violent. Efforts to close down works by force precipitated

riots; at Dowlais, Guest and some friends opened fire on the crowds; Crawshay and other ironmasters went into hiding. Troops suppressed the riots, but there were attacks on soldiers, attempts to suborn them and threats of a march under arms on the barracks at Brecon (which also became 'traditional'). Once again, a political bite registered in the final stages. Such actions were certainly violent and threatening, but they were selective and fairly well controlled and once again the objectives were defensive and limited, except for a minority of militants who were carried into nation-wide insurrectionary movements.[19]

Men clearly drew on their experiences of industry and on the traditions they brought with them from the villages, particularly in Cardiganshire and south-west Wales, where during these years public discipline and social control virtually broke down, removing whole rural areas and the town of Carmarthen from established order.[20] The *ceffyl pren*, the wooden cock-horse and mock village trial used to enforce communal discipline outside the law, was common and these rural influences became very visible in the marked divergence between Merthyr and Monmouthshire which characterised the 1820s.[21] Monmouthshire was growing in population at an even faster rate, particularly around the southerly sale-coal villages which lacked even such structure as Merthyr possessed. From 1820-22, colliers and miners began to take initiatives of their own and seem to have attained a more coherent and systematic form of organisation. In Monmouthshire, however, these were the years above all of the *Scotch Cattle*.[22] The Cattle were a highly organised secret society which might have originated in the Luddite troubles of the late war years (Ned Ludd was credited with their formation). They enforced solidarity through terror, by means of a developed system of warning notes, night meetings, signals by horn. Blacklegs and other offenders were visited by a Herd dressed in animal clothes, women's dresses, turn-coats, led by a horned Bull. Property was attacked, the window-sashes of the overly ambitious being a favourite target; there was some physical assault. The movement persisted into the 1830s.

It bore all the stigmata of a characteristically *rural* secret society similar to the Terryalts of Ireland. There was a *Scotch Law* and an alleged code of honour. Authority found it virtually impossible to get convictions; it was Luddite in its impenetrable secrecy. Its leader was said to be one Lolly, clearly a derivative of the Welsh *Lol* – lord of misrule, charivari, Punch.[23] The Bull talked of his 9,000 faithful children. He was the *Rebecca* of the Monmouth coalfield. Indeed, it is highly probable that the *ceffyl pren* secret societies of rebellious Cardiganshire were one root of the movement. What has to be stressed is that it was highly organised, effective, based largely on the colliery villages of the southern coalfield, which were to be strongholds of physical-force Chartism. During 1830, there seem to have been quasi-political overtones to the movement, even as fairly effective and consistent forms of trade unionism become visible in the county. In 1832 the Bull's warning notes carried the slogan *Reform.*[24]

Very striking, however, is the singular *absence* of the Cattle from the Merthyr district. Some forms of Cattle action, of course, were common to all industrial struggles, but there is no trace whatever of any Scotch Cattle organisation in Merthyr, just as there was to be little physical-force Chartism. One explanation no doubt was the general prosperity of Merthyr during the 1820s, another was the relative weakness of truck and the relative availability of money, the visibly improved supply position during the 1820s. Colliers were less numerous and were not segregated.

Another explanation, however, may well be the very presence of democratic groups and a tradition of democratic thinking and agitation. During the grain troubles of 1800, magistrates certainly suspected *Jacobinism*; Thelwall was present. The troubles coincided with a national campaign of petitioning sponsored by the revived *Jacobins*. Similarly in the spring of 1801 a broadsheet distributed at Merthyr clearly linked the area with the insurrectionary movements of the United Britons and others which were to culminate in the abortive Despard conspiracy.[25] A similar pattern was visible in 1816-17. Local insurrectionary strikes and food actions were followed by the sending down of Cobbett's papers, a speech of Henry Hunt in Welsh translation, the appearance of other radical tracts and in the aftermath of 1817 by a pamphlet which linked local militants with national insurrectionary movements of which the Pentridge Rising was a symptom.[26]

During these times of trouble, then, Merthyr workers *were* in fact influenced by a radicalism of which the local *Jacobins* could have been a channel and their movements generally ended in an epilogue during which some militants at least were caught up in insurrectionary plans national in scope. There followed, however, the long 'silence' of the 1820s. There is no evidence that Merthyr shared in the enterprises which characterised many nuclei of militant workers in that 'decade of silent insurrection', though there *is* evidence that there was some qualitative change in the nature of living in the town during these years. What distinguished the crisis which opened in 1829 however was the fact that the area (and clearly Monmouthshire) was drenched in radical propaganda and political debate *before* any local trouble erupted. Whatever the mental equipment of Merthyr workers, in 1830 in particular, they were abruptly politicised by exposure to the full blast of a national social and political crisis of major significance.

The degree of previous politicisation can be underestimated. The very instruments of informal social control on which authority relied in a normally rowdy community may well have proved double-edged. Friendly societies were generally favoured by ironmasters and magistrates as agents of respectability, and with reason. The major national societies were represented in the town.[27] The funeral of an Oddfellow in Merthyr in 1832 was attended by 170 brethren from four lodges 'excellent and chaste' in their deportment. So were those small-scale local organisations which, under an act of 1793, were given the protection of the law if they registered their rules with Quarter Sessions and which in 1829 were subjected to the scrutiny of a registering barrister. Many such products of popular initiative refused to submit to this process, but a survey of 1831 lists 32 Merthyr clubs which had registered since 1793, second to Swansea's 47, of a Glamorgan total of 181. The majority were clearly respectable. They were strongly supported by the newly-formed Society for the Improvement of the Working Population in the County of Glamorgan, Josiah John Guest and the Tory *Merthyr Guardian*. William Lewis, stock-taker to the Plymouth works, was secretary to most of them. They were an orthodox lot in title: Sons of Vulcan, True Blue, Ancient Britons (probably a Welsh-language society); both Dowlais and Cyfarthfa made regular contributions to their Firemen's Benefit. Some were regional: a Pembrokeshire society kept forming and re-forming. Few carried any trade name, though there were variants on Gentlemen, Tradesmen and Others. While there was evidently some confusion and breakdown, most seem to have been effective. The Old Star held at the Crown, oldest society in Merthyr, was paying five shillings a week at the age of 70 and one miner was drawing £13 a year, figures which compare with those of London clubs.

Closer examination, however, suggests that some of them may not have been as innocuous as they look. The Vulcan at the Swan Inn, Dowlais, excluded Oddfellows and was run by William Teague who was a political radical. The Jameses and their friends were prominent in the friendly society world.[28] Bursts of society formation, like bursts of trade combination, seem to have occurred at the point where a boom broke. There were such flurries in 1826 and in 1830, when several women's societies were formed and the radical Patriot produced a couple. The most striking was in 1807, when radicalism revived nationally. This was the very year of the formation of the Philosophical Society at the Dynevor Arms. Simultaneously eight friendly societies were formed and most of them were located at the Iron Bridge in the same area. The clientele of the Hirwaun Castle registered themselves as Hand-in-Hand a few months before Hirwaun puddlers made their village a storm-centre of the Merthyr Rising. The new colliers' union of 1831, after all, called itself the Friendly Society of Coal Mining.

More complex and difficult to locate within the contemporary discussion of the social and political role of Dissent, Methodism and popular culture is the intensely Nonconformist and intensely Welsh character of that populist Merthyr which was articulate.[29]

The town was Dissenter from birth. The Church had been crippled in the seventeenth century and even after its major revival in the 1830s, remained very much a minority force. During these frontier years, it was negligible. In a parish which had already fallen to Independency and its Unitarian offshoot, no fewer than 23 Dissenting meeting places in Merthyr and Dowlais were registered with the bishop's court alone between 1792 and 1836 and the real number was probably double that, even as congregations constantly split, formed and re-formed. A fastidious traveller in the early 1800s asserted that 'almost all the exclusively Welsh sects among the lower orders of the people have . . . degenerated into habits of the most pitiable lunacy . . . The various subdivisions of methodists, jumpers and I know not what, who meet in fields and houses, prove how low fanaticism may degrade human reason . . .' The justice who hanged the two workmen in 1801 blamed their revolt on this 'fanaticism'.[30]

In denominational terms, the traveller was very wrong. A striking feature of Merthyr (and of much of south Wales) was the relative weakness of the essentially Welsh Calvinistic Methodists. Indeed, the Wesleyans, introduced first to serve some Yorkshiremen whom Homfray imported, offered them a serious challenge. Both, however, were completely overshadowed by Independents and Baptists who built some of the greatest chapels in Wales, Zoar for the former, Zion for the latter, clusters of lesser but still vigorous sisters, a whole nest of singing birds in Dowlais.

It is true, however, that many of these strongholds of the Old Dissent were in fact heavily influenced by the enthusiastic, evangelical, 'methodised' modes of the revival, imported above all by immigrants from west Wales. Chapels split over the issue. This evangelicalism, often but not invariably accompanied by a narrow doctrinal and social sectarianism, was essentially populist in its inward self. It certainly bore familiar stigmata. Ministers' memoirs, which were growing into a distinct genre of Welsh writing, modelled on Bunyan, invariably have the hero struggling with the hordes of Satan, suffering a relapse, fighting through again to grace. This feeling is often reflected in random quotation from ordinary members of congregations reported in chapel histories. Quite clearly, many chapel people felt themselves an embattled minority, struggling out of the sinful world of 'the roughs' towards grace and respectability. Some congregations, at least, could be quite repulsively narrow. Moses Davies, a 'father' of chapel choral music in Merthyr, was repeatedly haled before the deacons of Pontmorlais Calvinistic Methodist chapel, once for taking his children for a walk on Sunday after service, once for going on a picnic to Vaynor. In the same chapel, 48 youngsters stopped wearing their hair in the correct Puritan fashion, brushed down over the forehead and ears, and adopted the *QP style*, brushing it back from the forehead; they were promptly summoned before the Big Seat. Nor was this inquisitorial censoriousness restricted to Calvinistic Methodists. Zoar Independent once lined up no fewer than 98 members in the aisles for wearing Temperance medals and succumbing to vanity (though one may suspect that the motives here were not entirely doctrinal). What has also to be noted, however, is that those who were subjected to discipline promptly rejected it; they seceded, the 48 from Pontmorlais presumably to form the QP Methodists.[31]

Equally as real as the respectability and the sectarianism, both without doubt vehicles for 'middle-class values', was the extraordinary democratic energy of the chapels, with their lively and strong Sunday schools, their eisteddfodau, their opening to literary and musical ability, their self-management. In these years, the Independents and Baptists were recovering their radical tradition, if they had ever lost it. David Saunders the Baptist was the son of a *Jacobin* minister and an ardent radical. Samuel Evans of Zoar was described in the customary terms by his biographer: 'If he lets down his hand, Amalek prevails . . .'; he was also a confirmed political democrat, a competent Welsh poet like David Saunders, a pillar of the eisteddfod and the Welsh revival and he taught a generation of Chartists.

The surge of Dissenting enterprise in these years, which was particularly strong in Dowlais, was *both* a separatist drive for respectability, objectively a vehicle for absorption and subjection, *and* a mass campaign for democratic education, objectively a vehicle for populist radicalism. Edward Thompson's brilliant characterisation of the permanent tension within Dissent, between rendering unto Caesar and going out with God's sword to build a New Jerusalem, is reflected in the early history of practically every chapel in Merthyr, most of which were strongly working-class from their first days. The one possible exception is precisely Pontmorlais, which was to be so ardent against Chartism that it got a grant from Josiah John Guest. An Independent minister in Dowlais, however, he had to summon before him to explain his presence at a trade union meeting in 1831.[32] In many ways, the really decisive shift in Merthyr does not occur until the Temperance movement. It began in 1837, very appropriately in a mass demonstration, with banners and marching hymns, from the chapels of Dowlais down into Satan's Strongholds in Merthyr, rallying God's fifth column at Pontmorlais on the way. In 1848 the great series of Temperance Eisteddfodau were launched and the eisteddfod was wrenched out of the public house. This shift, however, was itself perhaps the most visible popular symptom of the major process of re-stabilisation and re-alignment which characterised the 1840s. In these earlier years, no simple categorisation will work.

It is not even very helpful to apply a more characteristically Welsh distinction between *pobl y capel* and *pobl y tafarn* (chapel people and tavern people). Since Welsh nationality formed in the nineteenth century along a religious and language line which was also a class line, it considered itself classless. The distinction by 'pub or chapel people' is therefore both a useful tool of analysis of Welsh society in its characteristic modes of self-expression and itself a vehicle of illusion. In Merthyr, at least before the impact of Temperance, this tool breaks in your hand. Most of the first congregations in fact met in pubs. Zoar itself began in 1794 in the Long Room of the Crown. And while chapel opinion was certainly hostile to the mode of living of the *cwrw bachs*, it was simply not possible to construct a separate world. The vivid and rich cultural life of popular Merthyr in the 1820s of necessity focused on the pub, as did so much else . . .

Mae uffern yn y tafarn, medda'nhw . . . Hell is in the Tavern, so they say . . . Mae'r nefoedd yn y seiat, medda'nhw . . . Heaven is in the Chapel, so they say . . . Ond mae'r seiat yn y tafarn, medda'nhw . . . But the Chapel's in the Tavern . . .[33]

The chapel world which was beginning to rib and shape an important sector of Merthyr's working class had to confront not only the realities of an industrial society with all its grotesque inequalities and exploitation and a political society which was hostile; it had to operate in the face of a numerically weak but culturally and politically influential Unitarian inheritor of an older tradition of Dissent and an essentially un-evangelical popular culture which in the Merthyr area was rich and strong both in its native practitioners and in the immigrants it drew in.[34]

The ballad singers were the most immediate and direct agents of that culture, composing their own verses more often than they sang old ones, to any tune that took their fancy, Dafydd Bowen and Hugh Bach from Dowlais, the Blind Boy of Penydarren, John Jones who *lived* on the Morlais Tip. Street and fair men they were, 'patterers'. The most famous was *Dic Dywyll*, Dic Dark, blind Richard Williams, originally from north Wales. He lived at Riverside, a *China* man. *Bardd Gwagedd* he was called, Bard of Vanity, directing his shafts against Temperance, the Work-house, the police. He wrote one on the Merthyr Rising and the hanging of Dic Penderyn. He was said, single-handed, to have kept the Workhouse out of Merthyr for years . . .

> Bydd hwch y Crown yn dyrnu haidd
> A Benny'r gwaydd yn geffyl
> Cyn delo'r Workhouse byth i ben
> I fod ym Merthyr Tydfil.

(Basically untranslatable but goes with a lilt in Welsh. Roughly: The Crown's old sow will a barley-thresher be, and Benny the Weaver a horse, before they'll ever get their Workhouse up, in the town of Merthyr Tydfil.)

Selling his sheets at a penny a time on Saturday nights, he was said to make £3 a week which, if true, would have given him a higher income than a furnace manager.[35]

There were singers of a more traditional kind, experts at *pennillion*, the complex, subtle and strict form, and practitioners of the more free 'folk-songs' particularly of Glamorgan, Gwent and Dyfed: William Davies, *Grawerth*, popular in the clubs, is said to have been the first to sing a non-*pennillion* solo in an eisteddfod. William Morgan, *Billy Full Moon*,[36] was so good that Lady Charlotte Guest snapped him up, but he was a prickly man and went back to the clubs. His son, Dai o'r Nant, became a celebrated miners' agent in Aberdare. The best *pennillion* singers came from Dowlais, Thomas Jenkins and John Roberts, *Shoni o'r North*, though they were challenged by a skilled shingler called *Twmmi Hamburg*. Harpists, often blind, were common, though they were not so good, often mixing north and south Wales styles to the detriment of both. The Harri family of Vaynor, weaver trustees of Cefn Unitarian, were harpists, so were some of Morgan Williams's family. The best were a celebrated family called Frost, long established in Twyn-yr-odyn.

This 'traditional' group, when they were not packing into the *Coach Mawr* for the great eisteddfodau in Abergavenny,[37] moved easily, unlike the ballad singers, not only from eisteddfod to pub but from chapel to chapel. For the other populist thrust into music and poetry was the choral music of the chapels. Essentially a rival to the tavern song, its leaders had nevertheless to follow the same routes of exploration, striving for technical improvement, authenticity, a popular excellence. For while the people had a wealth of superb lyric poetry to draw on, notably that of the Methodist William Williams Pantycelyn, their stock of music and of skill was meagre. Though it was Temperance which gave birth to the really great choirs, the foundations of Merthyr's pre-eminence both in this field and in that of music instruction (it became one of the three recognised centres of this kind of excellence in Wales) were laid by working men in these frontier years. Moses Davies, for example, was a plasterer who often went on tramp through England.[38] He ran the Pontmorlais daughter cause in Dowlais, where he first encountered staff notation. He taught the principles of music by the Bell and Lancaster system, using large printed cards. He wrote two dozen mediocre hymns, 'too frequent consecutive fifths and eighths' said his son, a 'sculptor', but anticipated the democratisation of music in Tonic Solfa by introducing the 'movable doh' which apparently enthused the Dowlais choirs. The famous Rosser Beynon was more radical.[39] His family came to Merthyr from Neath in 1815; three of his brothers were literary lions at the local eisteddfod. He himself was a Dowlais collier from the age of eight. An Independent, he conducted the Zoar choir and published *Telyn Seion*, a collection of hymns which drew quite freely on any number of tunes then current. He raided the tavern world for his melodies. One of his hymns, angrily denounced by his rival music conductors, a mason and a cobbler, as *Jac-y-Jumper*, had women running from Zoar as the Devil entered; he was rumoured to have set a hymn to the English comic song *Tom and Jerry*! In his old age, however, he was reckoned to have ranked Merthyr with Llanidloes and Bethesda as a music centre; he initiated the school of musicians which was to make Dowlais celebrated, established a choral tradition. It was perhaps inevitable that both Rosser Beynon and Moses Davies were swept up by Temperance. Rosser had his first lessons, however, from one of the finest musical scholars in south Wales at this time, and he was a Unitarian.

It was perhaps inevitable that the Unitarians took the lead in launching the eisteddfod. Iolo Morganwg had been one of the pioneers in its 'revival'; he dominated one in Cefn in 1816. It was in 1820 that an eisteddfod was first recorded in Merthyr, but the real beginning of the campaign was St David's Day 1821 when the *Cymreigyddion* society was formed. The original *Cymreigyddion* had been decidedly *Jacobin* and it was appropriately in the Patriot Inn that they met every month.[40] Branches were soon flourishing in other pubs, the Bell, the Swan, the George, the Duffryn, the Glove and Shears. They were followed by *Cymmrodorion* in 1827, *Gomerians* in 1828; Dowlais produced its own *Brythoniaid* in 1834. Essentially literary, in both languages, these active and popular societies, each of which tended to hold three eisteddfodau a year, created a lively coterie of local poets and essayists in Merthyr, out of which world came Thomas Stephens who was to write the first critical history of Welsh literature. Thomas Price the historian, *Carnhuanawc*, was a frequent visitor. From 1824 in their Chair Eisteddfod at the Boot, they tapped a wider field, publishing their prize peoms. They were respectable, marching to church on St David's Day and attracting the attention of Lady Charlotte Guest. In the score or so eisteddfodau on record in the 1820s, however, they attracted a wider range of support, working-class harpists like the celebrated David Davies of Gelligaer, local poets like William Moses, *Gwilym Tew o Lan Daf*, a lock-keeper on the Canal and *Cawr Cynon*, William Evans, a poor miner from the Iron Bridge,[41] chapel poets like David Saunders the Baptist. Iolo's son Taliesin Williams presided; the James's cousin Henry Jones was prominent, so was Walter Morgan Georgetown and members of Morgan Williams's family. A bilingual clerisy of local intellectuals formed around the eisteddfod, notably at the Lamb Inn near *China*, the Boot and the White Horse (most innkeepers were themselves poets, notably the main sponsor, David Jones a watchmaker).[42] This intelligentsia, in the next decade, when it was not Chartist itself, was deeply sympathetic to Chartism.

The growth of music within the eisteddfod was the work of another, and remarkable, member of the Unitarian fraternity, the man who taught Rosser Beynon, John Thomas, *Ieuan Ddu*.[43] A skilled apprentice painter in Carmarthenshire, his hopes of becoming an artist were frustrated by the death of a patron uncle. He taught school in Carmarthen, moved to Merthyr in 1830 and returned after a brief stay in Monmouthshire, to take over from Taliesin. He was a genuine scholar and a man of sensibility and skill. He is generally credited with the foundation of the most rigorous choral tradition in Merthyr.[44] He was a Greek enthusiast, a folklorist, a poet (he translated Pope's Essay on Man into Welsh). He published a deal, notably some satires on the eisteddfod and *The Cambrian Minstrel*, a rather purist collection of folksongs supplemented by fifty of his own composing.

In one sense, the drive of John Thomas cut clean through the competing and overlapping worlds of populist cultural effort; in another, he brought them together. No great chapel man himself, he nevertheless taught music in a Baptist chapel and was a teacher of teachers. He bears a heavy historical responsibility. He is said to have been the first man to introduce Handel's *Messiah* into Wales.[45]

There was another, equally significant side, to John Thomas. The man he worked for as a clerk in Monmouthshire was Zephaniah Williams, butty and mineral agent who kept a pub in Nant-y-Glo in which there was a picture of the Crucifixion with the enigmatic caption: 'This is the man who stole the ass'. Zephaniah Williams was a notorious Deist. In 1830, he launched a Political Union in Tredegar; in 1831 it was almost certainly he who formed the Humanists/ *Dynolwyr* of Nant-y-Glo. Zephaniah was to be one of the three leaders of the Chartist march on Newport in 1839 and was transported to Australia for his pains (where he made a fortune).[46]

It was John Thomas who launched a wholly new eisteddfod society in Merthyr in 1831: the Free Enquirers, who held at least four major eisteddfodau at the Swan between 1831 and 1834. Free Enquirers or in its Greek form *Zetetics* (John Thomas knew his Greeks) was the title adopted by those freethinking and republican groups who were affiliated during the 1820s to the journals of Richard Carlile and the republican headquarters of the Rotunda in London. We do not know whether John Thomas or Zephaniah Williams was in direct contact with the Rotunda, whether Carlile's journals were some of the 'dangerous trash' which magistrates said flooded into Merthyr from 1830, but their meetings were devoted wholly to political themes. Theirs was the only eisteddfod in which Dic Dywyll is known to have won a prize; their chief literary prize-winner carried the *Jacobin* pen-name *Horne Tooke*.[47] Moreover, in 1834, John Thomas, with Morgan Williams, became the editor of Wales's first working-class newspaper, the *Gweithiwr*/The Workman; dedicated to the cause of Owenite

socialism. Thomas was responsible for the Welsh section. In [
number of the paper which survives, that section is devoted to the
Tolpuddle Martyrs.[48]

Out of the bubbling, contradictory world of the Welsh popular
culture of Merthyr Tydfil, John Thomas emerges as a central and
formative personality. It seems peculiarly apposite that the man
who introduced the *Messiah* into Wales also edited its first working-
class newspaper and was a Unitarian democrat from Carmarthen who
settled behind the Lamb Inn near Georgetown.

Unitarians could provide a political education of a different kind.
The president of the Court of Requests was one of theirs: Joseph
Coffin, who became the most hated man in Merthyr during 1831 was
also a political democrat!

That court had been operating since 1809. It had operated through
the terrible years of 1813 and 1816. No-one rebelled against it then.
What made it so intolerable in 1831? By that date, in large part because
of the Unitarians' own enterprise, working men in Merthyr had been
drenched in argument and propaganda over political rights and obliga-
tions, the nature of the just society, the real nature of the Whigs'
Reform Bill, the labour theory of value.

For a striking feature of the Reform crisis, and of 1830 in particular,
was the relatively sudden rise of movements of plebeian self-assertion
which aspired to be national. Established radical spokesmen of national
reputation, Henry Hunt and above all William Cobbett, at the peak of
his popularity, were both challenged and reinforced by relatively new
movements. The Political Unions which found a headquarters in
Birmingham, the kind of radicals who rallied around Francis Place, the
tougher and self-consciously 'working-class' militants who formed the
National Union of the Working Classes, the free-thinking republicans
who organised themselves around Richard Carlile's journals and shared
the Rotunda meeting hall, hub of London populism, all sent out their
missionaries and their literature. An even more remarkable movement
in the North, associated with John Doherty and operating at first
in virtual independence of the political campaigns, was the National
Association for the Protection of Labour, *The Union* to the Home
Office. Actively and successfully organising trade union federations, it
was committed to an Owenite co-operative socialism and the labour
theory of value. It was in this world, not that of the political nation,
that the French Revolution of July 1830 registered. John Betts, a
tough NAPL organiser in the North and Midlands, used to preface
meetings called to form a trade union with the raising of the tricolour.

At such meetings, old men stood up to recall how they had buried the *Rights of Man* during the war and to assert that the French 1830 had proved Tom Paine right after all.[49]

One major force within the NAPL was a new colliers' union with a highly sophisticated technique. From its headquarters in Bolton, it penetrated north Wales late in 1830. The response was millenarian; its progress was punctuated by riot. By the spring of 1831, it had affiliated to the NAPL and sent its Preacher back into north-east Wales. This was a young, fair, rather effeminate but eloquent man who had been destined for the Church and who called himself William Twiss (though according to the Bolton magistrates the real Twiss had left for America). According to a Ruabon correspondent who wrote anonymously to the Home Office on 29 June 1831, Twiss and his Welsh interpreters raised thousands of pounds and moved on to Merthyr, reaching the town *before* the outbreak of the Rising.[50] Magistrates in later recollections talked of delegates from Birmingham and Wigan in Merthyr, of Cobbett's papers and other radical tracts flooding in. The peculiar intensity of the crisis in Merthyr was precisely the product of this unprecedented impact of national forces on a local situation which was already tense.

The first and most immediate tensions were those of a severe economic depression, which deepened from 1829 right through and beyond 1832 as the market price of bar iron fell to an appalling £5 a ton.[51] Magistrates after the Rising professed themselves bewildered. Ironmasters and townsmen generally recognised that wages were lower than they had been and that there was widespread distress. They asserted, however, that many men were still in work and earning good pay; this was particularly true of the militants who actually led the Rising; many were earning 20 shillings a week, one Dowlais man had £9 on him. Evan Thomas, Chairman of the Glamorgan magistrates, said that the situation was much less severe than he had known it in 1816; in particular far fewer people were applying for relief and being shipped off to their native parishes.[52]

These judgements are half-truths. What is true is that the Rising broke out before the depression had reached its nadir; indeed the revolt and the terrible struggle over trade unions which ensued may well have aggravated it; by the end of 1832 certainly misery was rampant over the whole of south Wales. The depression passed through a number of phases. During 1829, all the ironworks went through an agonising process of cutting down wage rates while trying to maintain production and fulfil contracts. It was in the midst of this process that they appointed their stipendiary magistrate. The wage reductions had been worked through by the September of 1829, and as their effect registered, there was an increase in debt and probably in unemployment and short time. The stipendiary's court was almost certainly used to hold the labour force together through the slump.[53]

So was the Court of Requests, and even while Crawshay and Hill launched a campaign against the truck system now on the increase in rival Dowlais and Penydarren, the Court itself seems to have operated something akin to a form of 'public truck'. This complex situation became serious during 1830. Wage cuts proved insufficient. All the firms except Cyfarthfa started to reduce the make, even while struggling to meet orders in the pipe-line. By the end of 1830, a quarter of the furnaces in the town had shut down and even Crawshay had been forced to close one.[54] This process coincided with the parish reforms which probably tightened up the operation of the Court of Requests. The credit which the Court had extended to many working-class families now caused a profound social crisis. Shopkeepers themselves were getting desperate and there were waves of executions under writ, distraints and seizures of the property of the poor. Furniture and watches went first, to be followed by essentials like beds.[55] A whole sector of the working population was oppressed, while those at work on reduced wages lived in a dreadful uncertainty. Moreover this was happening at a time when the town was drenched in political propaganda and debate focusing on the rights, the dignity the worth of working men and controversy over the labour theory of value. The president of the debtors' court, Joseph Coffin, was himself one of the Unitarian fraternity. It would have been difficult to miss the contradiction.

During 1830 there were tides of working-class complaints against the Court of Requests and its ruthless bailiffs. One couple visited an old woman, Margaret Rees, who was ill in bed. They dragged the bed out from under her and she died on straw. Even the Swansea *Cambrian* talked of 'fiends in human form'. The two bailiffs were actually prosecuted in January 1831 but escaped on a legal technicality. Such cases, and there were several, were evidently the tip of an iceberg.[56]

Indeed, both debtors' and stipendiary's courts may have launched something of a law and order campaign. The *Cambrian* during 1830 reported a number of spectacular captures and trials of 'well-known' criminals, mainly petty traders and receivers. A family called Badger was taken, so was Elizabeth Morgan whom the *Cambrian* called 'the notorious Betsy Paul'.[57] Even as official pressure was plunging families into debt slavery and diminishing the marginal and extra-legal hinterland in which some relief might have been found, shopkeepers like the crooked wheelwright Thomas Lewis by Jackson's Bridge were exploiting the situation by advancing petty loans and capitalising on the Court of Requests distraints which followed and constables themselves were working rackets by blackmailing the beershops or *cwrw bachs* and other plebeian traders.[58] A great wave of hatred was building up of the Court, the bailiffs and of shopkeepers generally, in circumstances of high political tension, itself generated in large part by fervid political democrats within the shopocracy. Before 1830 was out, some ironmasters were talking of getting rid of the Court,[59] as the notion of *Reform* began to acquire a specific content among working people whom debt, industrial insecurity and legal repression were driving into an awareness of themselves *as a class* marked off from the rest of society.

Once again, as in his political radicalism, many workers could think of William Crawshay as an ally. The slump was made worse by the divergence between Crawshay, and to a lesser extent Guest, and the other ironmasters. William Crawshay I in London, who resolutely held out for the traditional Crawshay policy of stockpiling, refused to reduce the make. The son could not sustain this entirely; he was forced to blow out one furnace. Dowlais however had shut down no fewer than three, Penydarren and Plymouth two each.[60] Crawshay certainly stockpiled. Having sent 25,000 tons down the canal in 1829, over 5,000 of them from Hirwaun, he cut down to 21,000 in 1830. In the same period Dowlais increased its shipments by nearly 5,000 tons but this may have been to meet orders.[61] By March 1831 Crawshay reported that he had no less than 50,000 tons of iron in stock.[62]

The most serious problem, however, was ironstone. Coal seems to have been rather more flexible. It is noteworthy that shipments of sale coal down the Glamorgan canal, never a major trade, increased from 60,000 to over 102,000 tons between 1829 and 1830.[63] Crawshay had been the last to reduce his ironstone miners' wages during 1829. At the rates he had been paying he claimed his men were not working hard. In all probability they were responding naturally to the crisis by sharing out work and running a 'stint'. He pushed through a cut by the end of 1829. He asserted that production of ironstone then increased so sharply that he was building up surplus stocks at over 1,500 tons a month. In fact, his claim that his miners' wages were still higher than his neighbours' and that men were 'flocking' to his works was almost certainly true in essentials. By 1831 Fothergill in Aberdare was publicly

saying that Crawshay miners' wages were 'too high' and by as much
as 5 shillings a week; Penydarren works could not get any miners and
was running out of stock by the end of the month.[64] Ruinous import
was the consequence. So, in a situation of shrinking production and
growing unemployment and misery, the ironstone sector was in a
tortured state of unbalance.

Wages were certainly lower than they had been while the price of
bread and other foodstuffs rose. Later in 1831, it was reported that
puddlers and other skilled men were earning from 18 to 25 shillings
a week, counted 'good'; these were lower than the rates of 1816. It may
be inferred from Crawshay's figures that his ironstone miners were
getting around 12 to 14 shillings. *Lewsyn yr Heliwr*, the major
personality of the Rising, claimed that as a miner for Penydarren he
was getting only 8 shillings.[65] Men at work, whether their pay was
good or not, lived in permanent uncertainty; all around they could see
the bailiffs of the Court with their carts. Margins of extra-legal relief
were eroding under the pressure of tribunals which on the one hand
were operating to keep workers in the town and on the other were
serving the equally threatened interests of the town middle class. Truck
was mushrooming at Penydarren and Dowlais, where Guest, while
reducing his labour force, was also active in his customary charity
and doing his best to shield his men. Through this situation throbbed
the beat of political campaigns in which middle-class and lower-middle-
class democrats found themselves moving into alliance with that
William Crawshay who was apparently turning his works into an
over-manned sanctuary for ironstone miners. No wonder the harassed
and increasingly irritable master of Cyfarthfa hurled himself angrily
into the management of a town which was coming apart at the seams.

The year 1830 opened with the explosive re-entry of Crawshay into
parish affairs. Painful wage-reductions effected, ironmasters were
confronted with the still bleaker prospect of shut-down. The immediate
crisis, however, was parochial. The parish was £660 in the red, accounts
a shambles. On 18 January, Crawshay chaired a protest meeting, writing
out the minutes in his own hand. The vestry clerk was dismissed, a
new scale of church fees summarily rejected. The rating of the ironworks was re-organised and a testy run of meetings ensued, as parish
accounts were transferred to the Dowlais Company bank and debts
were cleared off. Joseph Coffin, the Unitarian tanner, already president
of the Court of Requests, became churchwarden and resumed his
familiar role as iron man. By April, Plymouth works had blown out
two furnaces and the poor rate had begun its climb from 3s 6d

towards the unprecedented 8 shillings it reached in the following year.[66]

This was the moment when E.J. Littleton of Staffordshire introduced his bill against truck into the Commons. Truck had engulfed Monmouthshire and was once more engrossing Dowlais and Penydarren. Crawshay and Anthony Hill mobilised their workers against this 'unfair competition'; they got up petitions and the Crawshay London House set to work in the capital. An alliance began to shape between Crawshay and the Unitarian democrats, in whose hatred of truck ideals and interests fused. While Hume rallied to the defence of Dowlais in the Commons, Littleton drew heavily on the Merthyr material sent him by the radicals; Job James transmitted medical evidence. William Milburne James, then at Lincoln's Inn and Edward Lewis Richards at Gray's, gave the MP their professional assistance.[67]

In June, Richards made a play for support through the friendly *Cambrian*. Attributing much of the tumult and famine of the past in south Wales to the truckmasters and warning that the slump threatened a recurrence, he denounced masters who built chapels for their workmen while denying them freedom. This scarcely veiled attack on Guest he accompanied with praise for 'honourable' ironmasters. He addressed himself specifically to that 'useful and industrious class of society, the Retail Tradesmen, who are fast giving way to the towering monopoly of the Truck Capitalist'.[68]

There was little immediate response in a summer made wretched by the close-down of three furnaces at Dowlais and another at Penydarren. The parish reform was breaking down. During the summer, Merthyr actually ran out of funds for the poor and there were emergency levies.[69] As more and more workers, their families strangled by debt, raised their voices against the Court of Requests and its bailiffs, worried ironmasters talked of drafting a parliamentary bill to get rid of it. Crawshay saw his ironstone stocks rising towards 50,000 tons and Hirwaun slithering deeper and deeper into the red, while Penydarren and Aberdare were running down before the month's end from shortages.[70] It must have been about this time that the tide of radical propaganda came flooding into Merthyr, for when the truck campaign was resumed in the autumn, it exploded into a violent and intensely political conflict in the columns of the *Cambrian*.[71]

The campaign opened on 18 September with a vitriolic attack on the 'truck-doctors' of Merthyr by XYZ, almost certainly William Milburne James. His uncle Job, at that moment busily distributing Cobbett's *Twopenny Trash* and other radical tracts, was the only doctor not connected with the works. He was supported by Edward Richards, writing as E. A major antagonist was unmistakably William Thomas the Court, a leading Merthyr Tory. Back came counter-blasts from ABC and ET; the controversy, which raged to the end of the year, immediately nose-dived into scurrility, charges of quackery and the threat of a libel action from Job James.

More significant is its tone and cross-reference. Rhymney, Bute, Dowlais, Penydarren and Plymouth, thundered XYZ, were served by one surgeon, a 'medical pluralist' with a bunch of half-baked apprentices. At Dowlais alone, 4,000 workers with their families, perhaps 15,000 people, lived at his mercy, fifteen miles away from the other extremity of his 'practice'. Had readers seen Josiah John Guest's speech on the evils of monopoly to the electors of Honiton? Back home, Job's son Christopher was denouncing the Dowlais master as an enemy of the working man.[72] W.M. James's attack was nakedly populist; he was defending those people who were treated like cattle 'because they are poor and only workmen'.

ABC, scarcely bothering to conceal his target, denounced Job James as a thick-skull who had sneaked a quack licence only through war service; he dwelt with loving care on his alleged malpractices. What sort of a doctor sold books and ballads? Who but readers of Paine, Hunt and Cobbett would think of going to him? Cobbett is a 'great political writer', retorted Richards; that the people of Merthyr were readers of him and Hunt demonstrated 'their well-known liberality of sentiment, talent, information . . . quickness of thought, soundness of judgement and superior cultivation of general principle . . .' ABC snapped back at this 'mean catering for the applause of the rabble by adulation of an unprincipled demagogue'. To charges of having inherited his practice, he replied, 'I, too, am a genealogist'; he knew what interests, what incomes from certain tenements were at stake. He would not be silenced by 'the diction and frothy declamation of a spouting club . . .'

This clearly indicates that the Political Union of Merthyr, singled out in governmental analyses of the Rising and certainly still operative at the election of 1835, must have been formed by the autumn of 1830; it strongly suggests that it appealed to working men from the beginning. Another flourished briefly at Aberdare. Early in 1831, the Free Enquirers started their political eisteddfodau in Merthyr, probably in alliance with Zephaniah Williams's Humanists/*Dynolwyr* in Nant-y-Glo and his Political Union in Tredegar, possibly in affiliation to Richard Carlile's journals and the Rotunda radicals in London. After the Rising, Colonel Brotherton spoke of Cobbett's *Twopenny Trash* reaching a monthly circulation of about a hundred; Job James was a devoted admirer of the radical. Brotherton talked of violent newspapers, 'much dangerous trash' disseminated among workers and 'eagerly read and listened to'. 'One would suppose that these cyclopes were little interested in politics, had they not given evident and violent signs to the contrary . . .' They had been encouraged by some of their masters; they had their Agitators, too, 'the chief of whom, of a better class, has lately been attempting a branch union political society amongst them . . .'[73]

There may have been several sources of propaganda and leadership. The NUWC was sending out delegates and there was talk later of an 'agitator' having come from Birmingham, headquarters of the more moderate Political Union movement. It seems certain, however, that the major channel was the Merthyr Union and its Unitarian radical core. About this time, young Morgan Williams started to appear in vestry; it was probably now that the future Chartist leader served his political apprenticeship.[74]

The occasion for the organisation of the Union was probably the mounting excitement of the late summer and autumn of 1830. One king succeeded another, an election cut the government's majority; in the November, Wellington fell to let in Whigs pledged to Reform and to unleash the popular movements. The activities of the James connection and the radicals through the autumn and over the winter bear all the hallmarks of an organised campaign. It is intriguing, too, to hear Brotherton talk of ironmasters encouraging their workers. For the campaign brought the radicals into alignment, slowly and hesitatingly, with a politically mobile Guest and, more visibly and dramatically, with William Crawshay himself.

The renewed drive against truck rallied Cyfarthfa once more; its London agents were devoting much of their time to Littleton's bill.[75] The Merthyr radicals launched a series of public demonstrations. On 13 November, they called a meeting in the parish church, with the curate's consent. Chaired by William James, it denounced the truck system and sponsored a petition to parliament which collected over 5,000 signatures in a matter of days. In December, when the bill had its second reading, the petitions of Crawshay, Hill, workmen and townspeople were presented together. Guest countered with an independent ballot at Dowlais which recorded a majority in favour of truck. The alliance between Crawshay and the radicals held firm to the end. The bill finally became law in the autumn of 1831. The Crawshay

London agent, while gloating over Guest's discomfiture, repeatedly stressed the need for follow-up action. As if in response, a town meeting chaired by Christopher James in January 1832 established a *Society for the Abolition of the Truck System* and raised over £200 the same night.

The Merthyr radicals kept up the pressure. Before November 1830 was out, they organised a petition against the Corn Laws which attracted over 9,000 signatures.[76] Here, William Crawshay would not follow them. While a supporter of universal suffrage and the ballot and a radical reform of the Church, he was a maverick among the ironmasters in that he defended the Corn Laws — 'he that knocks down corn knocks down iron'.[77] Josiah John Guest, however, was in agreement. At this time, Guest was clearly moving on the new seats which Glamorgan could expect from the Reform Bill.[78] Early in 1831, he spoke up strongly in the Commons in favour of the representation of the county's industrial region. He rejected universal suffrage and disliked the idea of the ballot. On the other hand he was at one with the radicals in his stand for free trade and his opposition to monopoly and the 'taxes on knowledge'. He was to vote for the Reform Bill and to lose his seat in Honiton as a result. He offered himself as a candidate for the second Glamorgan seat in May 1831, as soon as the election was over. He repeated his offer in June, when the second Reform Bill was published, but withdrew it temporarily when the bill was rejected by the Lords. When he was finally chosen as Merthyr's MP he gave up his truck shop.

This progression seems to have registered on political minds, not least that of the Marquess of Bute, over the winter of 1830-31. About the time of the Free Trade petition, Edward Richards's scarcely veiled attacks on the Dowlais master in the *Cambrian* came to an end, with hints of a 'reformation of character' on the part of hitherto misguided men. In the December of 1830 Guest's own nephew, E.L. Hutchins, rallied to the next of the radicals' campaigns. For on 23 December, two days after Newport had started the ball rolling in Wales, they called a meeting to the Bush Inn in support of parliamentary reform.

Over 800 people turned up and 'never more respectable' according to one observer. The Bush could not hold them. They asked W.D. Jenkins a churchwarden for permission to use the parish church again; an Anglican, he refused. His fellow-churchwarden, however, was the Unitarian Joseph Coffin and he 'saw no harm'. They swept into the church, brushing aside the clerk and the cleaners who were in for Christmas. The chief constable took the chair; Christopher James,

THE POLYTECHNIC OF WALES
LIBRARY
TREFOREST

Henry Jones, William Perkins, Hutchins, Dr Rees former Unitarian minister, David John the current pastor and Samuel Evans, minister of Zoar, all spoke. The petition they drafted called for the dismissal of placemen from the Commons, annual parliaments, abolition of rotten boroughs, representation of large towns, the ballot, and the vote for all who contributed, directly or indirectly, to national or local taxation. This was probably the programme which could secure maximum unity and it was in fact pretty radical. In the House, Croker the Tory took it as text for a sermon on the contradiction between the Whigs and their radical supporters in the country.

The meeting, however, broke up in confusion. Henry Jones decided not to speak on the need for reform in church as well as state, in deference to the locale. No such scruples deterred David John the Unitarian minister, a blacksmith and a blunt man. Evidently well-versed in John Wade's *Black Book* of the Reformers and probably in the more anti-clerical tracts which were beginning to circulate, he burst into a fiery denunciation of bishops who starved their clergy, proclaimed that the poor were living on carrion and preached revolution. Walter Morgan walked out in protest; Oakey the naval captain, William Jones and Perkins's own partner were incensed. Anglicans, however, were maddened beyond words. The dean of Llandaff, Bruce's brother, considered taking action against Coffin and David John, the latter for 'brawling', but afraid of strengthening the *Socinians* still further, contented himself with an apology from Coffin in the papers.[79]

William Crawshay, however, would not have been too disturbed, and it was over this winter that a working alliance, conscious or unconscious, was formed between him and these radicals who were now clearly flexing their muscles. During November and December they virtually packed parish meetings, in what looks very like a caucus. In November, a dismal vestry which wrote off £200 of rate arrears and confirmed the exemption of no fewer than eight furnaces now shut down, was monopolised by them. In December, the new beershop keepers brought a protest against constables who were harassing and blackmailing them. These new *cwrw bachs* were radical in temper. The Unitarians promptly sent the constables for trial at Quarter Sessions. By February 1831 they were threatening the new vestry clerk with dismissal as the poor rate climbed over 5 shillings and although Anthony Hill chaired the critical reform meeting in March, it was clearly a joint effort by Crawshay and the Jameses which imposed a new parish constitution and installed the Unitarians in local power alongside the ironmasters.[80]

Their local victory came at a singularly apt moment, for on 1 March 1831 (St David's Day, as no reformer in Wales failed to remark) the Reform Bill was published. On 9 March, the James brothers, Taliesin Williams, Richards and Hutchins called a meeting to express support for the Bill even though it fell far short of their hopes. They ran a private census of the town, which put its population at over 27,000 and collected data on housing. They prepared a petition for Guest to submit and on 8 April, called a more general meeting, attended by the iron-masters and the Tories Bruce and William Thomas as well as radicals. They had clearly decided to concentrate on getting a seat for Merthyr as a minimum programme.[81]

Several of the radicals were not present at these meetings; possibly they disapproved of the compromise. Certainly there was the possibility of a take-over by the ironmasters, by Guest in particular. It was Alder-man Thompson who led their deputation to the Chancellor Althorp. It proved fruitless: ministers had decided to retain the Welsh contribu-tory borough system and saw no reason to give Merthyr special treatment. Thompson, however, was still hopeful, but he was frightened by Guest's progress. He warned Crawshay that the Dowlais master was on the alert and would probably *start* for the *county* . . . (as he did). He suspected Guest of collusion with Bute in a share-out of seats and wanted the other ironmasters to combine against him. If anything, however, the Marquess and the Tories were even more disconcerted and began to conceive that hostility towards Guest which was to characterise their actions over the next few years. These divisions were lost in the sudden surge of excitement when the Bill (for which Guest duly voted) was halted and the country went to the polls, but the Dowlais master's shift towards his critics may well have helped to propel Crawshay into a renewed surge of truculent radicalism.[82]

With the election, the Reform crisis mounted to its first climax. All over the country, newly-stirring working-class groups moved into loud and sometimes violent action; so did Dissenters. Tricolours flew. William Crawshay went about vehemently declaring his readiness to die in the street fighting for the Bill. On 27 April, Christopher James and his son David William, Taliesin ab Iolo and William Perkins (perhaps significantly in view of his contact with working men) harangued a large meeting at the Bush. It was incumbent upon Merthyr as principal town of the Principality to take the lead in rescuing the land from thraldom and misery. In this high rhetoric, they promised to carry Reform voters to the poll in Glamorgan, Carmarthen and Brecon! With the more radical democrats moving into action once more, they translated this into a decision to work against Colonel Wood the Breconshire member who had voted for a spoiling amendment. The decision had local relevance, for several Merthyr men had votes in Brecon.

Yet more decisive was the action of William Crawshay. Sharing this crusading temper to the full, he pledged his support for the Brecon venture. He went further. He rallied his own workmen and helped them to draft a petition for parliamentary reform; he committed 'Cyfarthfa' to the cause. Knowing the spirit of 'his miners', he turned them loose.[83]

It was this decision which unleashed the pent-up power of working-class anger. The impact was immediate and dramatic and triggered an instant collapse of public order.

A mass meeting of workers was held on 2 May at Riverside, hard by the radical quarter and what was becoming *China*. This is the first recorded political initiative by working men. As usual, we know nothing about it, except that people thought that it was dominated by ironstone miners. It seems to have decided to enforce an illumination on the town the next day in honour of Reform. There were demonstrations, the burning of effigies, argument and fist fights in the street.[84]

On 9 May crowds paraded the town, burning effigies as they had done in Brecon. They singled out three Merthyr Tories known to be supporters of Wood in Brecon, so devoted were they to himself and to Reform, Crawshay said. Some 5,000 men massed outside the house of James Stephens, a well known trader and vestryman. Thomas Llewellyn, a Cyfarthfa miner, made a speech. Every one who was an enemy to Reform should be hanged on a gallows and he would be the man to do it, free of charge. They menaced Stephens, abused William Meyrick, attacked the Court of William Thomas. In the evening they went back to Stephens's house, stoned it and broke the windows.

Incensed, Stephens summoned the magistrate, J.B. Bruce, another Tory. Llewellyn and another man were taken on 10 May and hauled before Bruce in the Bush Inn, where the magistrate committed them to prison, since they lacked the money for bail. Three thousand people stormed to the Bush and rescued the prisoners. They forced Bruce to give them up and compelled Stephens to sign a quittance. Thomas Llewellyn they carried through the town in triumph, with the quittance stuck in his cap.[85]

At that point, authority lost its grip on Merthyr. Crowds marched nightly, burning effigies and demonstrating for Reform. It was about this time that a traveller, whose words were remembered three weeks later, reported that 'something extraordinary' was going to happen in Merthyr.[86] Bruce, appalled at the turbulence in the streets, did not dare send for soldiers, because the trouble was 'political', he explained to Bute — and probably because Crawshay might have become embroiled. He was evidently in total ignorance about the men's intentions. What happened for certain is that they summoned another mass meeting to Bryn Gwyn near Aberdare, probably for Sunday, 15 May. There, they took the fateful decision to call the men of Monmouthshire to a great rally above Dowlais on 30 May, to coincide with the annual Waun Fair.[87] They clearly meant to do *something*.

As soon as these workers enter the scene, every other performer shrinks. All the noisy, arguing figures and groups in the foreground suddenly disappear. A kind of silence falls, tense with foreboding. It is perfectly clear, from magistrates' correspondence and from later comments, that no-one had any idea of what the workers meant to *do*.

It was nearly a week before J.B. Bruce learned of the plan to hold a mass rally at the Waun Fair. He thought it had been engineered in Monmouthshire, where colliers were in struggle. His immediate reaction was to write urgent letters to Crawshay and Anthony Hill, asking them to forbid their men to attend.[88] He did not see fit to write such letters to Guest in Dowlais or to the managers of Penydarren. Crawshay's Cyfarthfa and Hill's Plymouth, of course, had made the running in the campaign against truck; William the Volcanic had gone much further. The mass meeting of 2 May at Riverside evidently marks the beginning of an emancipation of workers' action from outside control and manipulation. No less evidently, Bruce's letters indicate that their emancipation was incomplete. They had begun to act only when they got a 'warrant' from their 'betters'.

Here, too, they encountered disillusion. For, on 28 March, long before the 2 May meeting, William Crawshay had given his ironstone miners notice of a wage cut.[89]

After the Rising, practically everybody blamed it on this action. The Cyfarthfa ironmaster published a special pamphlet in self-defence. In it, he stressed the intimacy which had always characterised the relations between himself and 'his miners'. He had supported their campaign for political rights; he had helped to draft their petition (which was to be presented to the Waun Fair assembly). He had kept his works going, kept up the wages of his miners. Workers had 'flocked' to his plant leaving men like Fothergill and Thompson stranded.

His argument carries weight; he had in fact done all this. What had changed were 'his miners'. By March 1831, he claimed, and probably with justice, that his 'surplus' stocks of ironstone had reached 78,000 tons. He *had* to do something. He was careful. He introduced a sliding scale of cuts. On 28 March he informed his miners that, on some veins of ironstone, he would reduce by 1d a ton when 'little was got', rising to 7d a ton when 'the quantities raised by the men shewed that better work existed'. He calculated that on much work, there would be no reduction at all and that, on average, the cut would amount to no more than 3d a ton; that is, 3d in every 6 or 7 shillings or an average of no more than 1d a day for 'each man working'. He further asserted that no one had challenged this. No one had asked him for an increase in wages. When the reduction was effected and the notice ran out on 25 April, no-one had complained.

After the Rising, however, Robert Beaumont, mineral agent to the Marquess of Bute, said that the workers had been very disturbed by this cut. Probably, each in his own way, both men were correct.[90] What Crawshay seems to have been blind to was the *psychological* effect of his 'trifling' reduction. His action in March/April and his responses during May must have seemed to many workers a kind of *betrayal*. A few years later, they were to wave a weathercock in his face.

Nor was this all. After the notice expired on 25 April, said Crawshay, no-one left his works. Where could they have gone? To Fothergill's, at 5 shillings a week less? Workers, led by the miners, held their political meetings on 2 and 15 May. On 23 May, those miners received their new and lower pay. The very next day, Crawshay dismissed 84 puddlers.[91]

We do not know why they were dismissed or what works they served. There had clearly been some trouble; the elder Crawshay in London had urged his son to stand firm against 'trouble-makers'. Hirwaun was certainly a problem. It was running at a crippling loss; there was trouble over the shop there which the company had leased out. Perhaps the nervous puddlers were Hirwaun men. We do not know. What is clear is that workers, after the 23-4 May, must have realised that whatever 'warrant' they got from superiors, they could depend on no-one but themselves. Were they to get democracy from the radical Joseph Coffin whose bailiffs were dragging beds out from under sick old women? Were they to get security, dignity, the proper hire of labour from the democrat William Crawshay? In the last days of May, 'his miners' learned from William Crawshay that, if they wanted *Reform*, they had to get it themselves.

When Bruce heard of the dismissal of the puddlers, he was appalled.

This was six days before the rally at the Waun. Crawshay was away in Carleon, Guest in London. He wrote an anxious letter to Bute on 25 May. He was very uneasy over the Waun meeting; he was not clear whether it was a political meeting or a wages movement inspired by the Monmouthshire men. Should he alert the garrison at Brecon? Clearly, if the motives were political, the last thing he wanted was a Peterloo. Bute replied that there was no call for a preliminary notice to Brecon. He had, however, sent a 'secret order' to Major Rickards of the East Glamorgan Yeomanry to stand by and he passed the correspondence to the Home Office.[92]

The faces of authority at the windows of the Castle Inn were therefore anxious as they watched, on Monday, 30 May, while hundreds of men, behind a great white banner inscribed *Reform*, marched through Merthyr and headed out for the Waun.[93]

Notes

1. *Merthyr Guardian*, 23 April, 23 January 1836.
2. My mind has been formed by the Lancashire letters in HO 40/27, 52/13; the *United Trades Co-operative Journal*, 1830; the *Republican* and the *Lion; Report of the Proceedings of a Delegate Meeting of the Operative Spinners of England, Ireland and Scotland, Isle of Man, Ramsay* (Manchester, 1829); *Poor Man's Guardian*, 1831; G.D.H. Cole, *Attempts at General Union* (1953) set in the context of Edward Thompson, *The Making of the English Working Class* (Pelican, 1968) and John Foster, *Class Struggle and the Industrial Revolution*. I have touched on some aspects of the theme in my *Rowland Detrosier, a working-class infidel 1800-34* (Borthwick, York, 1965) and 'Merthyr 1831: Lord Melbourne and the trade unions', *Llafur* (Welsh Labour History Society), i (1972), pp. 3-15.
3. Llandaff Diocesan Records (NLW) Queries and Answers, LL/QA/4.
4. This is a wide field which I have partly explored in *Frontier of Illusion* and will be examining in depth in the forthcoming text on the *Jacobins*. I have touched on aspects of it in 'South Wales radicalism: the first phase', Stewart Williams (ed.), *Glamorgan Historian*, ii (1965); 'John Evans's mission to the Madogwys 1792-99', *Bulletin of the Board of Celtic Studies*, to be published 1978; 'Morgan John Rhees and his Beula', *Welsh History Review*, iii (1967) and 'Welsh Indians: the Madoc legend and the first Welsh radicalism', *History Workshop*, i (1976). The quickest entry without Welsh is Prys Morgan, *Iolo Morganwg* (Cardiff, 1975) and the work of Professor David Williams; bibliography in the special number of *Welsh History Review* in his honour, 1967.
5. Charles Wilkins, *History of Merthyr Tydfil*, pp. 142-3, 307-9; Rhys Howell Rhys, a member of the Philosophical Society, is said to have 'made a duck which did everything but quack'. On Flower and his paper, Edward P. Thompson, *The Making of the English Working Class*, pp. 166, 197, 519, 798; Unitarianism was one connection.
6. J.J. Evans, *Dylanwad y Chwyldro Ffrengig ar Lenyddiaeth Cymru*

(Liverpool, 1928), p. 96; John Thelwall, *Poems written chiefly in retirement* (1801); David Jones, *Before Rebecca*, pp. 28, 208; Thelwall was in touch with Iolo Morganwg and spoke to groups of workers during the troubles of September 1800.

7.   Tom Lewis, *History of the Hen Dŷ Cwrdd Cefn*, pp. 137-8; Charles Wilkins, op. cit., pp. 66-8, 307-9.

8.   *Merthyr Guardian*, 3 January 1835: letter from Taliesin of 19 December 1834, with recollections; Tom Lewis, op. cit.

9.   MT Minutes, 3, 16 October 1815; the movers were Henry Jones, Richard Jenkins and William Williams the clockmaker; the last two, with whom Iolo Morganwg used to lodge, were specifically called 'republicans': J.J. Evans, op. cit., p. 96.

10. This remarkable geographical continuity in radical tradition was maintained even as Georgetown was engulfed in *China*; respectable Heolgerrig nearby became a stronghold of Unitarians grouped around Evan Evans a coalowner of Six Bells, who used to drive to Cefn in a brougham: Tom Lewis, op. cit., p. 148.

11. Critical to the understanding of this conflict is R.T. Jenkins, 'William Richards o Lynn', *Trafodion Cymdeithas Hanes Bedyddwyr Cymru* (Welsh Baptist Historical Society) 1930; '. . . some of the Baptists deny the divinity of our Saviour' said the Methodist William Williams during the former's crisis of explosive growth; J.J. Evans, *Morgan John Rhys a'i amserau* (University of Wales, Cardiff, 1935), p. 143. On the essential background, Bernard Bailyn, *Ideological Origins of the American Revolution* (Harvard, 1967) and Caroline Robbins, *The Eighteenth Century Commonwealthman* (Harvard, 1959); the American dimension was central to the first Welsh radicalism and nationalism.

12. I do not intend here a full analysis of Merthyr Dissent; there is material in the standard histories and in Charles Wilkins, op. cit. I have found most useful D. Jacob Davis, *Crefydd a Gweriniaeth yn Hanes yr Hen Dŷ Cwrdd Aberdâr 1751–1951* (Llandysul, 1951); Tom Lewis, op. cit.; R.T. Jenkins, op. cit., and *Bardd a'i Cefndir* (Cardiff, 1949, on an Aberdare minister-craftsman-poet); *Bywgraffiadur* and *DWB* for individuals; the records of Zoar and Zion cited earlier and H.D. Emanuel, 'Dissent in the counties of Glamorgan and Monmouth', *NLWJ*, viii (1954), ix (1955).

13. Tom Lewis, op. cit., pp. 71, 147-8; Charles Wilkins, op. cit., pp. 173, 269-70.

14. Trust Deed of 28 October 1834 in Tom Lewis, op. cit., pp. 217-21.

15. Recorded speeches during the Reform crisis in the *Cambrian* and the election of 1834-5 in *Merthyr Guardian* and performance in vestry in MT Minutes.

16. Quoted by W.W. Price, 'Y Cefndir', *Hen Dŷ Cwrdd Aberdâr*, pp. 10-11.

17. The best and most convenient source is David Jones, *Before Rebecca*, chs. 3, 4 and appendix 1; also useful is E.W. Evans, *The Miners of South Wales* (University of Wales, Cardiff, 1961), an able book with which I often disagree.

18. This is *my* reading of the evidence presented by David Jones, *Before Rebecca*.

19. For example, when a marching gang from Merthyr reached Beaufort works and learned that the men were content with their master Kendall, they gave three cheers and marched on: David Jones, *Before Rebecca*, p. 77; for the revolutionary epilogue, the paper found at Penydarren works in January 1817, in David Jones, appendix 3, pp. 231-4.

20. This again is *my* reading, influenced by John Foster's chronology of de-

and re-stabilisation at Oldham (which, however, seems rather too abrupt to my mind in the latter case), of the evidence presented by David Jones, op. cit., chs. 2 and 5 and in David Williams's classic, *The Rebecca Riots*: I will develop the theme in the forthcoming study of the *Jacobins*.

21. On the *ceffyl pren*, David Williams, *The Rebecca Riots*, pp. 53-6; David Jones, op. cit., pp. 105 ff; the practice is found in many places.

22. David Jones's brilliant essay, op. cit., ch. 4, supersedes everything else ever written on the subject.

23. A recent Welsh-language periodical, racy, radical and lewd, which introduced nudes into the Eisteddfod and was the first public (I stress *public*) pornography in Welsh for centuries, bore the title *Lol* and was published at the *Lolfa* (the lounge, but also the lol-place). The dictionary meaning is nonsense. It seems a reasonable guess; there was still plenty of Welsh in Monmouthshire then.

24. *Reform* was written into the splendidly ghastly drawing of Bull's Head with hearts impaled on the horns in 'blood' from Hoarfrost Castle reproduced from April 1832 in Ness Edwards, *The Industrial Revolution in south Wales* (Labour Publishing Company, 1924), p. 97 (from HO 52/21).

25. David Jones, op. cit., appendix 1, pp. 206-20, in particular the Address on pp. 213-15; further confirmation, massively warranted in my friend and colleague Roger A.E. Wells's forthcoming thesis on the crises of 1795–1803, of Edward Thompson's thesis.

26. David Jones, op. cit., the Penydarren paper on pp. 231-4, in support of Edward Thompson.

27. I have published evidence on friendly societies in 'Friendly Societies in Glamorgan 1793–1832', *BBCS*, xviii (1959).

28. They colonised the Sympathetic Society, mother-society to many others, when it was re-organised in 1830: *Cambrian*, 13 February 1830.

29. Apart from works cited above, the whole of what follows is based on a remarkable local study, David Morgans, *Music and Musicians of Merthyr and District* (Merthyr, 1922). Based on local material now hard to come by, it is without doubt authentic and supported by much piecemeal and oral evidence. It may be supplemented by the commonplace books of *Talfrydydd*, antiquarian commentator of the *Merthyr Express* before World War I: CPL Ms. 1.725. The source of what follows is essentially David Morgans.

30. H.D. Emanuel, 'Dissent in the Counties of Glamorgan and Monmouth'; David Jones, op. cit., p. 207.

31. David Morgans, op. cit., pp. 24, 41-2.

32. *Iron in the Making*, p. 61.

33. The song belongs to a later date (we used to sing it after mid-week Band of Hope meetings in fact) but seems singularly apt for the 1820s.

34. What follows is based almost wholly on David Morgans, op. cit.

35. Charles Herbert James, op. cit., also describes the impact of Dic Dywyll.

36. He took his name from an Aberdare pub.

37. David Morgans, op. cit., pp. 12, 13, 30 and passim. When the Great Coach was not available, they went in the big cart of 'old Susan Morley' who traded weekly at Abergavenny market. The Abergavenny eisteddfodau were at their peak from 1838 to 1845, or at least, they were at their Merthyr peak then, since John Thomas's rigorously trained and often classical choirs took all the choral prizes! (Below.) From Abergavenny, *Y Fenni*, also came the most dreaded eisteddfod adjudicators.

38. David Morgans, op. cit., pp. 19-27.

39. David Morgans, ibid., pp. 38-49.

40. On the national societies, see R.T. Jenkins and Helen Ramage, *A History of the Honourable Society of Cymmrodorion and of the Gwyneddigion and Cymreigyddion Societies* (Hon. Soc. Cymmrodorion, London, 1951): R.T. was responsible for the section on the Cymreigyddion. William Howell of the Patriot, Gwilym Howell, was another Unitarian and host to Iolo Morganwg; from the beginning the eisteddfod was also a centre of political debate (as it had been since the *Jacobins* revived it in the 1790s, when their eisteddfod medals were struck by the engraver to the French National Assembly); Charles Wilkins, op. cit., pp. 310-11.

41. At least, he was poor until he wrote a poem to Josiah John Guest and got promoted (traditional, medieval bardic style!); he was a prime founder of the new Cymmrodorion in 1827 which may have been a shade more 'respectable' than the originals; he ended his days a Plymouth agent; Charles Wilkins, *History*, pp. 313-15 and David Morgans, op. cit., pp. 206 ff.

42. Among the Cymreigyddion societies, that at the Bush seems to have been the most successful and long-lived. All societies seem to have combined to launch the Chair Eisteddfod at the Boot, though it was the Cymreigyddion which published *Awenyddion Morganwg*. David Jones the watchmaker kept the Boot and the major figures seem simply to have followed him when he moved to the White Horse in Twynyrodyn. The Cymmrodorion started at the Lamb Inn and the Bush group moved there as well, to be followed by the Gomerians, who appear to have been English-language. The Lamb, Boot, Bush and White Horse were the central foci, though there was much fluidity as there was in the chapels at this time; as in the chapels, there was an intensification in this fluidity and multiplicity from the late 1820s into the 1830s and some of the causes might well have been 'political'; the subject calls for investigation. The major source is David Morgans's list, op. cit., pp. 205 ff.

43. David Morgans, op. cit., pp. 28-33; he is not aware of the significance of Zephaniah Williams and the Zetetics, or at least does not reveal any awareness.

44. The triumph of the Welsh Choir at the Crystal Palace in 1872 and 1873 was widely attributed to him.

45. The score was so expensive that, having bought one, he copied out all the choruses for a choir of forty, who are said to have given the first performance of the oratorio in Wales: David Morgans, op. cit., p. 30.

46. On the link with Zephaniah Williams, David Morgans, ibid., p. 28; on Williams, David Williams, *John Frost*.

47. David Morgans, op. cit., pp. 210-11; for the reference to the *Dynolwyr* of Nant-y-Glo, I thank my friend and colleague Jenkyn Beverly Smith of Aberystwyth.

48. R.D. Rees, 'Glamorgan newspapers under the Stamp Acts', *Morganwg*, iii (1959), p. 76.

49. Thomas Nightingale, Audenshaw to Peel, 8 November 1830, reporting Betts at a meeting to form a union, HO 40/27; Betts said, 'Trades Unions and Political Ones were now so intimately blended together that they must be looked upon as one'; also *United Trades' Co-operative Journal*, passim. More generally, Peel and Melbourne correspondence, HO 40/27 and HO 52/13; *Character, objects and effects of Trade Unions* (1834), Looker-On, *On the Oaths taken in the Union Clubs* (1831); G.D.H. Cole, *Attempts at General Union* (1953); papers in the Webb Trade Union Collection, LSE.

50. The key letter is: Notes relative to the Colliers Union Society in the parish

of Ruabon in Denbighshire, Anon to Melbourne, 29 June 1831, HO 52/16; the union's articles, denounced in the pamphlet by Looker-On and sent to the Home Office from Lancashire and north Wales, were published in the *Cambrian*, 12 November 1831.

51. Important sources on the slump are the pamphlet which W. Crawshay II wrote in self-defence after the Rising, *The Late Riots at Merthyr Tydfil* (Merthyr, 23 June 1831), correspondence in late 1830 and 1831 in Crawshay Papers, Box 2 (NLW) and MT Minutes, where rate exonerations and crises over poor relief register the onward march of depression.

52. Evan Thomas to Bute and Melbourne, 16 and 18 June 1831: HO 52/16.

53. Whereas Evan Thomas on 16 June 1831 reported that no ironmaster had received an application for a wage increase for a twelvemonth, Crawshay, on 23 June 1831, after stating that the iron industry had been in 'a most ruinous state' for two years, added that 'until 20 months ago', wage reductions and every economy had been resorted to and exhausted . . . 'For the last 19 months, no reduction whatsoever of wages in any department had been made by myself or any other Iron Master in this parish': Thomas, HO 52/16; Crawshay, *The Late Riots . . .*; on the use of the stipendiary's court to hold the labour force in Merthyr by raising support funds from the home parishes of the distressed, see *Merthyr Guardian*, 13 February 1836.

54. MT Minutes, 15 April, 9 July, 5 November 1830, 4 February, 27 May 1831. There seems to have been an acceleration in the slump's effects in three months early in 1831, when over £126 of rates arrears were expunged. In those few months, 5 pubs, 6 shops, a smithy and 13 houses were abandoned: MT Minutes, 4 February, 27 May 1831. By May 1830 Crawshay was telling a London buyer that he could quote no iron prices because all his make was bespoke for two months. W. Crawshay II to Adam Murray, 17 May 1830: Crawshay Papers (NLW), Letter-book 3 (6).

55. Inference (rather an obvious one) from the natural-justice action of 2 June 1831: see ch. 4. John Phelps's property, recovered by the rebels, had been distrained *two years earlier*, i.e. in June 1829; ch. 4.

56. *Cambrian*, 8 January 1831; see also issues for March 1831 and January 1830.

57. *Cambrian*, January 1830 and passim and retrospective reference to 'the notorious Betsy Paul' on 18 June 1831.

58. For Thomas Lewis, *Merthyr Guardian*, 2 March 1833, reporting on his transportation for a stabbing and on his character in general, and the popular action against him during the Rising, ch. 4 below; for the black-mailing constables, MT Minutes, 9 December 1830; *Cambrian* for March 1831 and chs. 4 and 8 below.

59. Bute to Melbourne, 8 June 1831: HO 52/16.

60. MT Minutes, 5 November 1830; Crawshay Papers (NLW), Box 2, 1830-1.

61. Record of Iron and Coal delivered at Cardiff, 1829-30, Bute Papers (CPL), XIV/54.

62. W. Crawshay II, *The Late Riots . . .*

63. Record of Iron and Coal delivered at Cardiff, 1829-30, Bute Papers (CPL), XIV/54.

64. W. Crawshay II, *The Late Riots . . .*; *Cambrian*, 11 June 1831 (for the sum of 5 shillings); Evan Thomas to Melbourne, 18 June 1831, HO 52/16, where Fothergill is reported to have said that Crawshay's wages 'were so high he could not get his complement of miners'.

65. *Cambrian*, 26 November 1831; W. Crawshay II, *The Late Riots . . .*; Petition of Lewis Lewis, 27 July 1831: HO 17/128 (part 2); Evan Thomas

reported that 'profligate' rebels on the first day of the Rising, 'chiefly miners', were earning 'perhaps 14 shillings a week only', but that puddlers and others who joined later were earning 'much higher wages'; one puddler was getting 20 shillings and his son 15 (E. Thomas to Bute, 16 June 1831: HO 52/16). This was Richard Evans, one of those tried at the Assizes; David Richards, another, and a miner, was getting £3 a month: *Cambrian*, 18 June 1831. The *Cambrian* said, 'These men truly had not wages to complain of'. Much the same line was taken by two military men after the Rising: 'On the whole we do not find that there is any serious general distress among the Miners. The wages are low rather in comparison with what they have been than with wages in any other parts of the Kingdom: Some large families no doubt suffer . . .' and they went on to talk of habits of 'comparative luxury among many' which had been 'unwillingly relinquished . . .' Col. Brotherton and Major Mackworth to Lord Fitzroy Somerset, 20 June 1831: HO 52/16.

66. MT Minutes, 18 January, 28 January, 4 February, 11 February, 25 March, 8, 15 April 1830.

67. *Cambrian*, 20, 27 March, 1 May 1830.

68. *Cambrian*, 19 June 1830: letter from E of Gray's Inn.

69. MT Minutes, 29 April 1830.

70. By this time, Hirwaun was running at a crippling loss and had become a serious burden. The shop there which the Crawshays had leased out was also giving trouble: 'I may be like a Dog with an old tin Pan tied to his Tail,' said Crawshay: correspondence in Crawshay Papers (NLW), Letter-book 3 (61-107 passim) and Box 2.

71. This controversy ran over *Cambrian*, 18, 25 September, 2, 9, 16, 23, 30 October, 20, 27 November, 4, 18, 25 December 1830; 1, 22, 29 January, 5, 12, 19 February 1831; with a postscript offering the 'calumet of peace' from Richards after the bill passed, in *Cambrian*, 15 October 1831.

72. *Merthyr Guardian*, 24 January 1835; reference back.

73. Col. Brotherton to Lord Fitzroy Somerset, 14 June and Brotherton and Major Digby Mackworth to the same, 20 June 1831; Evan Thomas on 18 June, talked of a 'series of very inflammatory placards . . . exhibited in Merthyr for a considerable period writing in Large Letters Reform and Downfall of Oppression, others explaining that the Rich were the oppressors, the Poor the Oppressed, in those very words . . .': all in HO 52/16. The soldiers spoke of political unions among 'shopkeepers and miners'; Evan Thomas said the Aberdare club had been given up, but blamed it for its effect on 'the better class of workmen' there, who on the third day of the Rising, were busy commandeering weapons.

74. MT Minutes, 18 February 1831.

75. W. Routh to W. Crawshay II, 13 December 1830, Crawshay Papers (NLW), Box 2 (539); *Cambrian*, 27 November, 25 December 1830; W. Crawshay I to W. Crawshay II, 7 September, 6 December 1831, 13, 23 May 1832, Crawshay Papers, Box 2 (587, 588, 620, 622); *Cambrian*, 28 January 1832; E.J. Jones, *Some contributions to the economic history of Wales*, pp. 107-9.

76. *Cambrian*, 20 November, 4 December 1830.

77. For Crawshay's politics, his speeches, *Cambrian*, 14 July, 22, 29 December 1832; his letter in *Merthyr Guardian*, 20 December 1834 and his *The Late Riots* of 23 June 1831.

78. For his public politics in Merthyr, see his speech at his election dinner, *Cambrian*, 22 December 1832; his Commons speech, *Monmouthshire Merlin*, 11 February 1831; for his moves on the Glamorgan seat, *Cambrian*,

14 May, 25 June, 22 October 1831. His relations with the Merthyr radicals had not always been easy; he had threatened the Unitarians with legal penalties for their use of the vestry room and the truck campaign had been directed against himself in a personal manner: *Merthyr Guardian*, 13 December 1834: letter with retrospective reference.

79.   The fullest account of this meeting is in Llandaff Records (NLW), LL/CC/G, 2050 a-n; see also *Cambrian*, 1 January 1831, *Seren Gomer*, Chwefror 1831, *Hansard*, 3rd series, ii, 206; on Croker's use of the Merthyr petition, *Annual Register*, 1831, p. 60 and *Cambrian*, 12 March 1831; Anglican protests and Coffin's apology appear in *Cambrian*, 15, 22 January, 5 March 1831.

80.   MT Minutes, 5 November, 9 December 1830, 4 February, 4, 25 March 183 1831; *Cambrian*, 8 January 1831.

81.   *Cambrian*, 12, 19 March, 23 April 1831; *Monmouthshire Merlin*, 26 March, 2 April 1831.

82.   W. Thompson to W. Crawshay II, 19 April 1831, Crawshay Papers (NLW), Box 2 (569). They knew Glamorgan was to have a 'second' member, i.e. the borough seat was to be divided between Cardiff and Swansea. Thompson, however, seized on some straws in one of Althorp's Commons speeches to assume that Merthyr would in the end get a seat of its own. He refused to commit himself to Guest and wanted the other ironmasters to confer; he 'clearly perceived' an electoral arrangement between Guest and Bute.

83.   *Cambrian*, 30 April 1831; W. Crawshay II, *The Late Riots*.

84.   This 2 May meeting is reported by Col. Brotherton and Major Mackworth to Fitzroy Somerset, 20 June 1831 and referred to by William Thomas the Court, second inquest on John Hughes, 20 June, in T. Thomas (coroner) to Melbourne, 26 June 1831, all in HO 52/16; on the fist fights: Petitions on behalf of Richard Lewis, 27 July and 5 August 1831 with covering letters from Joseph T. Price, HO 17/128, part 2, bundle Zp37, printed in part in Alexander Cordell, *The Fire People* (1972), pp. 369-80.

85.   These incidents were singled out as central by every commentator on the Rising. W. Crawshay II, *The Late Riots*; Col. Brotherton, 14 June and Brotherton and Major Mackworth 20 June to Lord Fitzroy Somerset; Evan Thomas to Bute, 16 June 1831; for immediate comment, J.B. Bruce to Bute, 25 May, Bute to Bruce, 26 May, Bute to Melbourne, 26 May and Melbourne to Bute 30 May 1831: HO 52/16; Melbourne's answer in HO 41/10. 'From that moment, the people thought that they were irresistible', said Bute to Melbourne on 15 June 1831 (HO 52/16).

86.   *Monmouthshire Merlin*, 11 June 1831.

87.   Evan Thomas to Bute, 16 June 1831 (HO 52/16) refers to this meeting at Bryn Gwyn; William Thomas the Court placed it at Hirwaun (the same area) at second inquest on John Hughes, 20 June (in T. Thomas to Melbourne, 26 June: HO 52/16). Evan Thomas said this meeting was a 'fortnight previous' to the 30 May meeting at the Waun; he also said the town had been in a state of much excitement for a considerable period 'but more particularly since 13 May' (ibid.). Clearly, some decisions were taken after the startling events of 9-10 May; I guess at 15 May for the Aberdare-Hirwaun meeting precisely because it was a Sunday. Perhaps it was at that point that the Aberdare Political Union was 'given up'? There were signs of 'moderate' alarm at the Waun.

88.   Bruce to Bute, 25 May 1831, HO 52/16. At that date, awareness of the Waun meeting was still based on 'rumours'; Bruce had written to Hill and Crawshay 'some days ago'.

89.   What follows is based on a critical reading of W. Crawshay, *The Late Riots*,
       which gives 'the facts' from Crawshay's point of view.
90.   Robert Beaumont to Bute, 11 June 1831: HO 52/16. Talking of the
       month's experience of lower wages (i.e. May essentially) Beaumont said:
       'During that month the workmen became dissatisfied.' But he added that
       the dissatisfaction had been increased by the 'late agitated state of the
       Country', i.e. by political motives. When my friend David Jones dismisses
       Crawshay's account as 'wrong' (David Jones, *Before Rebecca*, pp. 138-9)
       I think he is being a little hard on the Cyfarthfa master, but interpretation
       here is bound to be based on nuances of opinion and speculation.
91.   Bruce to Bute, 25 May 1831: HO 52/16. Bruce here called this action
       'rather unfortunate . . . every little addition to the distress will add to the
       risk of tumult'. In fact, it is clear that Crawshay's actions, in supporting
       political action by his men, in cutting the miners' wages, in dismissing
       puddlers, were alarming his peers. Within a few days, he was widely
       regarded as being responsible for the outbreak. Lt-Col. Richard Morgan of
       the Royal Glamorgan Militia, in a letter to Bute on 3 June at the height of
       the troubles, said: 'I much fear the principal cause of these disturbances
       originates in the injudicious conduct of Mr Crawshay who discharged a
       number of his people in a very hasty manner' (HO 52/16). The energetic
       magistrate, Rev. William Powell of Abergavenny, warmly praised
       Thompson and Guest for their role during 'the violent effervescence, which
       I am afraid the imprudence of another ironmaster had contributed to
       create . . .' (Powell to Melbourne, 7 June 1831: HO 52/16). These
       attitudes, however, partly reflect Crawshay's conduct in the mass
       confrontation with the men outside the Castle Inn on 3 June (see below).
       I am certain that Crawshay's dismissal of the puddlers was an important
       cause or occasion of the outbreak, but I do not think his reduction of the
       miners' wages was so significant in itself, and I consider his defence of his
       own actions largely justified, *except*, of course, for the vital point that the
       wage cut, followed by the sacking of the puddlers and by his intransigence
       once trouble had broken out, must have seemed a kind of volte-face to
       his men. 'Political' attitudes defined in a loose and broad sense were,
       I think, central (Evan Thomas certainly thought so and even the military
       men, while stressing plunder and economic motives, also emphasised the
       political 'cover' for it all). It should be remembered that J.B. Bruce
       and other commentators were Tories.
92.   Bruce to Bute, 25 May; Bute to Bruce, 26 May; Bute to Melbourne, 26
       May, Melbourne to Bute, 30 May; Bute to Melbourne, 1 June, with Home
       Office endorsement: HO 52/16 and 41/10.
93.   The preliminary march through Merthyr is indicated by the testimony of
       William Rowland, special constable, at the trial of Lewis Lewis and
       Richard Lewis, Glamorgan Summer Assizes, 14 July 1831: transcript of
       prosecution evidence by William Meyrick, sent by Justice Bosanquet to
       Melbourne on 1 August 1831 (HO 17/128, part 2, bundle Zp37; Alexander
       Cordell, *The Fire People*, p. 366): 'There had been a meeting before, a
       Reform meeting, I saw people passing through Merthyr with a flag on
       30 May . . .' For the nature of the flag, testimony of John Petherick,
       at second inquest on John Hughes, 21 June in T. Thomas to Melbourne,
       26 June 1831: HO 52/16, plus that of Adam Newell on 20 June.

4 REFORM

The meeting on the Waun on Monday, 30 May, was critical.[1] As usual, we have to look at the people who were there — 'chiefly of the working class of miners', according to John Petherick the Agent of Penydarren Works who attended — through a middle-class filter.[2]

About 2,000 people turned up, Petherick said, though this tended to be his standard assessment of any large crowd. Others put it at 8,000 to 10,000.[3] They held their meeting about a hundred yards from the Waun Fair itself and some were disappointed because more people had not come from Monmouthshire.

It is possible to detect three trends of opinion, or to be more precise, two broad political attitudes in which national perspectives were deeply refracted through violent local passions, both dislocated by a decisive third-party intervention. These were variations on the single, novel and intoxicating theme of worker self-assertion and it would be a mistake to see the meeting in terms of 'programmes' put forward by rival 'factions', though as it progressed, it did take on something of this character.

Its ostensible purpose was political. They unfurled their great white banner, which carried a Crown, a 'God Save William IV' and a 'Reform in Parliament'. One of the stated objects of the meeting was to prepare an Address to thank the King for 'his' Reform. Petherick noted that some called it a Petition. The difference is one of substance! One does not, after all, 'petition' in 'thanks' even to a Reformer King! One man, for example, spoke to the theme of an Address and called upon the meeting promptly to adjourn to prepare it; this, notes Petherick, was 'but partially agreed to'; it is hardly surprising!

Other speeches, to a Petition, went down much better. A blind man (Dic Dywyll) made a 'long and inflammatory speech', calculating the number of people who could be maintained at 15 shillings a week from a nobleman's income of £70,000 a year. Another spoke, from notes, on the expenses of government, on corrupt sinecures, on the income of bishops. This would have been meat and drink to the Political Union in Merthyr (and in Aberdare). David John the Unitarian had spoken to precisely this point in the parish church at Christmas. It very strongly suggests the use of the second, anti-clerical edition of John Wade's *Black Book* of the Reformers, which had been advertised in the *Cambrian* as recently as February.[4]

Few of those middle-class radicals, however (a David John, a Morgan Williams, perhaps a William Perkins) would have been sympathetic to the four-point resolution presented to the meeting by what was presumably a dissident group or at least a group independent of its official sponsors. The four planks of their platform were:

1. the abolition of the Court of Requests;
2. the abolition of all distraint and imprisonment for debt;
3. the enforcement of the old laws against forestalling and regrating (i.e. buying in the cheapest market and selling in the dearest for grains and foodstuffs);
4. the adoption of a rule that no miner or collier should take a stall vacated by another except at an increased price.

The demand for the enforcement of the old laws against forestalling and regrating (which a Chief Justice of England had pronounced still operative, in defiance of the market economy, during the food shortages of the 1790s) was of course something of a 'traditional' popular demand, an assertion of the 'moral economy' against the new man-made 'laws' of the market. The two resolutions on debt were more novel, but could easily be incorporated within the same moral universe. Their local relevance to a Merthyr in slump, with Court of Requests bailiffs ripping beds from under poor old women and poverty-stricken families being shipped back to their bleak upland parishes while men in work at shrinking pay waited for the chopper, was painfully obvious. The great debate on the Corn Laws and Free Trade which possessed the meeting was conducted largely in these terms; speaker after speaker denounced the Court of Requests, the corruption of local officials, the crookedness and heartlessness of local authority.

It is the fourth resolution which is intriguing, however. This was to be adopted as a standard demand in later years, but standards have to be established and this one was in fact being established at that very moment throughout industrial England by the National Association for the Protection of Labour and the new colliers' union which had conquered the north-eastern coalfield of Wales and which had affiliated to the NAPL in April.[5] It may reflect the deliberate policy of trade-union missionaries. The NAPL was a master of the technique of harnessing local grievances and national pre-occupations to union promotion; John Betts, unfurling his French tricolour in the North, was a grand-master.

For the decisive moment in the meeting came when a man stood up and said they 'must and would have the Court of Requests down'. Petherick noted (uniquely for him) that this man was a 'stranger'. His speech must have registered, because the Penydarren agent was able to quote freely from it (again uniquely in this instance) three weeks later:

> You have been petitioning Parliament several times for years and there is no notice taken of them. My plan is to bring the matter to a short conclusion and I advise every one of you to refrain from working any longer . . .

He told them to 'apply to the parish officers in the parishes you live in for the relief which is allowed by law. You will then be removed to the parishes to which you belong, in the case of you being strangers' (he evidently knew most of them would be precisely such) . . . 'all this and your support will cause very great expense, which must fall on the rate-payers, who are generally farmers and who cannot afford to pay more than they do now . . .'

The speaker took pains to add: 'Perhaps there may be some of them present and who hear me now, for I have no ill will against them, but only wish to reach the Great Men through them . . .' The farmers would be unable to pay their rents and taxes, so 'something decisive would take place for which otherwise they might go on petitioning for ever without obtaining any benefit . . .'

This speech evidently caused a sensation. The point to note is that, whatever the immediate context (it was directly linked, note, to the abolition of the Court of Requests) this very tactic was a standard practice of the new colliers' union and of the NAPL generally. It was actually put into effect in Merthyr four months later during the desperate struggle over the colliers' union, when the Union Preacher, William Twiss, or a man bearing his name, moved down to the town to supervise its implementation and drove the stipendiary magistrate, J.B. Bruce, with the connivance of Lord Melbourne, into an infraction of the law.[6] The first overt consequence of the Waun meeting was a march on Aberdare in the cause of the equalisation of miners' wages, the first major priority of every colliers' union and NAPL campaign. Union clubs were reported in Merthyr within two weeks of this meeting.[7] According to the informer in Ruabon who wrote to Melbourne, the union preachers had left north-east Wales with ample funds and had reached Merthyr shortly *before* the outbreak of the Merthyr Riots.[8]

This voice on the Waun was surely the voice of Twiss, the man bearing his name or one of his agents. As soon as it fell silent, a resolution to stop work was carried almost unanimously, with acclamation. Whereupon, another man got up to draw attention to what, he said, had been the original object of the meeting, to address the king on the subject of a reform in parliament (one can almost hear his pained accents!). He got little support and the meeting broke up.

The thrust of the Owenite trade-union movement was to be lost in the cataclysm which engulfed Merthyr within two days, but that it was present and might even have served as a detonator is clear.

The immediate response of authority, however, was relief. There had been no trouble, Bute wrote to Melbourne two days later . . . 'the cry principally resolved itself into free trade and no corn bill . . .'[9] It is surprising to find magistrates so blind to the hatred of the Court of Requests. In 1830, some of the ironmasters had proposed to get rid of it; after the troubles were over, everyone condemned it. They seem to have been unable to perceive, however, that hatred of the Court could serve as a common focus for working men suddenly seized by a new vision of their own dignity and worth, suddenly possessed by a dream of *Reform*, whether that reform was conceived in terms of the vote, the union or an older social morality at odds with that market economy of which the Court was an expression. As magistrates were to point out in tones of pained surprise, the Court of Requests had not changed. Precisely. It was not the Court which had changed. It was people who had changed, the people who suffered from the Court — or to be exact, the people who had suddenly perceived their experience of the Court as 'suffering'.[10]

To his letter to Melbourne of 1 June, however, Bute had to add a morning postscript. Bruce had just sent a worried note from Merthyr. People, 'some hundreds' of them, were again in motion . . . 'the magistrates are uneasy'. This was the first notice of the march on Aberdare. It is easy to see why it captured magisterial minds; the leader was Thomas Llewellyn, who had been the hero of the political riot of 9-10 May; the purpose of the march seemed subversive, 'outrageous'.[11] It seems completely to have blinded authority to an action which was in fact the first act of rebellion in Merthyr. For the previous day, on Tuesday 31 May, the very morrow of the Waun meeting, people in

Penderyn had, by physical force, stopped a Court of Requests distraint on one of their neighbours, Lewis Lewis, known as *Lewsyn yr Heliwr*, Lewis the Huntsman.[12]

The Merthyr Rising of 1831 had no 'leader'; it was precisely the absence of personalised 'leadership' which gave it its character. But if one has to look for a 'leader', there is only one candidate. Authority never had any doubts; the morning after Merthyr men had fought hand to hand with soldiers in their own High Street, ironmasters issued a proclamation directed wholly at one man. That man was *Lewsyn yr Heliwr*.[13]

He was a native of Penderyn, born in Blaen Cadlan in the Cwm Cadlan which, from Penderyn church perched on its dramatic knoll, would have looked in the spring of 1831 like a smudge of tufted green thumbed shallow into the barren but brilliant tawny sweep of moorland which beyond Blaen Cadlan drops down to the Taff as it curls out from under Pen-y-Fan through the Dan-y-Graig defile at Cefn. From Blaen Cadlan, with its standing stone, *Lewsyn* would have seen Penderyn church high above a straggling village which, on the plateau curving behind the quarries on Mynydd-y-Glôg, nudged the ironworks settlement of Hirwaun, clustered under the steep escarpment wall which blocks off the Rhonddas; beyond, the land falls away into the lush, lost tangle of woods, caves and waterfalls around Ystradfellte, where *Lewsyn* was to make his last stand this side of New South Wales.

Penderyn in 1831 was a parish of 1,385 people which looked rural but was not. It had 60 smallholders but 200 of its 280 families were engaged in industry, mostly in the works at Hirwaun, Aberdare and Merthyr. The Census credited it with eight 'capitalists, bankers, professional and other educated men' and its nearest approach to a squire was Morgan Morgan, whose miniature seat at Bodwigiad was as dwarfed by Mynydd-y-Glôg as Penderyn churchyard was by the Morgan funerary pillar at the church door. The paternalism attributed to Morgan on that pillar seems to have been more accurate than was customary; he exerted himself manfully on behalf of all Penderyn people, whether they were *Lewsyn* or the two constables who finally captured him after an epic struggle in Hendrebolon woods.[14]

In this parish of coal patches and quarries and ironworks ponds, Lewis's father, Jenkin Lewis, was officially and unromantically listed as a butcher, but father and son ran horses.[15] Lewis Jenkin Lewis, *Lewsyn Shanco Lewis*, a strong man, broke those horses in. Perhaps for that reason, he got involved with the local gentry like some Welsh Emiliano Zapata. Morgan Morgan thought well of him. He fetched a hunting dog for Mr Llewellyn of Rumney down on the coast, from Merthyr's surgeon 'squire', William Thomas the Court.[16] His nickname *heliwr* may well have been, originally, a corruption of the Welsh form of 'haulier', because that was how he had for a time earned his keep, hauling coal from the Llwydcoed pits to the lime-kilns at Penderyn, in a trade which was mobile, distinctive, artisan in character, set a man apart. By 1831, he was a miner for Penydarren, trying to keep a wife and four children on 8 shillings a week, he informed King William IV.[17] In a parish like Penderyn, this would have been only one of his occupations. Horses, hounds, gentry — no wonder legend was to make him the illegitimate son of any plausible gentleman within reach! From his first appearance in the records, everyone called him *The Huntsman (Heliwr)* and appropriately in both languages, for the man was bilingual, though his oratory was Welsh.

He was clearly a charismatic figure. Men listened to him; they followed him against muskets and bayonets. He waged war on the King's men; he put houses of 'enemies of the people' to the sack. But he was also, clearly, a man of *chware teg*, fair play, with a painful sense of honour. When he took a chest of drawers from a poor woman who had bought it from the debtors' court and restored it to its 'lawful' owner, he made sure the woman got her money back, even if he had to commit a capital offence to do so. He protected magistrates and a hated constable from his own men . . . 'Honour! Honour! he's had enough!' He was an unreconstructed man, straight out of an older morality.[18] He was no stranger to the Court; both he and his father had been relieved by it.[19] It was in the June of 1831 that he rejected the proper ritual of submission and supplication. The decision was probably made for him, for in that June he was no young turk, he was 38 years old.[20] He was one of those men which communities like his produce the world over, 'the man who makes himself respected'.[21] In the June of 1831, it was his neighbours who made him the man who would 'make the working people of Merthyr respected'.

For when the bailiffs came for his property, as usual for some of those 'best pieces' they always went for, on the very morning after those ringing resolutions at that Waun Fair where they sold fine horses (we do not know whether Lewsyn was there) people in Blaencadlan and Penderyn stopped them. This was the first resistance offered to the Court of Requests. The magistrate, J.B. Bruce, evidently treated it as one more of those squabbles which were plaguing him. He sent in the constables, haled the parties before him and hammered out a compromise. Lewis Lewis was to pay sixpence a week (towards a debt of

£18 19s 0d); his creditor took possession, as surety, of a cherished chest or trunk.[22]

Bruce had what he regarded as more serious trouble on his hands, in the march on Aberdare led by Thomas Llewellyn on 1 June. In fact on that Wednesday, two quite distinct and separate movements were in train. They were common in that both flowed from the new sense of dignity and unity and in that their theatre of action was the same, that critical zone of Bruce's bailiwick which embraced Hirwaun, Aberdare, the Cyfarthfa side of Merthyr – Merthyr's *Faubourg St Antoine*. In nature, however, they were radically different.

The occasion for Tom Llewellyn's march (the Orator, one magistrate called him) was the report that the Aberdare ironmaster Richard Forthergill had said the wages of Crawshay's ironstone miners were too high. Magistrates read this as meaning that Fothergill could get no miners; workers, that Fothergill thought he could get miners on the cheap. Tom Llewellyn and his men compelled Fothergill to sign a retraction; for good measure they attacked the Aberdare truck shop, and in traditional style, demanded beer for their trouble.[23] Crawshay's miners, of course, having worked their first month at the new and lower scales, would be peculiarly sensitive, but it went deeper than that. This was the kind of assertion of unity (and dignity) against sectional and corporate fragmentation and exploitation that the union delegates would have been preaching. The action might well have been planned at the Waun meeting. Certainly, it was to Aberdare that Bruce directed his meagre forces; it was Thomas Llewellyn's 'political' past which caught the mind of authority.

Bruce had neither resources nor mind to spare for the other movement, which was in fact the beginning of an insurrection. For, even as Llewellyn's men were marching, a crowd moved on the shopkeeper, apparently at Hirwaun, who had taken Lewis Lewis's trunk. They wrested it from him by force. They set it up in the highway and lifted Lewis Lewis on to it. He made a speech in Welsh. Shortly afterwards someone threw fire-balls through the windows of Joseph Coffin, president of the Court of Requests.[24] And, perhaps late that night, certainly early the next morning, what was obviously a planned insurrection broke on Merthyr.[25]

In the morning, a crowd gathered 'on the Kefan', near Cefn, natural rally point for the men of Crawshay's Cyfarthfa and Hirwaun. It was followed by some shadowy 'muster at the Castle Inn'.[26] Then, bands of men carrying banners moved through Merthyr from house to house. They first 'enquired', they identified and located goods which had been taken under legal process by the Court of Requests. They then restored those goods to the original owners. Their banners blazoned *Reform*; they shouted *Reform*. There had been direct action of all kinds in earlier years. This was a planned, premeditated, direct and sustained assault not only on the Court of Requests but on the whole system of property and human relationships which that Court represented. And, however generally, they were aware of the implications of what they were doing. 'Come with us,' shouted *Dai Llaw Haearn*, Dai Iron Hand, a skilled man, waving his pick-axe handle like a wand to a woman in servitude to the Court, 'We'll set you free, by the Devil!'[27]

Watches were a favourite target; Watkin Rees, a twenty-year-old collier, got his back from Thomas Davies in Merthyr while in Dowlais, Thomas Griffiths, a miner of 29, led a crowd against John Davies's shop to get his. They would have been the first cherished luxuries to go at a pinch; they were now the first to be recaptured. Furniture, too, was liberated on such a scale that some streets in Merthyr must have looked as if they were in the grip of a mass migration. Joan Jenkins, a woman of 62, took her two sons, Tom a labourer and Jenkin a smith, at the head of a crowd to Prothero Prothero's place and seized a clock, a box, two tables and a chair (in a revealing response, her victim pleaded for mercy for her at the Assizes six weeks later).[28]

The scale of the action was staggering.[29] Over a hundred houses and shops were visited on Thursday, in Merthyr, in Cefn, in Dowlais. One zealous bailiff assiduously listed the names of offenders and witnesses in 36 individual cases and had to be forcibly restrained by magistrates from taking legal action against a fair proportion of the population of Merthyr Tydfil. The crowds, of course, were not always nice in their discrimination. Not all the goods were being 'restored'; there was some looting on the margins, though surprisingly little in the circumstances (looting was rarely a feature of any south Wales riot). James Richards, known as James Schemer, a notorious thief, organised a gang which battened on shopkeepers in this collapse of one kind of order.[30] Even shopkeepers 'of an inferior grade' were hit and the movement threatened to grow into a wholesale expropriation of the shopocracy and a massive redistribution of movable property. When they heard of it in Monmouthshire, women got sacks ready.[31] Indeed, some of the leaders may have thought they were starting a national *Reform*. There was talk of simultaneous insurrection in Lancashire, Yorkshire, Staffordshire, the Forest of Dean, even the East End of London. Radical newspapers and delegates had been circulating for months. After it was all over, men remembered that a wandering pedlar had said three weeks earlier that something extraordinary was going to happen in Merthyr.[32] What is certainly true is that it was one of the most 'classic' of natural-justice actions in the tradition of 'primitive' rebellion.

The insurrection broke on authority like a thunderstorm out of a blue sky. Bruce at once began enrolling tradesmen as Specials. He installed himself in the Castle Inn and sent an urgent messenger to the depot of the 93rd Foot at Brecon; would the commander respond instantly should it prove necessary to send for the military?[33] The morning of Thursday, 2 June, was evidently a paralysing shock. It was after the dinner break, however, that the sheer scale of the revolt became clear. For, in the afternoon an *army of redressers* set out on its march, a long march which was to take some of them to death and transportation. John Petherick ran into them between two and three o'clock, marching down the Brecon Road and shouting 'Reform for ever!'; coming then from Cyfarthfa and Hirwaun works. J.B. Bruce, when he met them, thought they were Crawshay's men mostly and very young, but at their head was a handful of older workers who had made themselves respected.[34]

David Jones, a miner of 37, carried the expressive nickname *Dai Solomon*. One of Crawshay's managers was to give him a glowing testimonial at his trial, but he was a tough and obstinate man who 'knew his rights'. David Hughes was 40, another miner and much respected, though capable of arguing down magistrates when angry. He was angry now. Two of them were puddlers, skilled men. David Thomas, 24, made himself remembered on this Thursday. *Dai Llaw-Haearn* they called him, Dai Iron-Hand. He rarely entered a house himself, but he made sure those who ought to did. He carried a pick-handle as if it were an officer's baton. He was clearly the marshal of the host. The other puddler also bore insignia of authority. William Williams, 32, wrestled with the writhing banner-pole and sometimes needed a man to help him. For this was an army which marched behind a Red Flag with a loaf of bread impaled on the point. They had a horn, too, which they blew; good Scotch Cattle practice though hardly known in Merthyr. Perhaps they thought a Huntsman needed a horn, for at their head strode Lewis Lewis, *Lewsyn yr Heliwr*. They carried his rescued chest along with them.

Picking up crowds of women and young boys, they swept along the Brecon Road and turned off almost due west past Bethesda down towards Jackson's Bridge. They knew what they were about. Down there, nestling behind the Tip, a high cinder bank which looked from

the Morlais brook across the Glebeland field to the long back yard of
the Castle Inn, and settling their grip on the jugular of the huddled
houses and rabbit-warren cellars of Riverside and Ynysgau and the
cramped streets near the Taff, were a clutch of tradespeople, the three
clans of the Williams family of beadles and bailiffs of the Court of
Requests, David Rees the pawnbroker, above all the notorious and
hated huckster Thomas Lewis. Lewis, nominally a wheelwright, lived
in a shadow-land. He had been arrested once already for passing bad
coin. Eighteen months from this Thursday, he was to be transported for
life for stabbing a man. He was known to traffic in petty loans, and to
profit, largely in the cherished 'best pieces' of furniture of the poor,
from the Court confiscations which followed as regularly as lay-offs
of ironstone miners.[35] These people knew what was coming. Their
doors were locked. Thomas Lewis stood cocky outside his, the key in
his pocket. He had just buried two sovereigns in the garden.[36]

The marchers spilled out along the street. They set up Lewis Lewis
on his trunk, like some plebeian Welsh St Louis dispensing natural
justice under the oak tree. Out went their detachments, 'to enquire'
into oppressions by the Court of Requests. One of the most remarkable
of their encounters, and perhaps most revealing of the tone and temper
of the day, was their meeting with John Phelps.[37]

Phelps was a *Pensioner*, an old army man. He was working as a shoe-
maker with his mate William Davies at the Cardiff end of town when
they came for him. 'They were strangers and there were more than six
or seven,' said Davies. 'Come up and fetch your property from Tom of
the Balca (*Twm o'r Balca*),' they told Phelps. They did not know him
and he did not know them. His property was a watch, a Bible and
some other articles taken by the Court *two years earlier* . . . 'They told
him he was bound to go and fight for his property as well as themselves . . .'

Phelps would not go at first — or so he and Davies told the Assize
judge six weeks later. His wife was more resolute; she set off with the
crowd. 'Go with them, I'll finish the shoe,' Davies told him, 'for fear
your wife does something wrong.' When Phelps reached the house of
Thomas Williams the bailiff, near Bethesda, the crowd was outside,
thumping the door and shouting 'Reform!' They were beating sticks
together, said Martha Llewellyn, the Williams's servant who 'understood
a little English'. She was crouching in the back parlour, but she
'thought the door would have gone to pieces' and she couldn't keep her
bilingual nose out of the front room.

When they saw Phelps, the crowd roared — 'Why don't you go in, you damned lout, and get your goods!'[38] They smashed the door in and pushed Phelps and his wife across the threshold, straight into Jane, wife to *Twm o'r Balca* 'In the name of God, Phelps, what do you want?' she shouted. (A person could not be heard in the house unless he spoke loud, Martha Llewellyn explained to the judge; there were hundreds outside shouting 'Reform for ever!') 'I want the watch,' Phelps shouted back, 'and my Bible.' 'Out with the things!' shouted the crowd, 'Out with them!' (A South Walian can still hear them — 'Mâs â nhw!'). Jane Williams said she knew nothing of it, the watch had been sold two years ago (Phelps's Bible she'd bought at an auction).

At this, Mrs Phelps 'shut her fists' and said the mob would tear her to pieces. 'Damn your heart!' Phelps yelled, 'unless you bring me the watch, the mob shall come in.' His wife brushed past Jane into the parlour, took two pictures off the wall (never theirs, said Jane), went to a cupboard for two spoons and some tea. Phelps turned and shouted to the crowd, 'In with you! I can't have my watch!'

The crowd burst in and stamped all over the house. They found a chest of drawers belonging to somebody and out it went over their heads, to cheers in the street. Mrs Phelps found the Bible and the shoe-maker put it under his arm. Jane Williams fainted, as the crowd swarmed around her, shouting — 'Where's your husband? We're going to kill him.' 'Go and fetch a red hot poker,' Phelps told them (or so the clerk at the Assizes reported it), 'pass it from one end to the other of her and she'll soon come to herself. There's plenty of her sort left in the world.'

David Thomas, *Dai Llaw Haearn*, was outside, flourishing his pick-handle at the houses of Thomas Williams's brother and son.[39] 'Now is your time,' he was shouting, 'if they have anything belonging to you, take it!'[40] Furniture came out of the houses, every piece greeted by a great cheer. 'If you don't give me the teapot,' one man told Ann Williams, 'I'll pull you to pieces.' Young Tom Williams was out in the street, squaring up to Phelps — 'I'll remember you, Phelps' — when one of the crowd captains came over with a piece of paper and demanded that he sign a 'receipt' — else he'd 'lick him and pull the house down about his head'.[41]

John Petherick ran off to the Castle Inn to fetch the magistrates, as another crowd came out of David Rees's place and set up Lewis Lewis's box nearby. *Lewsyn yr Heliwr* spoke from it in Welsh. David Williams's widowed mother had a Court execution out against her, he said. The redressers had already taken from her a chest of drawers she'd bought from Thomas Lewis for two guineas. 'I do not see it right,' called out the Huntsman, 'for the poor widow to give the case of drawers back without having the two guineas returned ... If everyone is of the same mind as me [a favourite turn of phrase of his] rise up your hands and get the two guineas back from Lewis.' And as Thomas Lewis put it succinctly at the Assizes, 'They rose up their hands and came to my house.'[42]

Dai Solomon, David Jones, led them over. 'I've spent the two guineas,' Lewis said, 'on flour.' One grabbed him. 'The two guineas,' he said, 'or I'll give you to the throng and they'll pull you in quarters.' Lewis took out his key and opened the door. A group of them formed a cordon in the doorway to keep the crowd out, while *Dai Solomon* went in and started writing out a statement for Lewis to sign, promising to pay the money to Mrs Williams in the morning. It was at that point that John Petherick and William Thomas the Court came rushing up with the magistrates Bruce and Anthony Hill and a few Specials.[43]

The crowd greeted them with a roar of 'Reform!' The magistrates wrestled their way through to the door and stood on two of Thomas Lewis's chairs. Petherick thought the crowd was now 2,000 strong and 'very furious'. For half an hour Bruce and Hill shouted, pleaded, threatened.

'Down with them!' the crowd shouted. 'Several rather heavy pushes were made towards us or perhaps towards the door,' reported Bruce. Among all the women and boys and young men, he appealed to David Hughes as an older and perhaps familiar face. He got short shrift. 'It's no use to speak to us,' Hughes said, 'We're having the goods out and the Court of Requests down.'

Lewis Lewis intervened in person to push the crowd back from the magistrates, an act which may have helped to save his life six weeks later, but in the end, Bruce had to read the Riot Act. Hill explained it in English, the stipendiary in Welsh. They had used an out-of-date form. 'What have we to do with King George?' the crowd roared, 'King William is our king!' They shook the Red Flag in the magistrates' faces. Ann Evans, caught up in the crowd, an Irish woman married to a soldier, had never felt more scared on a battlefield. The crowd drove the magistrates off their chairs and down the street, John Petherick fighting his way out through a hail of kicks.[44]

Incensed, the people turned on the wretched Thomas Lewis. Thomas Vaughan, a miner of 21, burst in through the door and hit him sprawling. They hit his wife over on top of him. 'For God's sake, don't kill me!' Lewis shouted as his wife dug out her two long-lost watches for Gwenllian Pardoe.[45]

Dai Llaw Haearn went swinging his pick over to Mrs Williams's house and forced her reluctant son David out. 'He said he'd be damned if he wouldn't get everything back.' He saw Mary Phillips and asked her whether she was in the Court of Conscience. She said she was. 'Come with us then,' David Thomas said, as he frog-marched David Williams over to Lewis's, 'We'll set you free, by the Devil.'

Someone shouted from inside Lewis's that there was a cloak there belonging to another woman. David Williams ran away, but the crowd forced him back and *Dai Solomon* told Lewis he'd better pay up or he'd be dead and his house down. The coiner asked leave to go borrow the money, whispering to Williams that it was in the garden. He dug up the sovereigns, collected two shillings from his wife and handed them over, through David Jones. By this time, the leaders were circling around him, making out 'receipts' and demanding that he sign them. 'Give us no law,' they said, 'or you'll be killed.'[46]

At that moment, Thomas Llewellyn came down the street, returning from work and still in his working clothes. This was the leader of the march on Fothergill's, the hero of 10 May. Nothing better illustrates the autonomy of the natural-justice action than the fact that Thomas Llewellyn had known nothing about it. He ran into the crowd as it was breaking into Thomas Charles's. Carried to Lewis, he talked about a pack bedstead he had lost, but stood irresolute in the street and did nothing.[47]

Thomas Lewis's purgatory, however, was at last over, at least for a day. The captains drafted a letter to W.D. Jenkins the druggist warning him off his process against a poor man. The crowd picked up the Huntsman's trunk, gathered around their flag and marched off, like so many justices itinerant, on their way to Edward Morgan's place, to a circuit of the shopkeepers and to the hated Court itself, the house of its president, Joseph Coffin.[48]

At the Castle Inn, Bruce and Hill were paralysed. Guest and Crawshay had not yet returned. They had sworn in about 70 tradesmen as Specials, but could do nothing against the bands going about the town under their banners. They clung to the visible half-truth that these bands were a small minority; most workers were still in their jobs. Besides, what did the rebels want? At Thomas Lewis's, Petherick had heard no demand for increased wages, simply endless protests against the Court of Requests . . . 'they seemed to be looking generally for a better state of things . . . I cannot recollect their exact expression . . .' We cannot discover any distinct ground for their complaints, the magistrates reported to the Home Office. What they were doing, however, was clear enough. By the early evening, shopkeepers were running to the Castle and talking of a general expropriation. Forty-two of them met under the chairmanship of William Perkins; thirty-four of those voted to send for the troops at Brecon at once.[49]

In the next room, at 8.30, Bruce sat down to write a letter to Bute, at once a report and an interior dialogue. Horses were ready, saddled, for Brecon and for the East Glamorgan Yeomanry, but he was terribly reluctant to send for soldiers unless he had to. Were the Staff of the Glamorgan Militia ready? They had been first up in 1816 (there is an apostolic succession in such matters). Suddenly, he had to break off . . . 'Since writing this, they have broken Mr. Coffin's windows . . .' John Petherick had seen them through an inn window . . . 'a flag with the people assembled around it' outside Coffin's house further up the High Street . . . about 2,000 of them . . . cheering, shouting, a column of smoke . . .[50]

Luke Pearson had got to Coffin's house about eight; there was a crowd with their Flag.[51] Their temper was harder; they stretched ropes across the street to stop their people running away. David Thomas was there and *Lewsyn yr Heliwr* was up on his trunk. Pearson knew no Welsh and could not follow what the Huntsman said, but he saw him gesture with his hands and a volley of stones smashed Coffin's windows. The crowd began to shout for the Court's account-books. Coffin appeared in an upstairs window and threw some books down. They were obsolete. The crowd bayed with rage and tore them to pieces. Some of them broke in through the back door. They rampaged through the house, hurling the furniture through the window-sashes (a Scotch Cattle trick). They even ripped the wall-paper off the walls. Books and bottles of liquor went out of the windows. The crowd made a great bonfire outside the house; the flames climbed as high as the top storey windows. Pearson ran for 'young Mr. Bryant'.

The horrified faces at the Castle's windows swivelled round to confront William Crawshay who had just ridden in. Always a short-fuse man, he was beside himself; after all these were 'his miners'. They decided on the spot to send for the soldiers and the horsemen went clattering down the street, for Brecon and the Highlanders, for Llantrisant and the Yeomanry, for Neath and the High Sheriff. '9.40 . . .' scribbled Bruce into his letter, 'since the above . . . they have burst into Coffin's house, pulled out his furniture and *burned* it on the street . . .'[52]

Pearson and William Bryant battled their way into Coffin's. Mrs

Coffin was upstairs in bed with a scalded foot; the two children huddled around her. Coffin, warned by one of the rioters, had fled and men were shouting and kicking the furniture. Some threatened to pull the bed out from under her — revenge, no doubt, for Margaret Rees and all those other old women turfed out of their beds by the Court bailiffs (and who had probably grown into a generation in the telling). 'For God's sake, leave it,' shouted Pearson to the lady. The crowd ignored him, but objected to Bryant — so strongly that he jumped over the banisters and made his escape (the next day, David Hughes put a shot through his windows).[53] Pearson half-carried Mrs Coffin down the stairs. The crowd were shouting for a march on the ironworks to fetch the men out. They stormed out and headed for Cyfarthfa. When John Petherick came down, Coffin's house was a wreck; the leaves of his account-books were blowing down High Street like a snowstorm.[54]

During this brief respite, Bruce and Hill composed a formal letter to Lord Melbourne at the Home Office, justifying their request for troops. Shortly after 10.30, Josiah John Guest who had since arrived, took the letter, and Anthony Hill's brother Richard for company, and set off for Cardiff Castle.

About two hours later, the crowd came back from Cyfarthfa where they had stopped the works. Numbers of them again broke into Coffin's house, where Luke Pearson had shut himself up in Mrs Coffin's bedroom. He thought he heard them say 'Murder him!' in Welsh, because someone replied in English, 'No we won't hurt him; we want Coffin and the Specials, if we find them here, we'll kill them.' Many of them seemed drunk by this time. They ransacked the house and that of Ann Rees next door. Scooping up the papers and shreds of account-books, they snatched a candle from Pearson's hands, tried but failed to fire the house. They left, vowing vengeance on the Specials.

After milling about for some time, a great crowd set off up the road north, for the works at Penydarren and Dowlais. William Rowland, a Special in the Castle Inn, heard them go at about one in the morning, shouting and blowing a horn.[55] At about the same time, another party of about 30 to 40 went back into Coffin's house, looking for bailiffs and Specials in hiding. Pearson showed them an empty house and they left. John Petherick emerged and followed the crowd to his own works at Penydarren. There was a dramatic encounter as a large party under a banner entered the Puddling Forge shortly before two o'clock. 'Take hold of the flag', one of the men said to Petherick. 'Why?' 'It's Reform.' Petherick did so. 'Right,' said the man, 'now you're sworn in.'

The party stopped everything except the blast furnaces, where the workers refused to pull the iron out. The flag-party took the iron out themselves and the grates out of the fireplaces. 'Why are you doing this?' Petherick asked them. 'It is because we've taken it into our heads to do so,' answered one of them belligerently, 'it's to get better wages.' More calmly, he added, 'I am not in distress myself, but I know those that are so.' In fact, Petherick found them driven by fury against the Court of Requests and its officers, against all shopkeepers and others who had bought furniture under process of the Court and against any who had goods deposited with them as surety for debt.[56]

At about the time Petherick was being sworn in at the puddling forge, the Merthyr expresses were reaching Cardiff, with Guest and Hill at their heels. Bute at once sent orders to the Eastern and Central Yeomanry. By six, he'd heard from Major Rickards that the Merthyr message had reached him direct and that the Eastern Yeomanry were on their way. Guest and Hill, together with Guest's brother Thomas, left for Merthyr in the small hours. Bute had 52 men of the staff of the Glamorgan Militia trained in the musket ready to leave in coaches and light waggons under Captain Howells, but he held them in the hope of hearing better news by the early morning mail from Merthyr. He did not.[57]

Most of the Trade of Merthyr (though the hard core of the radical and Unitarian shopocracy virtually 'disappeared') spent the night in and around the Castle Inn as Specials. At half-past five in the morning, James Abbott, a barber, noticed men gathering at the market and around W.D. Jenkins's place.[58] There were soon several hundred. Four men broke into the ruin of Coffin's house yet again and searched the cellar for enemies. From seven o'clock, a massive demonstration began to march around Merthyr. William Rowland saw them coming, 'several thousands' of them. At their head went the Red Flag with the loaf on the point. Many of the men were carrying clubs and bludgeons. They had ropes and from time to time stretched them across the street to stop any of the recruits they scooped up running away. Ann Harries, a miner's wife, standing in her doorway right by the Castle Inn, saw the crowd filling the street 'as full as it could be' and stretching from far below to far above the Castle; she thought it well over a quarter of a mile long. Some time before 10 o'clock, to shouts and chants, they started to march out towards the Brecon Road.

At about that time, the Merthyr mail was reaching Cardiff. It brought a letter to Bute from the magistrates . . . We need every soldier we can get hold of . . . Off went the Royal Glamorgan in their coaches and waggons, without greatcoats or cartridge boxes, packing their ammunition into their haversacks.

Other men had been on the march for seven hours. The Merthyr horseman reached Brecon near midnight and at three in the morning, in the darkness, some eighty men of the 93rd Foot, the Argyll and Sutherland Highlanders, set off on a forced march, over the Beacons. Some time around ten o'clock, they came through Cefn, their kilts swinging, women lining the street and jeering . . . 'Go home and put your trousers on . . .'[59] At Tydfil's Well, they saw the magistrates waiting and behind them, the huge crowd marching to meet them.

Notes

1. The following two narrative chapters are based essentially on: emergency inquest on John Hughes by Evan Thomas, 17 June; testimonies in E. Thomas to Melbourne, 18 June; formal inquests on Hughes and Rowland Thomas by the Swansea coroner Thomas Thomas, 20-22 June; testimonies in T. Thomas to Melbourne, 26 June; reports on the inquests and on the Assizes in *Cambrian*, June-July; the Home Office and War Office correspondence in HO 52/16 and elsewhere; general accounts and analyses by Evan Thomas, the soldiers Brotherton and Mackworth, the agent Beaumont, Bute, Bruce, Hill and others, mostly in HO 52/16, two long accounts in *Cambrian*, 11 June, one by Crawshay (a gentleman of Merthyr) with the latter's *Late Riots*, petitions and transcripts in HO 17/128, part 2, bundle Zp37; transcript of trial of John Phelps in HO 6/16.
2. The fullest account of the Waun meeting is: testimony of John Petherick, second inquest on John Hughes, 21 June in T. Thomas to Melbourne, 26 June 1831: HO 52/16; this duly lodged in the reports by Evan Thomas and Brotherton-Mackworth and may be supplemented by detail from other testimonies.
3. Brotherton-Mackworth to Lord Fitzroy Somerset, 20 June 1831: HO 52/16.
4. *Cambrian*, February 1831; by July, the paper was advertising the radical *Alfred, Cambrian*, 30 July 1831.
5. Emlyn Rogers, 'Helyntion glowyr Dinbych a Fflint yn 1830-31', *Lleufer* (1946-7) and 'Labour struggles in Flintshire, 1830-50', *Flintshire Historical Society Publications* (1953-5); Notes relative to the Colliers Union Society in the parish of Ruabon in Denbighshire, Anon. to Melbourne, 29 June 1831: HO 52/16.
6. Ch. 9 below.
7. Evan Thomas to Melbourne, 18 June 1831: HO 52/16; *United Trades Co-operative Journal*, 1830; *Voice of the People*, 1831, passim.
8. Notes relative to the Colliers Union Society: HO 52/16.
9. Bute to Melbourne, 1 June 1831: HO 52/16.
10. 'The Court of Requests has existed more than 20 years administered in every respect, whether well or ill, in the same manner as it now is . . .'; Evan Thomas to Melbourne, 18 June 1831: HO 52/16.
11. Bute to Melbourne, 1 June 1831: on 3 July 1831, Bute, in reporting on

the formation of union lodges in the area, said he had been corresponding with Bruce about the man 'who had been foremost in the attack on Mr. Stevens' house and afterwards in a visit to Mr. Fothergill . . . *immediately previous* to the fatal riot . . .'. Bruce had replied that Thomas Llewellyn was 'well known' but that it would be difficult to get hard evidence against him. Bute referred Melbourne to Evan Thomas's account of the march on Aberdare and singled out Llewellyn in particular as 'showing the connexion of the tumultuous proceedings in that neighbourhood': HO 52/16.

12.   Evan Thomas to Bute, 16 June 1831: HO 52/16.

13.   Ch. 5 below.

14.   Personal observation and *Census 1831: Enumeration Abstract.*

15.   CPL Ms. 2.1086, D. Cynon Davies, Hanes Penderyn; David Davies, Dewi Cynon, *Hanes Plwyf Penderyn* (Aberdare, 1905, 1924); Jenkin Howell, 'Dyffryn Cynon', *Y Geninen*, xviii (1900), p. 211; Lewsyn was baptised 21 March 1793, son to Lewis Lewis and wife Margaret; Penderyn parish register, bishops' transcripts (NLW).

16.   Glamorgan Summer Assizes, 13 July 1831. During the third Merthyr case, the attack on the house of Thomas Lewis, while William Thomas the Court was being cross-examined, Lewis Lewis suddenly interrupted to say: 'Do you remember me coming for a hound from Mr Llewellyn of Rumney? *William Thomas*: No, I remember your coming there and stealing a dog from my kennel', *Cambrian*, 16 July 1831.

17.   Petition of Lewis Lewis, presented by Joseph T. Price and John Thomas, 27 July 1831: HO 17/128, part 2, bundle Zp37; quoted in full in ch. 8 below.

18.   Evidence cited below and in ch. 8.

19.   *Cambrian*, 11 June 1831: '. . . most desperate Rioter (known as Lewis Penderrin and Lewis the Huntsman) whose father had been relieved by Mr. Joseph Coffin in various instances of distress and who had been lent £10 at a time by him . . .'

20.   In the Assizes Sentence list, his age is given as 37; folk-heroes have to be permitted their vanity.

21.   For this telling phrase, which is 'classic' and 'familiar' in 'peasant' society, Eric J. Hobsbawm, *Bandits* (1969), pp. 28-30; men who stand up in a society of bent backs. Briefly, Lewsyn did in fact act like a 'social bandit' and in some respects he is reminiscent of the young Zapata.

22.   Evan Thomas to Bute, 16 June 1831: HO 52/16.

23.   Evan Thomas to Bute, 16 June 1831; *Cambrian*, 11 June 1831.

24.   Evan Thomas to Bute, 16 June 1831; I suggest Hirwaun, because when the crowd stopped the distraint the day before, the goods were being loaded into a cart for Hirwaun.

25.   Basic sources for this action, apart from reports in the *Cambrian* and the surveys by Evan Thomas and Brotherton-Mackworth: trial of John Phelps, transcript in HO 6/16; testimonies at the inquests of 17, 20-22 June in HO 52/16, reports of Glamorgan Summer Assizes in *Cambrian*, July 1831.

26.   Testimony of Jane Williams and Eleanor Williams, trial of John Phelps, Glamorgan Summer Assizes, 13 July 1831; transcript, HO 6/16; *Cambrian*, 16 July 1831.

27.   Testimony of Mary Phillips, trial of Lewis Lewis and six others for attack on house of Thomas Lewis, 13 July; *Cambrian*, 16 July 1831.

28.   Sentence List, Glamorgan Summer Assizes, July 1831 (Welsh Folk Museum, St Fagans); *Cambrian*, 23 July 1831.

29. The fullest account is in Evan Thomas to Bute and Melbourne, 16 and 18 June 1831: HO 52/16.

30. *Merthyr Guardian*, 15 November 1834, reporting arrest of Richards and a Swansea mason on suspicion of murder at Llandeilo Fair; reference back to the Merthyr Riots.

31. Evan Thomas to Melbourne, 18 June 1831: HO 52/16.

32. *Monmouthshire Merlin*, 11 June 1831.

33. J.B. Bruce to Bute and Bruce and A. Hill to Melbourne, 2 June 1831; in Bute to Melbourne 3 June 1831: HO 52/16. The letters were read by the King and circulated.

34. The best sources: testimony of John Petherick, at both inquests on John Hughes, in Evan Thomas to Melbourne and T. Thomas to Melbourne, 18 and 26 June 1831: HO 52/16; Bruce to Bute, 2 June 1831, ibid.; trials at Glamorgan Summer Assizes, 13 July 1831, *Cambrian*, 16 July 1831 together with its reports on the rising, 11 and 18 June 1831; Sentence List, Glamorgan Summer Assizes, July 1831. The *Cambrian* gives the nicknames.

35. *Merthyr Guardian*, 2 March 1833: retrospective reference; Thomas Lewis was 40 in 1831.

36. Testimony of Thomas Lewis at Assizes, *Cambrian*, 16 July 1831.

37. For all that follows, trial of John Phelps at Assizes: transcript in Circuit Letters, HO 6/16; report of trial in *Cambrian*, 16 July 1831.

38. The 'damned lout' was omitted in the official transcript sent up to London.

39. Trial of David Thomas at Assizes, *Cambrian*, 16 July 1831.

40. Testimony of Ann Williams at his trial, *Cambrian*, 16 July 1831; the testimony of David Rees, in the following trial, that David Thomas said this only after the magistrates had come and gone, seems mistaken (Rees had had his shop pillaged).

41. Testimony of Thomas Williams at trial of David Thomas, and of John Phelps at his own trial, *Cambrian*, 16 July 1831.

42. Testimony of Thomas Lewis and David Rees at Assizes, *Cambrian*, 16 July 1831.

43. Testimony of Thomas and Elizabeth Lewis at Assizes, *Cambrian*, 16 July 1831: Thomas says the magistrates arrived before Dai Solomon had finished writing his statement.

44. Bruce to Bute, 2 June 1831, Bruce and Hill to Melbourne, 2 June 1831; testimony of John Petherick, first inquest John Hughes, 17 June (on mix-up over Riot Act), second inquest, 21 June, in Evan Thomas to Melbourne, 18 June 1831, T. Thomas to Melbourne, 26 June 1831: all in HO 52/16; testimony of William Thomas the Court, Ann Evans and Thomas Lewis at Assizes, 13 July; *Cambrian*, 16 July 1831.

45. Testimony of Thomas and Elizabeth Lewis at Assizes, 13 July; *Cambrian*, 16 July 1831.

46. Testimony of David Rees and Mary Phillips (on David Thomas's remarks), of Thomas and Elizabeth Lewis on remainder, *Cambrian*, 16 July 1831.

47. Testimony of David Rees: 'I saw Thomas Llewellyn coming from work in his working clothes'; Thomas and Elizabeth Lewis said Llewellyn 'demanded' his pack bedstead and some pans but did nothing, *Cambrian*, 16 July 1831.

48. Testimony of John Petherick at second inquest on John Hughes, 21 June, in T. Thomas to Melbourne, 26 June 1831; Bruce to Bute, 2 June 1831: HO 52/16. At the trial, the exchange between William Thomas the Court and Lewis Lewis occurred when defence counsel Sockett was cross-examining the former on the crowd's attack on the magistrates. Bruce reported: 'There were some near us endeavouring to keep the pressure off

ourselves and in their own defence.' This seems to be a rather grudging acknowledgement of Lewis Lewis's effort to protect the magistrates: *Cambrian*, 16 July 1831.

49. Evan Thomas to Melbourne, 18 June 1831; testimony of John Petherick, 17 June 1831; Bruce and Hill to Melbourne, 2 June 1831: HO 52/16. The letter which Bruce started to write to Bute at 8.30 pm on 2 June (HO 52/16), repeatedly interrupted, is perhaps the most dramatic I have ever read in the public records.

50. Bruce to Bute, 2 June 1831; testimony of John Petherick, 17 June 1831: HO 52/16.

51. The fullest account of the action at Coffin's is the testimony of Luke Pearson at the first inquest on John Hughes, 17 June, in Evan Thomas to Melbourne, 18 June 1831: HO 52/16; for the wall-paper, *Cambrian*, 11 June 1831.

52. Bruce to Bute, 2 June 1831: HO 52/16.

53. Sentence List Glamorgan Summer Assizes, July 1831.

54. 'The street was covered with the leaves from his books.' John Petherick, 21 June 1831: HO 52/16.

55. Testimony of William Rowland, second inquest on John Hughes, 20 June 1831: HO 52/16.

56. John Petherick, 21 June 1831: HO 52/16.

57. Bute to Melbourne, 3 June 1831: HO 52/16. This letter and its enclosures were read by the King.

58. Testimony by the individuals named: James Abbott at the Assizes, 14 July 1831 (HO 17/128, part 2, bundle Zp37); Luke Pearson (Coffin's house), first inquest on John Hughes, 17 June 1831; William Rowland and Ann Harries, both inquests, 17 and 20 June 1831: HO 52/16.

59. Oral testimony: six women and girls in Cefn High Street, September 1975. They would not give their names because 'they did not want to get involved'! This may have had more to do with the then relations between Merthyr Labour councillors and Merthyr Civic Society than with an over-developed sense of the presence of the past!

5 RIOT[1]

On that oppressively hot and thundery Friday morning,[2] the vanguard of the crowd, with its banner, pulled into Forman's Field near the mansion of Penydarren House, to watch the eighty Highlanders go by, led by William Crawshay, who had greeted them at Cyfarthfa and by the magistrates Bruce and Hill, who had cut through side-streets to meet them at the Pandy by Tydfil's Well.[3] According to one observer, the people were 'sullen and sturdy and kept the sides of the road under the walls, not choosing to be driven before the soldiers into town'.[4]

In fact, with the banner and its cohorts looming behind, the detachment of the 93rd marched through lines of people who hissed and shouted 'Reform!'. Gangs of men and women and children paraded in front of them in mockery. 'Look at them! . . . See how few they are! . . . They're in our hands! . . . The game's ours!' Cries, insults, jeers in Welsh flew through the narrow streets at the uncomprehending heads of the soldiers. The crowd had come ready for trouble; hundreds of them carried makeshift weapons, clubs, bludgeons, mandrels, an iron bar, pit timber, hedge stakes, even the side of a wheelbarrow; the rearguard carried its ropes.[5] And now, here they were, the men whose coming had been awaited with a tautening of the stomach and a quickening of the breath: uniforms, commands, a drilled impersonality, the muskets and the bayonets. They were face to face now with the naked power of the State, the ultimate sanction of sovereignty, the men with the licence to kill. But they were so few! A dangerous exhilaration, a giddy sense of irresponsible power recharged the tension of the stifling day.

The troops halted outside the Castle Inn, where the Specials were assembled, while the head of the crowd swept on down the road and hundreds massed around the banner directly outside the front door on its tier of steps rising from the pavement. More and more joined; people packed the doors and windows of the surrounding houses, crowded on the roofs. Observers inside the Castle estimated them at anything from 7,000 to 10,000.[6] At the Castle were the bulk of the Trade of Merthyr, armed as special constables, the High Sheriff of Glamorgan, the magistrates of Merthyr and the communities around, three of the four ironmasters of the town. Outside were thousands of angry and excited demonstrators, ironstone miners, colliers, puddlers; women and

129

shouting children, hundreds of the curious and the expectant. The hard core were the men of yesterday, massed around their Red Flag with its loaf of bread.[7] Lewis Lewis was there, standing by William Williams and his banner; so were David Jones, *Dai Solomon*, and David Hughes. Others were to be singled out as scapegoats later: David Richards, a miner of 31 with whom 'the notorious Betsy Paul' had lived;[8] Richard Lewis, *Dic Penderyn*, a miner of 23, who had thrashed the constable *Shoni Crydd* (John the Shoemaker) and had fought with Tories on the night of the illumination,[9] a twenty-two year old puddler Thomas Richards, a cordwainer Joseph Prothero and two twenty-five year old labourers, Thomas Kinsey of Cefn and James Bird who had led the Reform raids in Dowlais. Of the ten men who were to answer to the law for their actions this day outside the Castle Inn, five were ironstone miners and two were puddlers.

So tense and urgent were the magistrates that they had the Riot Act read before the troops had been effectively deployed.[10] Bread and cheese were brought out to the tired and sweating soldiers as the crowd pressed around them on all sides. Major Falls, their commander, asked the people to fall back. For a moment they did, but then pressed forward again, trying to talk the Highlanders into sedition, mocking them, shouting. The Specials were ordered to drive the crowd back. They ran into the wall of hatred that now divided Village and Inhabitants of the Ironworks and utterly failed.[11] Bruce concentrated them in and around the passage of the Inn as the soldiers, by platoon, went into the Castle, took off their knapsacks and came out again with weapons at the ready.[12] It was while this manoeuvre was in train, that Richard Hoare Jenkins, High Sheriff of Glamorgan, got up on a chair on the Inn steps and read the Riot Act. After he'd started, Bruce asked William Rowland the time; it was 10.40 by the bar clock. When Jenkins finished, Bruce followed in Welsh and took up his station by the door. The crowd replied with a great roar of defiance and raised a forest of clubs.

At that moment, while a squad took up position inside the Inn, some soldiers came clattering down the steps with fixed bayonets. The crowd bubbled with excitement, rage and alarm. There were catcalls and yells as the Highlanders struggled to form two ranks along the wall of the Inn and in front of the door steps, with their bayonets fixed. They carried their weapons at the porte, with the bayonets pointing straight up in the air; those muskets were not loaded.[13] The crowd were not to know this, as they pressed forward upon them, while hundreds heaved behind. A loud voice at the Castle door (which several thought was Lewis Lewis) shouted in Welsh — 'There's no need to fear the soldiers. The game's ours. They're no more than a gooseberry in our hands.'[14] In a tumult of shouting, gentleman after gentleman tried to address the heaving, pushing, sweating, noisy crowd. Men were hoisted up on shoulders to shout back at the gentry. The crowd 'hurra'd . . . made a great noise . . . treated the speeches with contempt . . . treated the Riot Act with perfect indifference . . .'

Anthony Hill finally made himself heard, called on them to choose a dozen or so delegates and send them in to talk with the magistrates and ironmasters.[15] Somehow, a dozen men were picked out of the crowd and William Rowland led them into the conference. They talked for ten to twenty minutes.

In some ways this confrontation is the most opaque moment of all. Accounts of it are vague, confused and contradictory. The most precise (probably deceptively so) was that which Anthony Hill wrote for Lord Melbourne only a few hours later after a wild ride from Merthyr. He said the deputation wanted:

the Court of Requests suppressed
higher wages
a reduction in the cost of all articles and appliances which they used
    daily in their work (presumably a reference to the butty system
    of sub-contracting)
an immediate Reform 'which they expected would reduce the price
    of bread over half and by introducing a free trade immediately
    advance the price of iron' . . . and hence wages.

Evan Thomas the Glamorgan magistrate reported later that the deputation talked at length 'but in a very desultory manner . . . Alleging that they were starving under the want of food at the moment, to which it was replied that that could not possibly be the case, unless they had been neglecting their work for the purpose of carrying on their proceedings at Aberdare etc etc . . .' Talking of another deputation two days later whose spirit was certainly much the same, Evan Thomas said everyone agreed that the language and conduct of the delegate were those of a man expecting some direct individual advantage from political reformation and confident that physical force would shortly effect reform.[16]

These indications are important less in themselves than as symptoms of a much deeper disaffection. There are some obvious points of contact with the issues debated at the meeting on the Waun on 30 May and, less directly, with the actions against the town middle class on 2 June. Note that even the demand for higher wages (which would surely be an unavoidable ritual on such an occasion) was linked with a general Reform and Free Trade. On the one hand there are the broad, generic, near-millenarian expectations of profound change from the national crisis; on the other, the translation of this essentially revolutionary sensibility into intensely local and particular exigencies – the suppression of the Court of Requests, grievances over the butty system, a restoration of 'natural order' at the expense of the shopocracy. Essentially *absent* is a sense of reality about, of getting to grips with, the intermediate but determinant power of the ironmasters. Equally notable is the 'absence' on the one hand of the hard-core radical democrats of the town middle class with their active political consciousness (where were Christopher James, Job James, David John? One Unitarian minister was manhandled by a crowd) and on the other of the kind of working-class activism which magistrates associated with such as Thomas Llewellyn (who seems to have disappeared).

The power of the ironmasters was, of course, visible and omnipresent. Their hegemony ran deep. Consider the manner in which Cyfarthfa and Dowlais workers reflected the attitudes of their masters. It was Crawshay's men who followed their leader into radical action, at least in the beginning; at that very moment of confrontation, hundreds of Guest's Dowlais workmen were holding aloof from the struggle. But in the realities of working and living in Merthyr that power of the ironmasters was refracted, mediated through a hundred multiple and often divergent channels, diffused through a hundred contradictions. When workers came to 'translate' their general and near-millenarian sense of revolutionary change into direct action, they rebelled against enemies they could see, with whom they were in daily friction; they smashed the Court of Requests, they virtually rebelled against the shopocracy and the middle class. The natural-justice action directed essentially against the middle class was, in fact, an effort to assert *control*. It was to establish some control over their own lives in the face of apparently impersonal powers that they took local control of Merthyr. In so doing, they ripped the fabric of order and had to confront the real agents of control – the soldier and the ironmaster. At that point, communication was hardly possible. What is very striking about the reports of this confrontation, as of others, is the *gigantic disproportion* between the spirit which obviously moved these people and the small change of ritual negotiation into which they had to translate it. They found no adequate vocabulary; there probably was none to find.

This is why their masters and their magistrates found it so hard to discover what they actually *wanted*. In the last resort they wanted nothing that those masters could give them, because they wanted everything. They wanted a renovation of all things. They wanted *Reform*.

It was a traditional confrontation of the irresistible and the immovable. The masters and magistrates would concede nothing while a crowd remained in arms; they promised to consider 'grievances' if they were properly presented. The delegates, on the other hand, *had* to go back with something. Anthony Hill, with a characteristic blindness, thought the delegates were 'satisfied' (it was the mob which would be unreasonable, naturally); James Abbott, who saw them go out, said they looked very dissatisfied. One rumour repeated much later was probably a myth and an effort to smear Richard Lewis, *Dic Penderyn*, who was one of the delegation and the only rioter to be formally executed, but it is closer to Abbott than to Hill. One of the delegates is alleged to have said, 'Damn them, I wish my knife was three or four inches in their bellies.' William Rowland certainly heard them say 'there was nothing settled'.[17]

He added . . . 'Everyone wanted to know the result of what the gentlemen had said . . .' People crowded around the delegates as they threaded their way through and there was uproar. It was suddenly stilled, when Rowland told Bruce that it was 11.42. The Riot Act's hour was up. Sheriff Jenkins got on his chair by the door and explained in English that they had to disperse on pain of death; Bruce followed in Welsh.[18]

Rowland reports that the crowd greeted this with 'the utmost contempt'. John Petherick saw its ranks seethe with excitement and start pressing on the soldiers. Major Falls again begged them to fall back; once again pressure eased momentarily only to start again almost at once. Men began to work their way round the soldiers' backs, between them and the wall. Donald Black, one of the Highlanders, became very uneasy when he saw Lewis Lewis and the flagbearer trying to get between him and the door. Captain Sparks grabbed one man who had got through and forced him back. 'You wouldn't do so to me,' Lewis Lewis told him belligerently in English.[19] Petherick, going into the passage, heard a soldier complain that the crowd had insulted him. 'Do your duty and hold your tongue,' an officer replied. The soldier went on grumbling and the officer snapped, 'If you don't be quiet and obey orders implicitly, I'll cut you down.'[20]

At this tense moment, according to William Thomas, a painter, who was at the parlour window, the people began to call for Josiah John Guest.[21]

Guest had a good paternalist record at Dowlais. At that moment, many of his men were quiet about his works. Anthony Hill was 'a gentleman' according to Lady Charlotte Guest, but rather quirky, a Tory of the old school and a dry stick of a man. Guest was rarely loved, as Crawshay quite often was, but he was never hated, as Crawshay equally often was; he was respected. Now they began to shout for him.

Guest refused to stand on a chair at the head of the steps. He went, with Crawshay and Petherick, to the upstairs window over the front door. He did not fear personal violence, he told them. His men would acknowledge that he had done everything to ameliorate their condition. If the people came to him when this moment of excitement had passed, he would see what he could do.

A man clamoured to speak and was hoisted on people's shoulders. Their wages were too low, he said. For himself, if he could get enough bread for himself and his family, he'd be content. At once, the crowd gave a great roar. 'Down with him!' Another man was lifted up. They wouldn't be satisfied with bread only, he said. And at that point, the crowd suddenly broke into a great cry — *'Caws gyda bara!'* Cheese with the Bread! They took it up as a chant . . . *Caws gyda bara!*[22]

Only a fool could think that men would attack soldiers and risk bayonetting, hanging and transportation for a piece of cheese. This was precisely the same dialogue of the deaf that had baffled Bruce on the Thursday and the masters a few minutes earlier. The language of a crowd has to be read as the instinctively symbolic language it is: what these men were shouting was that men do not live by bread alone.[23] Characteristically, the speaker tried to follow through with a clumsy list of 'essentials' . . . cheese, shoes, clothes, rent, beer . . . He wanted an answer: were they to have these things or not? The crowd got impatient and pulled him down. Lewis Lewis, *Lewsyn yr Heliwr*, who had been trying vainly to speak for some time, had himself hoisted up by the door and shouted 'Stick together till we get these terms!'[24] He was at once replaced by a young man, who addressed himself directly to the window where Guest and Crawshay stood. He called for an answer.

By this time, the crowd was in movement. They were thrusting themselves between the soldiers and the Castle Inn. 'Keep the wall,' they shouted, 'whatever you do, keep the wall . . . Squeeze on . . .

press on . . .' One observer thought they were getting three deep between the soldiers and the wall. The ranks were breaking up. Donald Black saw *Lewsyn yr Heliwr* behind him. The Red Flag got behind the front rank. 'Press on . . . press on . . . don't let them back into the Inn' the crowd was shouting.[25] At this point, soldiers went upstairs at the Castle and took their stance at the windows, with loaded muskets, two to each window. 'Recollect men,' said an officer in a very loud voice, 'your orders are not to fire unless commanded by an officer, by an officer, mind . . .'[26] On the pavement, crowd and soldiers were locked: the Highlanders could not get their bayonets down. 'If the Commanding Officer had understood Welsh,' Bruce said later, 'no musket would have been seized.'[27]

The young man who had called for an answer, called again, in Welsh. This time, he called Guest by name . . . 'We have waited for your answer a long time. We have waited long enough. Come, we must have your answer.'

Guest came to the window. He was sorry they had not listened to him. It was their own violent behaviour which had led the Inhabitants to send for the soldiers. If any lamentable consequences followed, no man would regret it more than he. 'I have done all in my power; you must take the consequences upon yourselves.'

Then Crawshay came to the window. Within hours, the legend had reached Monmouthshire that he had fired a pistol into the crowd. The effect was comparable: 'So help me God,' he shouted, 'I will not listen to people coming in arms in this violent manner.' But if his men elected one or more delegates from every level and came to see him in a fortnight, he'd pledge himself to redress their grievances . . .[28]

There was a roar of anger from the crowd and they surged around the soldiers . . . 'Don't let them go in,' they shouted, 'press on . . . press on.' The crowd around Lewis Lewis hoisted him up on their shoulders and he held on to the lamp-iron by the Inn door . . . 'Listen, boys,' he shouted in Welsh, 'We wanted bread but the masters have brought the soldiers against us. They say they've brought the soldiers here for their protection. We'll show them they're not protection enough. Boys, if you are all of the same mind as me, fall on them and take their arms away. Off with their guns!'[29]

He jumped down. Henry Jones, a gentleman, from the Castle windows, saw Lewis Lewis and the men around him thrust forward at the soldiers. Ann Harries, standing by her door, saw him, 'a man dressed like a miner', jump down and then heard 'the crashing and rattling of guns . . .' Richard Lambert, further up High Street, saw bayonets moving and shaking backwards and forwards over the heads of the crowd. Petherick, from his upstairs window, saw what he called 'a heavy swell of men' move forward, as if driven by those behind. There was a momentary check as they hit the soldiers, then loud shouts of 'Press on . . .' and 'Bread! Bread!' and a blinding hail of missiles as they hurled their clubs, bludgeons, stones, at the Castle. On the roofs opposite men stood up and threw a volley of stones and brickbats. The windows of the Castle Inn splintered as the crowd surged forward again (Henry Jones thought it was like a great wave of the sea). They seized the muskets of the front rank of soldiers, three or four men to every soldier.[30]

In seizing those muskets, they were seizing 'the property of our Sovereign Lord the King'; they were laying hands on the sovereignty.

Those hands were violent, almost beyond the telling. Petherick saw three men struggle so violently with a sergeant that they broke his pontoon. Samuel Thomas, from the upstairs room next door, saw a man hit a soldier in the grip of two attackers so hard that he snapped the stock of his captured musket. A shoemaker downstairs, probably brother to that Shoni Crydd whom Dic Penderyn had fought, said he saw *Lewsyn yr Heliwr* twice thrust with a bayonet at the Highlanders.[31]

In the first onslaught, the crowd laid out four or five soldiers, seized most of the muskets of the front rank and went surging at the windows and into the front passageway. The Specials hammered at them and the soldiers there could level their bayonets. The attackers were driven out. They returned to the attack, again and again. They dragged William Rowland into the crowd. He had to fight his way back alongside the disarmed Highlanders struggling up the steps and lugging their wounded into the packed, panting and swearing passage. William Williams led a sortie down the steps to snatch a rioter with a musket in his hand. James Abbott thought he heard a shot here though no-one else reported it. But men were already dead. One rebel fell with a bayonet sticking right through him and out of his back; another took a bayonet through the heart. Donald Black, fighting his way back up the steps, lost his musket and was stabbed through the thigh. Major Falls reeled in with blood pouring from his head and neck. Again and again, the crowd fought their way up the steps and into the Inn; again and again they were driven out.[32]

'Oh God!' shouted one soldier by an upstairs window as he saw a comrade clubbed senseless on the pavement, 'can't we fire?' 'No!' shouted his companion, 'we dare not until we get orders!'[33] In the adjoining room, an officer watched in agony as the sergeant went down. He turned to Crawshay and asked whether he was a magistrate. The ironmaster said he was not. The officer turned and looked through the window to see a man floor a soldier with the barrel of his own musket.[34] At that moment William Howell of the Patriot Inn in the passage downstairs heard an officer yell at the soldiers in the street to load and fire.[35] Someone, perhaps the same man, ran to the stairs and shouted up them, 'Fire, men, fire!'[36] Almost simultaneously, the officer at Crawshay's window cried 'Fire!'[37] A volley crashed out, mostly from the soldiers upstairs, straight into the heaving mass below.

At the first shock, the crowd reeled back. As the smoke cleared, Petherick saw four or five bodies lying bleeding in the street. William Davies, trapped in the crowd opposite the Castle and a little below, was carried by the frightened surge of people up against the line of men stretching the rearguard rope across the street. 'Stand back! Stand back!' shouted the men with bludgeons, 'they have nothing but powder!' The crowd recoiled, reeled back towards those deadly muzzles. Davies heard a shriek and the word 'killed!' and the people lurched forwards, trampling dozens underfoot as the rope gave way and men, women and children ran off in every direction.[38]

Even as hundreds fled and the soldiers fired shot after shot, scores of others came storming back through the firing to attack the doorway and the windows yet again. Ann Harries saw two men carried off to the Tramroad and down the High Street, saw John Hughes, a miner who had fought as a soldier in six battles and never suffered a scratch, fall mortally wounded. Men picked up his stolen musket and turned back to face the Inn.[39] Petherick saw one man aim a musket directly at him and pull the trigger; it misfired. David Jones, *Dai Solomon*, and David Hughes were two of those who fired back at the Castle.[40] As the ground in front of the Inn cleared, more and more soldiers brought their muskets into play, but William Thomas the Court was horrified to see men return to attack the doorway even as the shooting went on. According to Crawshay, it took a quarter of an hour of the most desperate and determined fighting on both sides to clear the street.[41]

And even as the first volley crashed out at the front, a thunder of stones came drumming on the back wall of the Castle. In a sudden alarm William Thomas, with William Rowland, led an officer and three men to the back door. Men were already half-way up the long stable yard. When they ran into the soldiers, they drew back and let fly with stones. The Highlanders opened fire and two or three men fell. But they went on fighting. One man got within three yards of a soldier to smash a stone into him before he was shot. The soldiers fought their way down the long yard and out into the street. The battle went on raging there, even as the front of the Castle was cleared and troops spilled out into the highway.[42]

Suddenly, there was another shout. A crowd was coming at the Castle from Riverside. Every soldier with a gun (some thirty stand of arms had been lost) turned out into the street to meet them. William Thomas went through the yard into the field to see if they were coming that way. He ran head-on into Lewis Lewis, running with a musket in his hand. 'Stand your ground! Stand your ground!' he was shouting as men with captured guns went racing round the rear of the Inn.[43]

Outside the yard the struggle was still going on, even though the firing 'had rather abated' according to Richard Lambert. One group dragged a soldier a hundred yards from the Inn up the lane leading to William Perkins's house. They got hold of his musket and belted him across the head with it. He ran back to the Inn, holding his head, as his assailants dispersed. Rowland Thomas, a sick man of 47 who worked for Perkins, passed at that point on his way home to dinner. He picked up the Highlander's cap and threw it over the wall. A soldier shot him down.[44]

There was a short silence, as John Petherick and William Rowland picked their way through the caps, bludgeons, two-pound stones which littered the street, among the eight or nine corpses lying there, like slates after a thunderstorm, past the people being carried off, the weeping woman with her dead son in her arms. Suddenly there was the whine of a shot whipping into the Castle and narrowly missing Crawshay and the High Sheriff.[45]

Men with guns had run down to the Morlais brook and the Tip, the cinder bank whose towering height commanded the entire rear of the Inn. Four of them broke into the shop of the wretched Thomas Lewis, who went through his second day of hell. They demanded powder and shot. He had no shot, but they took a can of marbles. Lewis hid in the garden as the men lay on the Tip and opened fire at the Castle. The soldiers in the street fired back. William Thomas had to make a desperate detour through Ynysgau to keep out of the line of fire.

Thomas Lewis gingerly ventured out into the street. There, among the men running with guns, was *Lewsyn yr Heliwr*. He demanded powder. When Thomas said there was none, *Lewsyn* pointed the musket at him. 'If you don't come with us to the Tip,' he said, 'you're a dead man.' They forced Thomas Lewis to hold a can of powder as they lay along the Tip and sent shot after shot at the Castle Inn. Petherick could see their heads and shoulders moving on the cinder bank. William Rowland said they kept up the fire for twelve or thirteen minutes. When they ran out of shot, they fired the marbles.[46]

The guns of the soldiers fell silent. Major Falls, bleeding and bewildered, kept shouting, 'Cease firing, men, cease firing' until Rowland told him that it was not his men but the rebels on the Tip. William Thomas the painter, who had made his way up into the stable loft, saw one man emerge on to the field and fire a shot at the Inn. He pointed him out to the soldiers who opened fire. The man fell. Thomas said this was the last shot the soldiers fired.[47] After a while, there was silence.

Two weeks later, the magistrate Evan Thomas was to exclaim, in understandably fractured grammar . . . 'The circumstances and duration of the conflict with the soldiers on Friday morning were such as seldom, I believe, never occurred in England before . . .'[48] It is certainly difficult to think of anything comparable. The determination and sheer blind courage of many in the crowd were matched by the bravery and discipline of the soldiers, who no doubt shared their desperation. No soldier was killed but sixteen were wounded, six of them severely.[49]

The clock-watcher William Rowland said the shooting could not have started before 12.10.[50] He is broadly confirmed by John Garnons the gardener who left his work just before noon, walked 150 yards up a lane to be blocked by the crowd and walked back down before he heard the firing.[51] John Petherick said the soldiers upstairs went on firing for about five minutes before the cease-fire while those downstairs kept on a little longer. The time-conscious William Rowland made it seven or eight minutes. Both William Thomas the Court and Petherick said the soldiers they were with fired 'two or three shots' each; none of these estimates seems to include those moments when every soldier who could carry a gun was out in the street firing at the people at the Riverside and on the Tip, among other targets. At first, only the dozen or so men upstairs would have been able to shoot but the volume of firing would have increased rapidly; the *Cambrian* spoke of 'rapid firing'. There could well have been over a hundred shots. In the early stages, it would have been difficult to miss.

Rowland saw the bodies of six men, a woman and a young boy of 12 to 14 in the street. They were carried into the coach-house but were taken away by their families by six o'clock. Many men were dragged or dragged themselves off to die in corners. Crawshay gave the rather odd total of 'nearly 16' killed; the *Cambrian* put it at 18. One woman was killed as she sat in her room knitting; a pauper on his way to pick up his poor relief died. Evan Thomas, on 16 June, gave the latest 'authentic list' as sixteen killed, three of them women and one a boy, but admitted there was much uncertainty. He thought five or six more had been killed. The wounded, he said, could not be estimated; the *Cambrian* put it at seventy. Individuals must have perished in secrecy. Both Thomas and the *Cambrian* said the wounded kept themselves hidden unless they became desperate . . . 'The dead have been buried in the most quiet and silent way by their friends . . . bodies are daily found in the fields and hedges of the place . . .'[52]

As people died in ditches and scores more nursed their wounds in frightened and angry kitchens, bitter and militant men fanned out through the town and much of north Glamorgan, calling men to arms, hunting for weapons, raiding farmhouses for fowling pieces. David Hughes put a shot through William Bryant's windows. That night, Cyfarthfa Castle came under fire for a couple of hours. Even as the guns at the Castle Inn fell silent, survivors from the crowd had rallied near the canal bridge. *Lewsyn yr Heliwr* spoke to them from the parapet. He told them to distribute the guns among the men who could use them.[53] That capacity for planning, for a quasi-military discipline which the *Reform* actions of Thursday had hinted at, soon registered on the startled minds of authority. The hard core of Crawshay men began to set up an armed camp near Cefn, on the Brecon Road and to establish an outpost near Hirwaun on the road to Swansea.

The men at the Castle Inn were in desperate predicament and every one of them knew it. They were in deadly fear of a mass insurrection in vengeance which would engulf the whole coalfield. A breathless Anthony Hill told Melbourne that evening of their dread at the thought of a population of some 120,000 to 150,000 within a fourteen-mile radius, nearly all of them working-men and lacking in the 'intermediate grade' of a middle class. He left the Castle Inn at once, on a desperate search for troops, galloping on a mad ride to Cardiff where he got letters from Bute to the commanding officers of every unit within reach, to Newport where he persuaded the officer in charge of the 93rd's detachment there to move. Twenty-eight men piled into coaches, smashing the windows with their bayonets, and careered off along the valleys road. Hill rode on, to Trowbridge, but failed to move the commander of the 3rd Dragoons there, so he had to spur on all the way to London. After an evening exchange with Melbourne alarm gripped the government. The Merthyr correspondence was passed to the

King and in the morning, Lord Hill at the War Office ordered out the 3rd Dragoons from Wotton-under-Edge and instructed 150 men of the 98th Foot at Plymouth to embark on the new steam packet *Albion* for Cardiff. Anthony Hill had already set off for Merthyr late the previous evening.[54]

Lieutenant-Colonel Richard Morgan, of the Royal Glamorgan Militia, got there first. As soon as he heard that Major Falls had been severely wounded, he volunteered to take command and Bute let him go. He reached Merthyr at seven o'clock on the day of the shooting. He found the town had been abandoned.[55]

At the Castle Inn, in hourly fear of a renewed attack, they had decided to pull out to the more defensible station of Penydarren House, a mansion in its own grounds set back from the main north-south road and within easy reach of Cyfarthfa Castle. Crawshay reported that the men of the 93rd left at five o'clock, carrying their wounded in the coaches which had just brought up the staff of the Glamorgan Militia. An anonymous correspondent to the *Cambrian*, however, claims that the 93rd had left 'long before'; it was the Royal Glamorgan who escorted the wounded through crowded and hostile streets, and through the torrential rain which finally broke late in the afternoon. The key was obviously the arrival of Major Rickards and some 70 men of the East Glamorgan Yeomanry, who were the first to get through, followed by 50 more, probably from the Central Division, in the evening. Edward Purchase, keeper of the Castle Inn, supplied 'lunches' (a unique service) for 80 Highlanders and 70 of 'the Cardiff cavalry' before giving them the regulation 'dinner' (normally a mid-day meal) in the evening. It was these cavalrymen who were the shield for the withdrawal of the 93rd and for Captain Howells and his 52 men of the Royal Glamorgan carrying the six badly wounded Highlanders through the rain and the rioters to Penydarren House. An order for 27 quarts of ale later in the evening probably testifies to the arrival of the 93rd's detachment from Newport.[56] There were nearly 300 men at Penydarren by the evening of 3 June, but only some 60 to 70 of them were regulars who were fit to act. Their situation seemed as desperate as the hostility they encountered in the streets. They were glad to borrow a case of duelling pistols, three guns, three powder flasks, two shot belts and a canister of powder from William Marsden, draper and chief constable.[57]

They had reason. The crowds moving on the hills and drilling with their new weapons were more ominous than the thunder-clouds above them. At embattled Hirwaun, angry and determined men enacted a full ritual of vengeance. They sacrificed a calf and bathed a flag in its blood. The bearer carried the banner, still wet, with blood streaming down his arms. When it reached Merthyr, there was no-one to challenge it.[58]

Notes

1.   To avoid tedious repetition: henceforth, testimony will be cited by name and date only; unless otherwise stated, all correspondence, inquest testimony and accounts/analyses will be HO 52/16; all testimony at Assizes from *Cambrian* 16 or 23 July 1831; general narratives from *Cambrian* 11 and 18 June 1831.
2.   Charles Wilkins, *History of Merthyr Tydfil*, p. 303.
3.   The actual number of the Highlanders is a problem; some accounts put it at around 80, others in the upper sixties, not a matter of moment, but irritating. Anthony Hill gave Melbourne the deceptively precise figure of 'about 68' (Hill to Melbourne, 3 June), J.B. Bruce, at the Assizes, spoke of 'about 70' soldiers (HO 17/128); Crawshay said that, after the first attack on them, the 93rd were 'reduced to 50' (*Cambrian*, 11 June); some 16 of the Highlanders were wounded and this would suggest a total in the upper sixties. On the other hand, some 30 muskets had been seized and Crawshay might have meant 50 effectives, which would suggest a total of around 80. The *Cambrian* itself referred to 'two companies'.
           The lower assessments are directly contradicted by other estimates. At the final confrontation on the 6th, above Dowlais, there were 110 Highlanders. The only substantial reinforcements known to have got through were 27 Highlanders under one officer from Newport who reached Merthyr on the evening of 3 June; an ammunition train from Brecon had got through on the 5th; allowing for any men who might have accompanied this train (they could have been only a handful) and for the 16 wounded on the other hand, this would point to a total of about 80 on the morning of the 3rd.
           The most decisive evidence in favour of 80 is that of Edward Purchase, keeper of the Castle Inn. He supplied 'lunches' for 80 Highlanders and 70 of the 'Cardiff cavalry' on the 3rd followed by 'dinners' for a group of '81' men. Dinners for men were normally provided at mid-day; the 'lunches' seem to refer to the bread and cheese supplied to the 93rd soon after their arrival; the East Glamorgan Yeomanry arrived shortly after the shooting. Moreover, 81 quarts of ale for the 93rd were one of the first orders to come from Penydarren House after the military's withdrawal there (distinct from an order for 27 quarts later, which seems to announce the arrival of the 93rd's detachment from Newport).
           I have therefore plumped for a total of 'about 80' Highlanders on the not very bold assumption that, in such matters, an innkeeper would know what he was doing. (Riot Expenses, a roll of 125 items in Crawshay Papers (NLW), Box 12.) I have discussed this material (though I there mistimed the shooting) in 'The Merthyr Riots: settling the account', *NLWJ*, xi (1959), pp. 124-41.
4.   On the entry of the troops: testimony of William Thomas, painter, 17 June; Crawshay in *Cambrian*, 11 June; Evan Thomas to Bute, 16 June.

5.   Brotherton to Fitzroy Somerset, 14 June; J.B. Bruce, testimony at Assizes (HO 17/128); testimony of William Thomas Court, 20 June; testimony of Richard Lambert, inquest on Rowland Thomas, 22 June.

6.   Testimony of Ann Harries, 20 June; testimony of William Rowland, 20 June; testimony of Richard Lambert, 22 June; for the position of the Red Flag, testimony of William Rowland and Donald Black at Assizes (HO 17/128) and from a remark attributed to Lewis Lewis after execution of Dic Penderyn, *Cambrian*, 20 August 1831 and comment of *Man of Glamorgan*, ibid., 10 September; testimony of James Abbott at Assizes (HO 17/128) for estimate of 8,000 to 10,000; William Thomas Court, 20 June, put them at 7,000; Col. Morgan on 3 June, said 'upwards of 3,000' actually attacked the soldiers (letter to Bute on taking command at Penydarren House); for people standing on roofs opposite, testimony of William Thomas, painter, 17 June.

7.   These names derive from Sentence List, Glamorgan Summer Assizes, July 1831, correlated with reports of the Assizes, *Cambrian*, 16 and 23 July and HO 17/128.

8.   *Cambrian*, 18 June 1831.

9.   Chs. 7 and 8 below.

10. The chronology is a little difficult here, since testimonies are not easy to correlate. The Riot Act was read from 10.40 am (testimony of William Rowland, 17 and 20 June). Evan Thomas says the Act was read 'as soon as they [soldiers] arrived', while saying that bread and cheese were brought out and some of the soldiers went into the Inn (letter to Bute, 16 June). William Thomas Court says that the Act was read *before* soldiers 'moved to the pavement' in front of the Castle (17 June). William Thomas, painter, says the troops took up position in two ranks outside the Inn; the front rank went inside to take off their knapsacks, returned, and were followed by the second rank, and he then says bread and cheese were brought out and then that the Riot Act was read (17 June). My account in this paragraph and the first section of the next seems to me the best way to make sense of this evidence and the various general accounts. There can be no certainty, of course, but the general trend is clear.

11. Testimony of William Thomas, painter, 17 June; William Rowland, at the Assizes (HO 17/128) said the crowd was particularly furious against the Specials: '. . . they were determined to be revenged on the constables . . . particularly would play the devil with the constables . . . or words to that effect' (i.e. the shopocracy).

12. Testimony of J.B. Bruce at Assizes (HO 17/128) confirmed by that of William Williams at the Assizes and William Thomas, painter, 17 June.

13. For the unloaded muskets, testimony of Donald Black, a Highlander, at Assizes (HO 17/128): 'We had fixed bayonets . . . Our guns were not charged'; testimony of William Howell, the Patriot, deposition, 8 June (in A. Hill to Melbourne, 26 June); after the attack had begun, he heard an officer 'tell the soldiers who remained in the street to *load* and fire . . .' (my italics); on the bayonets pointing up in the air, testimony of John Petherick, 21 June; the soldiers were at 'Shoulder Arms' and could not use their weapons; testimony of James Abbott at Assizes: 'the bayonets were upright'; testimony of Richard Lambert, 22 June: after the attack began, he saw muskets and bayonets 'moving and shaking backwards and forwards' over the heads of the crowd.

14. There is some doubt as to precisely *when* this was said. Expressions of this nature were used from the moment the troops arrived, as is clear from many people's testimony; Evan Thomas (16 June) quoted the remark and

placed it *after* the deputation; William Thomas, painter, however, on 17 June, implied that it was said *before*; so did William Rowland at the inquest of 17 June, though at the Assizes (HO 17/128) his statement is indeterminate chronologically and could be construed as meaning that the gooseberry remark was made *after* the deputation. I have placed it here, after the Riot Act, but your guess is as good as mine.

On its attribution to Lewis Lewis: testimony of William Rowland at the Assizes: 'This was said opposite to the Castle door loud enough to be heard at a distance' (this is where Lewsyn was); Mr Maule, prosecutor at the Assizes, attributed it to Lewis Lewis.

The remark itself sounds like a current Welsh idiom, though I do not know it. In my youth 'goosegog' (gooseberry) was used as a term of abuse, in Welsh and English.

15.   Evan Thomas, 16 June; testimony of William Thomas, painter, 17 June; William Rowland, who said Hill asked for 10, 12 or 14 delegates, showed them into the room for talks, testimony 20 June and at the Assizes; James Abbott and Thomas Darker also spoke of the deputation at the Assizes, while in petitions on behalf of Dic Penderyn, several people spoke of his presence among the twelve (HO 17/128).

16.   A. Hill to Melbourne, 3 June 1831 (HO 52/16); Evan Thomas to Bute and Melbourne, 16 and 18 June.

17.   A. Hill to Melbourne, 3 June 1831; testimony of James Abbott and William Rowland at Assizes (HO 17/128); *Cambrian*, 27 August 1831: anonymous letter.

18.   Testimony of William Rowland, 17 and 20 June; of William Thomas Court, 20 June; Evan Thomas, 16 June.

19.   On the crowd pressing behind the soldiers, testimony of William Thomas Court, 17 June; testimony of John Petherick, 21 June; testimony of Donald Black at Assizes (HO 17/128).

20.   Testimony of John Petherick, 21 June. At this point, Petherick moved into the passage and went to the upstairs window over the front door of the Inn, with Crawshay and Guest. His testimony, particularly at the inquest of 21 June (in T. Thomas to Melbourne, 26 June) becomes very full and precise, particularly on the order of events and speeches, while others seem rather confused over chronology. I have therefore taken him as prime witness for the last few minutes before the attack.

21.   Testimony of William Thomas, painter, 17 June; Evan Thomas, 16 June, says Guest was listened to 'with great attention'; James Abbott at the Assizes says a man who addressed Guest from the crowd did so 'respect-fully'.

22.   The basis of this section is the testimony of John Petherick, 21 June. Others also referred to the 'bread and cheese' though not so succinctly as Petherick. William Thomas, painter, 17 June, also has a man calling for bread and being replaced by others saying 'they would not be content to work for bread alone'; James Abbott, at the Assizes, said he heard a man say 'in the presence of 10,000, he spoke as loud as he was able, I did not hear any threat, he did it respectfully, he said they wanted bread and cheese, that there were many families that had not sufficient . . . I did not hear Mr Guest promise them bread and cheese . . .' (HO 17/128). My guess is that the respectful speaker was the man who was pulled down and replaced. Lewis Lewis in his petition of 27 July 1831 (HO 17/128) said that he spoke of his poverty from the lamp iron and 'cried for bread', that another man 'took his place at the Lamp Post' and that this man called out 'We must have cheese too'. This suggests that it was Lewis

himself who was pulled down. This seems unlikely to me; not only was it out of character, no-one mentioned Lewis by name on this particular issue and they did not fail to, on other occasions! Petherick himself knew Lewis Lewis, of course – 'he knew his person before' he said on 17 June, and certainly did not credit him with the 'bread alone' speech. This supplementary evidence, however, confirms me in my reading of the incident – that the man who spoke respectfully calling for bread was denounced and pulled down, that his successor said bread alone was not enough and that then, it was the *crowd* which began to chant Cheese with the Bread, leaving the speaker to follow up (which is precisely what Petherick says).

23. Many years ago I heard Aneurin Bevan speak on the Waun above Tredegar; I forget what he was actually saying, but at one point, an old miner (blue scars) near me started to shout 'Give us bread, Aneurin!' The crowd around us took it up briefly as a chant. South Wales miners calling for 'bread' in the late 1950s, when their clubs were stocking Bacardi and coke and were loud with argument over the quality of various cars and the rival claims of the Costa Brava and the Costa del Sol! 1831 of course was not the 1950s, but I think the call for 'cheese' then had precisely the same quality as the call for 'bread' which I heard.

24. What 'terms'? There *were* no terms. The intervention, however, rings familiarly to anyone who has heard a speaker compete for the attention of an excited crowd.

25. Basis, once more, testimony of John Petherick, 21 June; Evan Thomas, 16 June; testimony of William Thomas Court, 17 June (where he said the crowd were three deep between the soldiers and the wall); testimony of Donald Black at the Assizes (HO 17/128).

26. Testimony of John Petherick, 21 June.

27. Testimony of J.B. Bruce at the Assizes: HO 17/128.

28. Testimony of John Petherick, 21 June; it is William Thomas, painter, 17 June, who has the 'So help me God!' which sounds both characteristic and plausible.

29. Practically every witness reports the speech in much the same terms, though their wording differs a little. One could think of a Welsh version but I lack the nerve to provide it; my version is an attempt to collate the reports into something credible; all evidence was an English translation of Welsh and reads more clumsily than the original would have sounded; William Thomas, painter, 17 June, says: 'The people were much pleased by the man's speech, they shouted loudly', though he is a little confused over precise order (understandably!).

30. All witnesses at the inquests of 17 and 20-22 June, all authors of depositions on 8 June (in A. Hill to Melbourne, 26 June) and all general accounts agree; the statement of Henry Jones comes from the second petition on behalf of Dic Penderyn, 5 August 1831, in HO 17/128; all other testimony under the persons named at inquests of 17 and 20-22 June.

31. Testimony of John Petherick, 21 June; deposition of Samuel Thomas Pont-y-Storehouse, 8 June (A. Hill to Melbourne, 26 June); Thomas had been ordered out of one upstairs window when the soldiers took up their positions, but moved to another, behind more soldiers; for the shoe-maker, Evan Thomas, 16 June.

32. Testimony of William Rowland and William Williams at the Assizes (HO 17/128); testimony of William Thomas the Court, 17 June, in particular, where he stresses that the crowd forced the inn three or four times; on the

deaths, James Abbott, testimony at the Assizes and *Cambrian*, 11 June; William Thomas, painter, rushing into the passage, ran into Major Falls with blood all over his neck: testimony, 17 June; testimony of Donald Black at the Assizes; Evan Thomas, 16 June.

33. Deposition of Samuel Thomas Pont-y-Storehouse, 8 June.
34. Testimony of John Petherick, 21 June.
35. Deposition of William Howell, the Patriot, 8 June.
36. Deposition of Samuel Thomas Pont-y-Storehouse, 8 June.
37. Testimony of John Petherick, 21 June.
38. Testimony of William Davies, 17 June; I do not know whether this is the same William Davies as John Phelps's mate; the name is not exactly rare in Wales!
39. Testimony of Ann Harries, 20 June; testimony of William Thomas Court, 17 and 20 June. He was called to Hughes an hour after the battle was over. Hughes claimed that he had been 'pressed' into the crowd, said he had served his country, fought six battles and never been wounded. He could have hoped for a better death. At the inquest of 21 June, his father William — 'I knew John Hughes, he was my son' — said his son had admitted that the crowd were more to blame than the soldiers: 'No one must blame the soldiers, they only did their duty.' Hughes had been hit in the back, the ball passing through his navel; he died shortly after Thomas had seen him.
40. Testimony of John Petherick, 21 June; Sentence List Glamorgan Summer Assizes, July 1831.
41. Testimony of William Thomas Court, 17 and 20 June; Crawshay in the *Cambrian*, 11 June; Evan Thomas, 16 June, also emphasised the persistence of these attacks even as the firing went on.
42. Testimony of William Thomas Court, 17 June and William Rowland, 20 June: the latter was stationed at the rear of the Inn, he only 'heard' the rush at the front, but he saw the rebel get within three yards of a soldier before being shot; Evan Thomas, 16 June.
43. Testimony of William Thomas Court, 17 June. Here, the official transcript sent to the Home Office is a complete muddle; it has the crowd coming by the field and Thomas encountering Lewis Lewis by the Riverside and then making a detour through Ynysgau. This makes no topographical sense. Evan Thomas warned the Home Office that the chairman of the inquest jury, who was Christopher James himself, was taking notes and that a report would appear in the press. (Evan Thomas to Melbourne, 18 June.) The report in the *Cambrian* of 25 June 1831 is in fact much more accurate (and is followed here); the official transcriber seems to have skipped whole sentences.
44. Testimony of Richard Lambert, 22 June. Four witnesses gave evidence on 22 June as well as the surgeon Job James. Thomas was hit in the leg, but he was sickly and died just before the inquest, probably preventing a resumption of the riots; see ch. 7 below. The evidence is in T. Thomas to Melbourne, 26 June.
45. Testimony of John Petherick, 21 June, of William Rowland, 17 and 20 June; Evan Thomas, 16 June.
46. Testimony of Thomas Lewis at the Assizes, *Cambrian*, 16 July 1831 and see *Merthyr Guardian*, 2 March 1833, for retrospective reference; testimony of John Petherick, 21 June; of William Rowland, 17 and 20 June; Evan Thomas, 16 June.
47. Testimony of William Rowland, 17 and 20 June; of William Thomas, painter, 17 June.
48. Evan Thomas, 16 June.

49. W. Crawshay in *Cambrian*, 11 June; he said two soldiers were severely
wounded from 'contusion of the brain'; he spoke of bad head wounds, of
a man stabbed in the thigh (Donald Black) and of others stabbed in the
chest and arms. An anonymous correspondent to the *Cambrian*, 18 June,
however, said that six badly wounded men had been left in the Inn, when
the 93rd pulled out to Penydarren House; they were carried to the House
in four coaches which had just brought up the 52 men and an officer of
the staff of the Royal Glamorgan Militia who escorted the wounded, under
cover of a screen provided by the East (and possibly the Central) Glamorgan
Yeomanry: see ch. 6 below.

50. Testimony by the people named at the inquests of 17 and 20-22 June.

51. Testimony of John Garnons, 22 June (on Rowland Thomas).

52. Testimony of William Rowland, 17 and 20 June, of William Thomas
Court, same dates; Crawshay in *Cambrian* and the paper itself, 11 June.

53. Sentence List Glamorgan Summer Assizes, July 1831, for David Hughes;
Crawshay in *Cambrian*, 11 June, who also says the rebels planned to
'pull down' Cyfarthfa Castle itself, an enterprise which would have
required a corps of engineers. Evan Thomas, 16 June, on Lewis Lewis
at the Canal bridge (Pont-y-Storehouse). The raids on houses and farms fill
the Home Office correspondence; they figure prominently in the Sentence
List; see ch. 6 below.

54. A. Hill to Melbourne, 3 June 1831 (HO 52/16): this letter was read by the
King and circulated; Bute to Melbourne, 4 June, ibid; Lord Hill, War
Office to Melbourne, 4 June (HO 50/14); on Newport detachment of 93rd,
Melbourne to Mayor of Newport and Lord Fitzroy Somerset, Horse
Guards, 4 June (HO 41/10); on the coach windows, transport bill of W.H.
Iggulden, keeper of the Westgate Hotel, Newport, with endorsements,
bills of Riot Expenses, Crawshay Papers (NLW), Box 12.

55. Bute to Melbourne, 4 June; Morgan to Bute, 3 June (HO 52/16).

56. Crawshay in *Cambrian*, 11 June; *Fair Play* in *Cambrian*, 18 June. *Fair Play*
said the 93rd had gone to Penydarren House earlier, leaving Major Falls
and six badly wounded Highlanders at the Inn, because it was 'too
hazardous' to take them through the streets. Captain Howells of the
Royal Glamorgan went to Penydarren House and then to the Castle to
confer with Major Falls. Rebels, it was said, were threatening to pull down
the Inn and kill the wounded soldiers; so the Royal Glamorgan's 52 men
who, in their hurry, had left their greatcoats behind, cleared the streets
around the Castle in the torrential rain while the wounded went up to
Penydarren in their four coaches. This dramatic story makes more sense
(what line regiment would abandon its wounded in such circumstances?)
when one considers the unique account presented by Purchase, keeper of
the Castle, for a 'lunch', not only for 80 Highlanders but for seventy of
the 'Cardiff cavalry'. The East Glamorgan Yeomanry under Major Rickards
had been the first non-regular troops to set out for Merthyr and their
own account also specifies a 'lunch' for 70 of their men. They also accounted
for 119 dinners and suppers supplied later the same day, independently of
the 80 dinners delivered by Purchase to the 93rd. Lieutenant Franklin of
the Central Division was already at Penydarren House by the early morning
of the next day, when Lieutenant Talbot's Bridgend troop of the same
division came (ch. 6); this suggests to me that 70 of the East Glamorgan
arrived while the 93rd were still at the Castle Inn and were the essential
shield for the withdrawal, whatever the miseries of the Royal Glamorgan;
50 of their colleagues from the Central Division must have followed soon
afterwards. Riot Expenses, Crawshay Papers (NLW), Box 12; and see my

'The Merthyr Riots: settling the account', *NLWJ*, xi (1959).

57.   Bills, W. Marsden, drapery, 5 June; Riot Expenses, op. cit. and my 'The Merthyr Riots: settling the account', op. cit.

58.   Crawshay in *Cambrian*, 11 June. This incident naturally caught people's minds. When the *Newgate Calendar* swooped on the trials of the Merthyr rebels, it adorned its account with a dramatic drawing of this ceremony in full sans-culotte style, complete with a Death or Liberty in the cap.

6 REBELLION

'The Ringleaders of the Tumult up to Friday,' reported Evan Thomas two weeks later, 'were mostly daring and profligate characters, but on the Saturday they were joined by most respectable workmen as to character . . . men of good and quiet character earning 20 shillings a week . . .' One leader was a householder in Dowlais with £9 on him when he was captured.[1]

All the evidence suggests that Evan Thomas was correct, at least in his second comment. Puddlers at Hirwaun and Aberdare joined the insurrection; two of them were very well known and highly-respected men. John Morgan, *John the Racer*, who led a crowd armed with guns, pistols and swords against Philip Taylor's shop at Hirwaun, to seize a pound of powder and 28 pounds of shot, was a man of 39. At the Assizes, the judge gave him a light sentence because 'I have received such an account of your character', not least from Philip Taylor himself, who said that Morgan's leadership had saved him from worse violence. A colleague, Richard Evans, who led an armed party to John Watkins's place to commandeer a gun, was 43, and well thought of. In 1813, he had assigned property in Merthyr to a woman who made him a loan of £160 and had deposited the agreement in Zoar Independent chapel. He was actually acquitted.[2]

Hirwaun and Aberdare, however, saw scenes of shattering violence. Squads of armed workers, 15 to 20 at a time, lined up opposite shops which were forced for guns, powder and ammunition. Evan Nicholas, a thirty-eight year old collier, organised an armed blockade of the King's Highway. While this area and the Cefn which looked on the Cyfarthfa works were the storm-centres, shops, houses, works, depots were raided wholesale for weapons, powder and ammunition. Bands of men scoured the whole countryside taking fowling pieces and some rifles from farmhouses. Within the day, they were reported to have 300 to 400 guns.[3]

Moreover, they deployed their forces with skill and system. 'The workmen to the number of some thousands are in a much more organized state than had been supposed,' reported a startled Bute. They had encampments, drill, a signals system, masses of arms. They were making pikes, possibly in those moortop caves which have gone down in local tradition as *Chartist Caves*. The hard core of armed men seem

149

to have organised themselves in detachments with their own commanders and red flags. Thomas Kinsey the labourer went about Cefn flourishing the sword of Mr Kins, surgeon to the 93rd. Kins, called to a wounded worker, had been given a 'sporting start' on his horse by the Cefn men before they opened fire on him.[4] Their aim was clearly to collect weapons and ammunition, concentrate their armed force, drill and train their men, isolate Merthyr, win support from Monmouthshire and the western valleys and destroy the military power at Penydarren House, probably in the hope of being imitated elsewhere.

Road-blocks were set up, farmers and their families turned back, markets stopped. They cut the Brecon and Swansea roads. The road into Dowlais remained open, perhaps for the Monmouthshire men. They failed to cut the one to Cardiff, which remained the last vital life-line for authority.

Their guerrilla *foco* was on the Brecon Road, near Cefn, beyond the Daren toll-gate. They posted their men in the Dan-y-Graig ravine and on the hills above, near the precipitous Grawen Rocks, a strategic and commanding site. Another base, linked to Cefn by an efficient signalling system, was established on the hill running down into Merthyr from Hirwaun, not far from the junction of the Swansea and Brecon roads. Here, they tried, but failed, to destroy a bridge. In the early morning of Saturday, however, they opened fire on the public coach at this point and one of Bute's agents saw 400 to 500 men armed with scythes and other makeshift weapons crossing over to the Cefn side.[5]

For around the armed core, thousands of men rallied. There was even a strong body of Irish labourers with clubs, a rally unique in south Wales in these years.[6] Cyfarthfa and Hirwaun works were clearly the strongholds but men and women of all works and trades joined. Many still remained quiet about the silent works and in the streets and their greatest weakness was Dowlais. Some hundreds of the Dowlais men, to avoid conscription, fled to Brecon, streaming over the Beacons and through The Gap along the drovers' road.[7] The rebels had their delegates out further afield. Before Friday had closed, Merthyr men were in Ebbw Vale, Nant-y-Glo and Tredegar.[8]

Confronting Dan-y-Graig was Penydarren House. It was a substantial place, shared between Alderman Thompson and the Forman family. The grounds were extensive with trees and five park seats. The house had a large front hall, complete with an organ, a drawing room, library, dining room and dressing room, all with white marble hearths. Upstairs there were seven bedrooms, four with their own dressing rooms, a schoolroom, governess's room and a maid's workroom; in the attic, five rooms for groom, butler, gardener and housekeeper. The soldiers overran the house and set up extensive bivouacs and temporary stabling.[9]

John Petherick took over the victualling.[10] A flow of requisitions to a handful of the town's most important and courageous tradesmen, Purchase, W.D. Jenkins, Thomas Darker, funnelled supplies under Yeomanry escort into the mansion on an increasingly massive scale as unit after unit threaded its way there through the crowds and the ambushes. They were scrawled on Penydarren Company receipt books, odd scraps of paper, one on a piece torn from a copy of the Riot Act. 'Please send up dinners for about 30 officers and gentlemen', ran the first, addressed to Purchase at the Castle Inn; eighty-one quarts of ale for the Highlanders followed, bulk orders for bread, cheese, hard tack, 1,000 copper caps and a bag of large shot ('large' underlined).

The basic necessity was food. Inn meals, ready dressed, were served from the Castle, officers and gentlemen getting breakfasts and dinners (in the evening), men dinners only (at mid-day and at half the price). Beer was soon coming in barrels, ten and twenty at a time; officers and gentlemen ordered 24 bottles of wine on the first day, 48 on the second, 72 on the third. The East Glamorgan ran a separate food and forage account and the officers of the Royal Glamorgan, who got twice as many blankets as anybody else, seem to have been markedly more regimental than the regulars; by Sunday they were ordering soap and pipe-clay. During the eight days of requisitioning, the troops at Penydarren consumed at least 7,792 pounds of bread, 1,637 pounds of cheese, 34 bottles of brandy, 208 bottles of wine, 15 gallons and a quart of porter and 950 gallons of beer.[11]

Penydarren was for eight days the seat of government in Merthyr. Its first, desperate need was information. As soon as Richard Morgan took over, he sent out Pensioners in plain clothes as scouts; Bute had his own 'confidential servants' among the workmen. From the tower of Cyfarthfa Castle the rebel strongholds could be kept under observation.[12] Their intelligence in fact proved reasonably good.

Almost as urgent a necessity was contact, however feeble, with men among the workers who could be persuaded to return to obedience. They had already ordered multiple copies of the Riot Act and the (mobilisation) Notice to Pensioners.[13] On the morning of Saturday, they issued a dramatic proclamation from the ironmasters to their men.[14]

WORKMEN OF MERTHYR TYDFIL

No one can lament more deeply than your Masters do the dreadful occurrences of Yesterday!

They are grieved beyond measure that the blood of their industrious Men should be spilled by the rash attempt [plural s deleted] you made to disarm the Soldiers brought here only to protect our Property and Persons, against your threatened Violence.

Good God! that you should have been led on by the Speech of one Violent Man to commit so daring an attack as you did, one which was sure to produce the melancholy and heartbreaking result which followed, and which we shall all of us, Masters and Men, regret to the end of our lives.

There are now ten times the number of Soldiers to protect us and our Property which were here Yesterday, and we implore you to consider the fatal effects of continuing your present unlawful Proceedings.

For your own, your Families' sakes, at once come in a small number and meet us, and assure us of your immediate reliance upon our Justice and Feelings.

Return to your Work and put an end to this dreadful state of things, which must and will be worse every hour it continues.

YOUR FRIENDS AND MASTERS

The 'one Violent Man', of course, was *Lewsyn yr Heliwr*, now an active leader at Cefn.[15]

'If any attempt is made to attack us here,' Morgan had reported on the Friday evening, 'we shall give them a lesson that will not soon be forgotten,' but the force was too small for offensive action. He sent a magistrate out that night to call the western, Swansea, division of the Yeomanry.[16]

The 93rd, however, was in desperate need of weapons and ammunition. Captain Moggridge, with 40 men of the East Glamorgan, was ordered out on Saturday morning to escort the ammunition train from Brecon. As they passed through the Cyfarthfa side of Merthyr, they were sniped at from houses, but got through Dan-y-Graig without trouble. When they returned with the convoy, however, they ran into great rocks rolled across the road and hundreds of armed men. A desperate message to Penydarren brought officers at the head of 100 Yeomanry. As they came up to Dan-y-Graig, the rebels rolled rocks down on them and opened heavy fire. The Yeomanry momentarily panicked. They were held by the courage and verve of Lieutenant

Franklin of the Central division. Four horses were injured but none of
the men, except, of course, in their self-esteem, for they had to beat a
humiliating retreat in full view of Cefn, Georgetown, Cyfarthfa and the
Village. The frustrated Moggridge turned back. He headed east on a
long and risky detour through Beaufort, up Llangynidr Mountain and
over the mountains and moors. At Penydarren, there was consterna-
tion.[17]

Captain Talbot's (Bridgend) troop of the Central Division was that
morning approaching from the south. At Quaker's Yard, at the
southern end of Merthyr parish, they ran in with J.B. Bruce, coming
back from Cardiff, where he had accompanied Hill the previous day.
A shaken Franklin sent an urgent warning; they might have to fight
their way through Merthyr. At Troedyrhiw, the troop halted and
loaded their weapons. They came into Merthyr like the vanguard of
an enemy army. There was no trouble, however, except from some
women who shouted that so many horses would eat up all the few
provisions left.[18]

The Swansea Yeomanry, however, ran into a disaster which was to
discredit them utterly. The overnight call from Merthyr came when
the horses were out to grass in Gower after a heavy day's work.
Nevertheless, Major Penrice set off at once with 34 men, ordering the
rest to follow as quickly as they could. In the early afternoon, their
approach was signalled to Dan-y-Graig, which had its own 'confidential
servants' and excellent communications. Bute heard that a woman
was sent up to Cefn on horseback. A strong detachment of armed men
crossed over.

As Penrice came down the hill from Hirwaun to Waun Coed
Meyrick, he entered the 'defiles', a warren of slag-heaps like a miniature
moonscape. Workmen appeared on the tips and made friendly noises.
Penrice advanced with one companion. Men suddenly sprang around
him, pointed a musket at his right ear, pistols at his chest. His arms
were pinioned. His troop promptly surrendered. Pistols, swords and
carbines were snatched and the Swansea Yeomanry were sent stumbling
back in disgrace to Neath.[19]

It is difficult to exaggerate the shock this action inflicted. The
workers at Hirwaun and Dan-y-Graig exploded into an ecstasy of
triumph. They fired in the air from one post to the other. Their cheers
could be heard in Penydarren. Reports came flooding in that the
workers meant to launch a mass attack on the mansion in the evening.

At Penydarren, faith in the Yeomanry abruptly vanished. When
Bruce reported to Cardiff late that night, he said they had hardly more

than 135 effective men. This when there were over 300 Yeomanry in the place! He simply ruled them out; the Yeomanry 'does not answer'. The rout echoed through press and parliament. 'Half a troop was disarmed . . . and the other half ran away . . .' jeered the radical Henry Hunt in the Commons. There was deep suspicion of treason. Colonel Brotherton who took over at Merthyr the following week, was scathing: '. . . the Shameful Conduct of the (mis-called) Yeomanry . . . vile Conduct . . . not a single plea or excuse in extenuation . . . more a willing than a compulsory surrender . . . they were influenced by a worse feeling even than intimidation . . .' Bute did his best to defend them; he quite seriously reported Penrice's statement that he had been ambushed by 1,200 men, most of them armed![20] But henceforth, the officers at Penydarren (unfairly in the event) were for ever looking uneasily over their shoulders at their own Yeomanry.

Certainly these defeats repeatedly inflicted by armed workers on regular and yeomanry troops seem without precedent in the history of civil conflict in eighteenth- and nineteenth-century Britain.[21]

How was Penydarren to ward off the looming onslaught? Bute was filtering Pensioners with good weapons up from Cardiff and about 40 got through during the day.[22] A desperate effort was made to break the workmen's unity. Josiah John Guest was particularly active in this, sometimes rather murky business, and a key role was played by the radical solicitor William Perkins. They managed no fewer than three meetings with delegates in the course of the afternoon. One, apparently with a solitary man, was chilling. He was utterly intransigent and made it clear that he lived in hourly expectation of a general insurrection. They seem to have had more success with a second delegation. At one stage, Guest took an answer to the very 'outposts of the insurgents'.[23]

At five o'clock, the talks became a matter of life and death. Rebels on the Aberdare side crossed over to join the armed men at Cefn. About this time, a deputation of twelve men, which sounds substantive, got through to Penydarren House. Accounts of this meeting are unclear. Apparently Crawshay let it be understood that he would stop his wage reductions; the men apparently agreed to hand in their weapons and return to work on the Monday. Bruce and Morgan reported, however, that just when agreement seemed at hand, the men increased their demands and broke off. Crawshay talks of a demand for a wage increase of 10 per cent which was unanimously rejected (and which in fact sounds more like a defiance, a *diffidatio*, than anything else). He nevertheless talked as if some kind of understanding had been reached.

These talks came in the nick of time. Before the deputation could have got back to their comrades, the great crowd set off from Cefn. 'Immense multitudes' came marching down the road, shouting, cheering, brandishing the Yeomanry's weapons, firing in the air. The troops at Penydarren turned out (they stood to arms three times that day). The cavalry massed front and rear of the mansion. They were a formidable sight.

The crowd reached the great gates of Cyfarthfa Castle and stopped. Apparently, they ran into the deputation. We do not know what happened then, but after a while, the great mass of men 'became loosened'. Many moved on into Merthyr; thousands stayed in the Brecon Road. They split up into detachments, which gradually dispersed. In an hour or so, firing was heard 'in fifty directions', especially from the men returning to Hirwaun and Aberdare. Bruce even reported, hopefully, that parties of workers opened fire on each other. At 9.30 the soldiers stood down. At 11, they were called out again by tumultuous shouting near the House; after an hour, all was quiet.[24]

This abortive march was clearly a critical moment. Quite evidently the deputation served to distract and divide the men. Many, no doubt, wanted to settle, many were losing their nerve. Dissension had obviously broken out. If they had ever seriously planned to attack Penydarren House, they had lost their best opportunity. It is from this point that initiative begins to slip back to their opponents.

Those were still nervous. In the early hours of Sunday, 5 June, Bruce and Morgan wrote to Cardiff. Morgan would be glad of the 27 Pensioners Bute planned to send up with 50 stand of arms, but he urged 'great circumspection' for fear they would be captured. He was sure of holding Penydarren but added 'we have no strength that we can depend on to act on the offensive'. Bruce suffered from the same gnawing anxiety over the Yeomanry. They would fight if supported by seasoned troops, he thought, but they could not be sent to points of danger. It is surely significant, however, that he added that they could not be used to single out and take the 'ringleaders'. For the capture of those 'ringleaders', he said, 'was now the main object'. This reflects a significant shift in the moral and strategic balance.[25]

What was obsessing the officers was the threat of a mass meeting on Monday. The militants, frustrated outside Penydarren House, had decided to concentrate on a great rally at the Waun on Monday, where they hoped thousands of men from Monmouthshire would join the insurrection. In response, Penydarren House resumed the psychological offensive it had started on Saturday. On Sunday, it issued a minatory

Proclamation: 'Divers ill-disposed Persons have against the Peace of our Lord the King, riotously and tumultuously assembled themselves together with *Fire Arms and other offensive weapons* and have been guilty of *felonious and HIGHLY TREASONABLE ACTS*, to the terror of our Majesty's Liege Subjects . . .' Six magistrates solemnly warned against carrying fire-arms or other offensive weapons, lest the bearers be considered guilty of *'HIGH TREASON AND REBELLION'*. All meetings of more than twelve people would be dispersed and offenders punished with the utmost rigour of the law. This intimidation was coupled with renewed efforts to contact moderates. A meeting with delegates was fixed for eight in the morning of Monday, presumably to pre-empt the mass assembly.[26]

During the Sunday, Colonel Bush managed to take up the Pensioners with the additional weapons and Moggridge finally got through to the mansion. The Swansea Yeomanry, 150 strong, was approaching by a circuitous route which avoided dread Hirwaun and cut north of Cardiff. Strenuous efforts were made to check the infection. Bute arrested two Merthyr men in their beds at Cardiff but could find nothing on them. Brecon mobilised Pensioners and Militia and assiduously cultivated the Dowlais refugees.[27]

Very striking was the workmen's failure to co-ordinate the Merthyr revolt with actions in Monmouthshire and the Neath and Swansea valleys. Merthyr delegates certainly scored some successes in the latter. Colliers were in rebellion against the truck system and during the following week, there were marches by colliers on Swansea and a strike at Neath. On this Sunday, however, the Swansea magistrates issued a well-timed statement denouncing truck and promising the men their wages in money. In fact, they reported that Merthyr delegates had more influence among the 'masons and other lower orders' of Swansea town than among the miners.[28] They took no chances; yeomanry were standing by and two revenue cutters were ordered to Swansea from Milford Haven.[29] In Neath, on this Sunday, all the chapel ministers, English and Welsh, preached sermons against rebellion.[30]

Such trouble as there was in the western valleys surfaced after the Merthyr action had ended. Much the same was true of Monmouthshire. The Merthyr men seem to have made no serious effort to contact the sale-coal colliery villages, strongholds of the Scotch Cattle as they were to be of physical-force Chartism. They were locked in their own struggle and again, climaxed after everything was over in Merthyr, whose delegates concentrated, in rather traditional manner, on the ironworks to the north. Here magistrates claimed that the men were quiet even if 'overawed' by the Merthyr men.[31]

This failure of effective communication became visible on Monday, 6 June. It was in the small hours that the Merthyr rebels made their serious effort in Monmouthshire. Parties of from 500 to 1,000 men and boys marched on the works at Nant-y-Glo, Llanelly (Breconshire), Blaenavon and down the valley to Abersychan and the Varteg near Pontypool. They certainly raised a crowd. Observers estimated that anything from 12,000 to 20,000 people, the women allegedly carrying sacks, set out for Merthyr. By 10 o'clock they were reported to be nearing Dowlais.

Morgan decided to prevent a junction with the armed men at Cefn. He mobilised the most effective striking force he could, 110 Highlanders, 53 Royal Glamorgan Militia and over 300 Yeomanry; Penydarren House was left to the Pensioners under Bush. They met the crowd at Dowlais Top. The confrontation was tense. Josiah John Guest once again threw himself into the action. Later versions had him, single-handed, preventing a massacre. Colonel Morgan makes no mention of this, but praised his 'great activity and zeal'. Guest's speeches had no visible effect. According to Crawshay the Riot Act was read. The crowd still did not move. Crawshay reports that the soldiers then actually levelled their muskets but that officers gave their orders with deliberate slowness. Morgan says nothing of this but reports that he ordered the soldiers to advance with fixed bayonets. The resentful crowd slowly gave way, getting behind some high walls to the side. The troops marched on to the Ponds above Dowlais where Guest managed to talk another big crowd into dispersal. Some crossed over to the Cefn, but many went home. Monmouthshire ironmasters reported them complaining bitterly that they had been left in the lurch by the Dan-y-Graig men.[32]

It is hopeless to try to lay hands on the reality that lay behind this dramatic, enigmatic and totally impenetrable encounter.[33]

The military were now clearly on the offensive, but there was still plenty of fight left in the rebels, at least in the morning. The Yeomanry (who had in fact been very steady) moved into Merthyr, clearing the streets of the crowds and disarming those with clubs 'by dint of a little force and much persuasion'. The watchers at Cyfarthfa, however, reported in alarm that the men at Dan-y-Graig were 'exercising in line' with the muskets of the 93rd, the sabres and pistols of the Yeomanry and their own fowling-pieces. Their numbers were 'immense' and by noon had increased 'to a most alarming extent'. There was continuous firing and two black flags suddenly appeared on the Daren toll-gate.

Then, abruptly, between twelve and two, the movement collapsed. Men began to disperse in such large numbers that Crawshay from Cyfarthfa urged the military to strike at once. Around six o'clock the irreducible core of intransigents itself seemed to split up in dissension. Men could be seen burying, breaking or throwing away their weapons. The soldiers had been back at Penydarren for four hours. By this time the Swansea Yeomanry had arrived and in the evening, the first troop of the 3rd Dragoons, 45 men under Captain Arthur, who came in time to break up a last effort by the rebels to rally.[34] It is possible only to report, not to explain these events.

Before eight o'clock, two of the rebel leaders had been taken and, as men fled in all directions, massive police raids swept through Merthyr during the night, rounding up 14 of the militants who had been marked down for retribution. Over the next few days there was a regular manhunt. At Brecon, the authorities issued a public testimonial in praise of the Dowlais workmen there and organised a fund for them. On the Tuesday, William Williams, who had carried the Red Flag, was caught in the queue for relief. David Thomas, *Dai Llaw Haearn*, was captured in Swansea on the 15th and constables went hunting as far afield as Carmarthenshire and Pembrokeshire.

By Tuesday night, 7 June, eighteen of the men's leaders were in custody as workmen streamed back to work, the colliers and miners more slowly than the forge and furnace men. It was on that day that Guest had the satisfaction of reporting the capture of 'the ringleader and author of all the mischief'. In fact it was a premature claim. Lewis Lewis was reported taken in the small hours of the 7th; a strong party went out into the very heart of Hirwaun to fetch him, but he got away. He was finally traced by Rees Rees (Rees Pant-y-cynferth) and a fellow constable Hywel Bryn Carnau, in the woods of Hendrebolon near his home and captured after a desperate struggle. They held him in the lonely Lamb Inn until gallant Lieutenant Franklin rode 'alone' with yeomanry, dragoons and a bevy of magistrates to fetch him at 1.30 on Wednesday morning. Morgan of Bodwigiad sent Rees Rees to Crawshay who gave him £5, a sum which the ironmaster promptly charged to the 3rd Dragoons.[35]

By this time Colonel Morgan had given up his command at Peny-darren, to be succeeded by Colonel Brotherton, who lived near Abergavenny and had been active against the rebellious labourers in southern England. The Militia staff and many of the East Glamorgan Yeomanry left on 7 June, when the 98th Foot landed at Cardiff from the *Albion*. On 8 June all the Yeomanry left, as the 98th, with its own field kitchens, marched in. During these few days, however, the number of troops at Merthyr must have fluctuated between 600 and 800, as prisoner after prisoner was subjected to long and gruelling interrogation. By 10 June, the first major investigations had been finished and there was another heavy concentration of troops as dragoons and infantry escorted prisoners to Cardiff, shackled with ironwork provided by the Cyfarthfa and Penydarren companies, rather an original way of supporting local industry. These included Lewis Lewis, Richard Lewis, *Dai Solomon*, William Williams, John Phelps and David Richards. The magistrates moved on to Hirwaun and Aberdare. By the end of the month there were 26 prisoners in Cardiff jail, where *Dai Solomon* was to lead them into a protest riot.[36]

In these circumstances, the atmosphere in Merthyr became poisonous. Alderman Thompson got home to Penydarren on the 7th and was at once struck by 'the desperate character of a vast number of persons'.[37] On the 9th, the magistrates broke off from their examination of prisoners to address a special letter to Melbourne — 'The present state of tranquillity existing here is entirely the effect of intimidation . . .' The stand-down of the Militia would actually add to the number of malcontents and it was absolutely essential to maintain a strong military force in the town.[38] In fact, the 98th Foot had 150 men in Merthyr and there were garrisons of dragoons at Dowlais and Cyfarthfa. They were very ready with their weapons and had cause to be.[39] But by the 10th, Millward the blacksmith was hauling stores from Penydarren House and the only order from the mansion on the 11th was for four bottles of brandy, presumably for the farewell toasts. For on that day, the 93rd, veterans of the struggle, finally returned to Brecon and a heroes' welcome.[40]

In Merthyr, however, tranquillity was a distant dream. As the town echoed to soldiers' boots and police raids, Evan Thomas of Sully, Chairman of the Glamorgan Quarter Sessions, came up to help the magistrates in their investigations. On 9 June, he wrote to Bute from the Talbot Inn in Penydarren . . . 'The depositions already made in Lewis Lewis's case have disclosed facts of so serious a nature that I think it would be very desirable to have the advice of some Legal Man on behalf of Government as to the Commitments . . .' The *Cambrian* had no doubt. It stated baldly that government was sending down a KC to conduct a trial for High Treason.[41]

Notes

1.   Evan Thomas to Melbourne, 18 June 1831: HO 52/16; the source for all official correspondence may be assumed to be HO 52/16, unless otherwise stated.

2.   Sentence List, Glamorgan Summer Assizes, July 1831; sentencing at the Assizes, *Cambrian*, 23 July 1831; for the property assignment, records of Zoar Independent chapel, Merthyr.

3.   *Cambrian*, 18 June; Sentence List, Glamorgan Summer Assizes, July 1831; Bute to Melbourne, 5, 6 and 8 June; J.B. Bruce to Bute, 5 June, said the rebels had 200 to 250 fowling-pieces and the general estimate was 300 to 400 guns; Evan Thomas to Bute on 16 June, after it was all over, reported that he had questioned a rebel who was an ex-serviceman; the latter 'made the best of their case', claiming that they had 78 guns and reckoned 28 swords and pistols taken from the cavalry (below). Thomas said that it was 'well known' that the rebels had swords and pistols before the disarming of the yeomanry. A 'most respectable man' in Aberdare computed the muskets and guns there to be 400. Crawshay by 11 June, was reporting 'great numbers of guns' being handed over: Henry Crawshay at Hirwaun had by that time received 14 sabres, 2 muskets, a carbine and 6 pistols, William himself 4 muskets, 2 sabres and a pistol (*Cambrian*, 11 June); these were clearly weapons taken from soldiers and yeomanry; fowling-pieces, rifles and other guns were also destroyed en masse (Crawshay, same account).

4.   Bute to Melbourne, 5 June; Crawshay, *Cambrian*, 11 June, spoke of 'red flags' being used on the Saturday; for Kinsey, see Sentence List, Glamorgan Summer Assizes, July 1831; on the Cefn incident, Tom Lewis, *Hen Dŷ Cwrdd Cefn*, pp. 205-7; the wounded worker was the author's great-gandfather, Dafydd Lewis, who was handy with a gun. He led the Cefn contingent on the slopes of Darren Fawr. The Cefn men thought Kins had come to take Dafydd Lewis away; they forced the surgeon to kneel in prayer, took his sword, and then gave him a start on horseback to Pen-y-Bryn; he turned to wave and they opened fire.

5.   Hugh Bold, Recorder of Brecon, reported the Brecon road cut on the Saturday, Bold to Melbourne, 4 June; he also said that 300 of them were armed and threatening an attack on the Brecon barracks (this letter was read by the King); Bute to Melbourne, 4 June (11.15 am) for the men with scythes; on the firing at the public coach and the attempt on the bridge on the Swansea road, Evan Thomas to Bute, 16 June; the outpost there was at Waun Coed Meyrick; Coed Meyrick was near the little settlement of Clwyd-y-fagwyr, about halfway up the hill running from Hirwaun common down into Merthyr town (personal observation). When my aunt was head-mistress of the little school there during the War, children still remembered the disarming of the Swansea Yeomanry at this point (see below). All the accounts, of course, give these details on armed camps, road cutting, market stopping, blockade, etc.; see, for example, *Cambrian*, 11 and 18 June. Aberdare, Hirwaun, Cefn, Penderyn were obviously the strongholds. The failure to cut the Cardiff road may represent some failure fully to mobilise the men of Plymouth works which were on the road and a little way south. Despite many changes, the Dan-y-Graig stretch is still very dramatic (and just across the river from the hill running up to Blaen Cadlan and Penderyn, *Lewsyn yr Heliwr*'s bailiwick).

6.   Bruce to Bute, 5 June 1831; the Irish as a whole held aloof from the Chartist troubles for example, and the Irish press preened itself on the

fact; the entire Cork police force volunteered to come over to teach rebellious Celts a lesson. Their short guns would be just as effective as the soldiers' muskets. Daniel O'Connell boasted that of the Specials enrolled at Cardiff against the Chartists, 100 were Irishmen: David Williams, *John Frost*, pp. 111, 225, 240. Relations between Welsh and Irish were generally very bad and the role of the latter vis-à-vis working-class movements was quite unlike that of their compatriots in Lancashire for example.

7. Proclamation of Borough of Brecon, 7 June 1831, in praise of Dowlais workmen; *Cambrian*, 11 June; 'several hundreds' were said to have gone; they could have gone down the Glyn through Tal-y-Bont, but the Roman road straight through the Beacons would have been quicker. A fund was raised for them in Brecon.

8. Harford (Ebbw Vale) to William Powell (Abergavenny), 3 June; these appear to have been miners; they said men should not work at Ebbw Vale, Nant-y-Glo and Tredegar 'except at the furnaces'. These delegates might represent some sub-group within the rebels; they were clearly miners and/or colliers and might perhaps have been a 'trade union' team operating in terms of a 'strike' as mooted at the Waun Fair; the serious effort to rally Monmouthshire men to a *rebellion* came two days later. The letter was enclosed in Powell to Melbourne, 6 June.

9. The description of Penydarren House derives from an inventory and valuation by Adam Murray on Alderman Thompson's claims for damages as a result of the military occupation; it is enclosed in Thompson to Home Office, 20 November 1832: HO 40/30; there was what seems an almost endless haggle over the claims, which drags its dreary length across 1831-3, in HO 52/16, 41/10 and 40/30.

10. The source for what follows is Riot Expenses, roll of 125 items in Crawshay Papers (NLW), Box 12; I have analysed the accounts in consider-able detail in 'The Merthyr Riots: settling the account', *NLWJ*, xi (1959).

11. One error I made in the article was to assume that 27 quarts of ale ordered the first day were for the Royal Glamorgan; I was then closer to Gwernllwyn chapel and thought there'd be a quart for two men. Clearly the 27 quarts were for the detachment of 27 of the 93rd coming from Newport; orders were for a quart per man at a time. In fact by the end of the first day, beer was coming in ten barrels at a time.

12. Morgan to Bute, 3 June; Bute to Morgan, 4 June and passim; I have confirmed by personal observation that the two rebel camps could be seen from the tower of Cyfarthfa Castle and I am grateful to Gillian Bale and Professor Harold Carter for their professional geographical comment.

13. Table 2, 'The Merthyr Riots: settling the account': 200 copies of each were ordered.

14. Address, 4 June 1831 in Bute to Melbourne, 6 June; the Riot Expenses cit, list 300 copies of a Proclamation, but this may refer to a proclamation threatening trials for High Treason issued the next day. Bute made the sensible suggestion that they be translated into Welsh (6 June).

15. For Lewsyn at Cefn, see Judge Bosanquet's sentencing on 16 July 1831, after the Assizes, in HO 17/128, part 2, bundle Zp37.

16. Morgan to Bute, 3 June; order confirmed by Bute, 4 June, when he hoped two-thirds of the Division would already have reached Merthyr; he was optimistic, see below n. 19.

17. Full account by Crawshay in *Cambrian*, 11 June; Bruce and Morgan to Bute, 5 June; Morgan gives the information that Moggridge was going to try to get through via Beaufort, which meant going up Llangynidr

Mountain (where several of the 'Chartist caves' are located). These despatches were read by the King.

18. Bruce to Bute, 5 June (read by the King).

19. Bruce and Morgan to Bute, 5 June; Morgan said that 400 armed men staged the ambush. Bute sent a long explanation of this incident (duly read by the King and circulated) on 9 June, quoting from a verbal report by Penrice's adjutant despatched to Cardiff as the Swansea Yeomanry passed by north of the town on its second and successful attempt to reach Merthyr on 5 June. Full account in *Cambrian*, 11 June, by the newspaper and by Crawshay and in the same paper for 18 June, a note in defence of the Yeomanry in reply to an attack by *The Age*, which gives further details; also letter of J.B. Bruce and the paper for 25 June.

20. Crawshay in *Cambrian*, 11 June; Bruce to Bute, 5 June (early morning); *Hansard*, 3rd series, iv, 397-400 (27 June); Brotherton to Lord Fitzroy Somerset, 13 June; Bute to Melbourne, 9 June; the *Cambrian*, 18 June, said the troop had been ambushed by 'several thousand armed rioters'. The Adjutant, Captain Jeffreys, and other officers, asked Bute to conduct an enquiry. *The Age*, implying treachery, said that the officers were owners of ironworks who were hostile to truck and supported Reform and hence 'went over' to the rebels. This is nonsense, but is an indication of the kind of feeling which had been created by Crawshay's actions, I think.

21. All material on these shattering incidents on 4 June, duly reported by Bute, was read by the King and circulated. The Crawshay representative in London wrote to Cyfarthfa on 15 June, promising to pass on to the Attorney-General and the Home Office a letter from William demanding a garrison of regulars at Merthyr. He added: 'They were very much frightened at the late affair at Merthyr and it appeared to us that they at first suspected something wrong with the military . . .', Crawshay Papers (NLW), Box 2 (575d).

22. Morgan to Bute, 5 June; Bute to Melbourne, 5 and 6 June; by the 6th some 60 Pensioners had got there.

23. Bruce to Bute, 5 June; Evan Thomas to Melbourne, 18 June; Crawshay in *Cambrian*, 11 June and *The Late Riots*.

24. Bruce to Bute, 5 June; full account by Crawshay in *Cambrian*, 11 June and argument in *The Late Riots*; Morgan to Bute, 5 June.

25. Bruce wrote at 5 am on the 5th, Morgan at 6 am. Crawshay in the *Cambrian*, 11 June, said it was only after the stand-down at 9.30 pm on the Saturday that the officers and gentlemen took their first refreshment of the day (though the Riot Expenses list breakfasts and dinners for the officers on the 4th 'as yesterday', together with 24 bottles of wine sent up to reinforce the 4 bottles of brandy on the Friday: 'The Merthyr Riots: settling the account').

26. Proclamation, 5 June, enclosed in Bute to Melbourne, 6 June, where he also reports the delegate meeting planned for 8 am on the 6th. Anthony Hill had reached Cardiff by the 5th, with news that troops were on the way. Bute thought them not enough and asked for 'some flying artillery'! (Bute to Melbourne, 5 June); by the 6th Bute's spies had told him that the workmen were going to hold a great meeting and were intending 'to attack today' (Monday, 6 June).

27. Bute to Melbourne, 5, 6 and 9 June; Morgan to Bute, 5 and 6 June; Hugh Bold (Brecon) to Melbourne, 7 and 8 June; Melbourne to Bold, 6 June: HO 41/10; *Cambrian*, 11 June; Table 3, 'The Merthyr Riots: settling the account'.

28. L.W. Dillwyn to Melbourne, 7 and 8 June; *Cambrian*, 11 and 18 June.

29.   Cdr. Edward Chappell, RN to Melbourne, 6 June. The gallant Chappell,
       in charge of the government packet service at Milford Haven, offered to
       lead 100 men drawn from the quarantine and packet services, 'to be
       thrown on shore' either in Glamorgan or Ireland. The Post Office steam
       packet could be used. Chappell, who had heard of the Merthyr troubles
       only that morning, had spent 22 years in the service and had been
       wounded, was 'ready at any time to lay down my life if required'. HO
       52/16.
30.   *Cambrian*, 18 June.
31.   Harford to William Powell, 3 June; Bute to Melbourne, 6 June; Morgan to
       Bute, 6 June, afternoon and evening letters, enclosed in Bute to
       Melbourne, 7 June (misdated 6 June). This correspondence was read by the
       King. A full account by Crawshay in *Cambrian*, 11 June; also eye-witness
       account by *Fair Play* in *Cambrian*, 18 June.
32.   The official account is in Morgan to Bute, 6 June (first letter); W. Powell to
       Melbourne, 6 June; account by Crawshay in *Cambrian*, 11 June; the
       Cambrian itself, 11 June, said the soldiers showed 'symptoms' of firing;
       Fair Play in the *Cambrian*, 18 June, an eye-witness, says the speeches of
       Guest and Morgan were treated with contempt and that soldiers advanced
       within a few paces of the crowd and were 'on the point of firing'; he adds
       that the crowd were armed with iron bars and bludgeons with nails. *Fair
       Play* says the military force marched to the Waun, to encounter the crowd
       at the top of Dowlais; Morgan places the encounter at a hill 'about
       Dowlais' called the Bryn (*bryn* means hill; there are several in the area,
       needless to say!). *Fair Play* was concerned to praise the Royal Glamorgan
       and Colonel Morgan; Crawshay, while saying that Guest read the Riot Act,
       also singles out Morgan; Guest, however, won much prestige by his conduct.
33.   David Jones, *Before Rebecca*, p. 149 also finds the incident puzzling,
       noting that some modern writers speculate on 'betrayal' and talk of
       'trickery' by Guest. On the complaints of Monmouthshire men, W. Powell
       to Melbourne, 7 June.
34.   Morgan to Bute, 6 June (second letter); Crawshay in *Cambrian*, 11 June;
       Morgan reported that two of the leaders had been captured by 8 pm; for
       the Dragoons and the Yeomanry, see W. Routh (Crawshay London House)
       to Home Office, 8 June and 'The Merthyr Riots: settling the account'.
35.   Morgan to Bute, 7 June; Guest to Bute, 7 June; Bute to Melbourne, 7 and
       8 June (read by the King); *Cambrian*, 11, 18 and 25 June; Hugh Bold
       (Brecon) to Melbourne, 7 June; replies by Melbourne in HO 41/10; on the
       capture of Lewis Lewis, Guest to Bute, 7 June; Riot Expenses, E. Purchase,
       transport 7-10 June, Penydarren and Crawshay companies, miscellaneous,
       8 June to 20 August, in 'The Merthyr Riots: settling the account', p. 132;
       on the reward to Rees Rees, M. Morgan to W. Crawshay II, 20 August,
       Crawshay Papers (NLW), Box 2 (583a); Riot Expenses, Bills, Crawshay
       and Sons, 20 August, ibid., Box 12, 'The Merthyr Riots: settling the
       account', p. 132; David Jones, *Before Rebecca*, p. 150.
36.   On Brotherton's command, W. Powell to Melbourne, 6 June; Guest to
       Bute, 7 June; Bute to Melbourne, 8 June; on troop movements, Table 3,
       'The Merthyr Riots: settling the account', based on Riot Expenses,
       Crawshay Papers (NLW), Box 12; departure of militia and yeomanry,
       Guest to Bute, 7 June and Table 3; arrival of Dragoons and 98th Foot,
       Bute to Melbourne, 8 June; for the field kitchens of the 98th, W. Crawshay
       II to J.C. Hobhouse, Secretary at War, 15 January 1832, Crawshay Papers
       (NLW), Box 2 (603a) and Riot Expenses, Receipts, 13 June; on prisoners,
       etc., *Cambrian*, 11, 18, 25 June; Morgan to Bute, 7 June; Riot Expenses,

Bills, Crawshay and Penydarren, miscellaneous, 8 June to 20 August, 'The Merthyr Riots: settling the account', p. 132. According to these accounts, the Dragoons accounted for forage for 350 horses with Crawshay on 8 June; since the 98th Foot marched to Merthyr on that day, when 150 Swansea Yeomanry and over 40 East Glamorgan Yeomanry were still there, at least in the morning, while the Highlanders were remaining, there must have been at least 800 soldiers in the town on that day. The Dragoons were still there on the 9th, though from the 10th they were reduced to garrisons of some 40 each at Dowlais and Cyfarthfa. On the 10th Dowlais had to find beds for 600 men (accounting with the Dragoons) while Purchase supplied dinners to two lots of soldiers totalling over 650 men. From the 11th, when the 93rd quit, there appear to have been stable garrisons of 150 or so of the 98th at Penydarren, with the two troops of Dragoons at Dowlais and Cyfarthfa; Table 3, 'The Merthyr Riots: settling the account', based on Riot Expenses, Crawshay Papers (NLW), Box 12.

37. Thompson to Melbourne, 7 June.

38. Hill, Guest, Bruce and George Thomas to Melbourne, 9 June; by this time Major Digby Mackworth had come down on mission from the War Office.

39. W. Crawshay II to W. Crawshay I, 20 August 1831, Crawshay Papers (NLW), Letter-book, 3 (132).

40. 'The Merthyr Riots: settling the account', pp. 128-9.

41. Evan Thomas to Bute, 9 June; he wrote at 1.30 in the morning; *Cambrian*, 2 July 1831.

7 RETRIBUTION

The *Cambrian* was mistaken. 'There seems to me no ground for this,' Melbourne commented on Evan Thomas's letter, 'the men may be committed for rioting (the simplest of all cases). If afterwards the charge is of a higher nature, they may be prosecuted accordingly . . . There is no reason for doing this.' When Evan Thomas renewed his request on 18 June, having conducted the first inquest into the riot deaths, the Home Office was firmer — 'Lord Melbourne does not consider this a case calling for the interference of Government.' The county should prosecute in the usual way but choose its man carefully.[1]

Melbourne had to walk a tight-rope. The Crawshay representative in London reported that the Government had been very frightened indeed.[2] The upheaval in Merthyr was clearly different in kind from the familiar spate of election troubles and the other outbreaks which had so far characterised the Reform crisis. It was 'out of phase' and alarming. The Home Office took pains to send the correspondence to the King.[3] Eight years later, at the time of the Chartist march on Newport, Melbourne wrote to the then Home Secretary — 'It is the worst and most formidable district in the kingdom. The affair we had there in 1831 was the most like a fight of anything that took place . . .'[4]

Moreover, it was soon associated in Melbourne's mind with the remorseless growth of *The Union* which tended to obsess him. On 8 June, before the dust had settled in Merthyr, Sir Watkin Williams Wynn wrote from north Wales: Robert Hughes a collier who had been interrogated by a local coalowner had said that he was going to Bolton (headquarters of the new colliers' union) 'to be employed as a captain by the union'. Hughes understood that there was to be a general strike of colliers in less than a month's time . . . 'I should not have troubled your Lordship with this detail did not the period fixed for turning out tally exactly with that mentioned in South Wales as the time for insurrection by the colliers throughout the kingdom.'[5]

In fact, lodges of the union began to emerge in Merthyr and the south Wales coalfield generally within days of the end of the rising. They first register in official correspondence on 18 June, when Evan Thomas referred to them. By 3 July, their shadowy presence was disturbing the Marquess of Bute who was finding it difficult to get information, so secretive were they. All he had been able to find was a placard, *The Workman's Manual*, which printed relevant clauses from the 1825 Act. It was on 29 June that the anonymous correspondent from Ruabon supplied detailed information on the activities of William Twiss there and warned that delegates had left for Merthyr *before* the riots.[6]

Melbourne took Williams Wynn's information seriously enough to alert every mining district in the kingdom and in his repeated requests for information to south Wales, he particularly stressed the problem of intimidation, which he associated with *The Union*. The ropes carried by the rioters occupied his mind and it is clear that he tended, perhaps half-unconsciously, to think that the unions were behind the revolt.[7] This may have influenced him when he had to consider appeals against death sentences in a few weeks' time.

What he was evidently anxious to avoid was unnecessary provocation of a still violently discontented working population. This was only one of the pressures, at a time already strenuous with the struggle over the Reform Bill. While the republican Richard Carlile hailed the news from Merthyr as the first attempt to fight the soldiers of a brutally repressive government, Henry Hunt rose in the Commons to pillory the administration for 'the slaughter . . . of 26 of our fellow-subjects'. Merthyr, which the Whigs had ignored and which they intended to make simply one of Cardiff's contributory boroughs in the Reform Bill, thrust itself upon public attention, even into the King's Speech at the opening of the session on 21 June. John Walsh, hammer of the Reformers, quoted Petherick at length; the sins of the Swansea Yeomanry were bruited around the Chamber. Croker took Merthyr's petition as text for a sermon on how the Whigs were betraying their radical supporters. In the memorable August debate on the proposed enfranchisement of Gateshead, Tory after Tory paraded Merthyr as a shameful contrast, victim of Whiggery, Cinderella to Durham's ugly northern sisters. Peel divided the House and Merthyr was the stick ready-made for Whig backs.[8]

It was essential to thrust the wretched place back into its well-merited obscurity. Its inhabitants had to be protected from further attack and Melbourne sent the 11th Foot by steamship from Portsmouth to Cardiff, as support for the 98th and the cavalry, though most of them had to be diverted immediately to deal with the riots in the Forest of Dean.[9] The Home Secretary urged local authorities to be firm, but to rely on their own resources, to mobilise the 'respectable' to defend their own property but also to be cautious and conciliatory.

He bombarded local magistrates with repeated demands for detailed information on the causes of the riots, the Court of Requests, the state of industry, the Swansea Yeomanry, on every aspect of the troubles.[10] He was anxious above all, to make *local* powers assume responsibility and show initiative, to be firm without being provocative, to take the town back to tranquillity and out of the public eye. Time after time, however, pressures from the Commons or the press forced him to jerk the Merthyr magistrates into action.

Protests began to be voiced because at least two dozen people had been killed and no proper inquest held. Melbourne's inevitable letter followed. He was horrified to learn that the East Glamorgan coroner had actually left the country since the riots. The Merthyr men had to explain that rebels had held the town for four days, that bodies had been buried in secret, that public feeling was still so bad that the very act of holding an inquest might provoke further trouble. The clamour of self-justification overflowed into the *Cambrian* and is in itself an indication of the state of the town.[11]

Evan Thomas was compelled to hold some kind of inquest on 17 June, in the absence of the coroner.[12] With great difficulty, he obtained details of a case *which did not need a view of the body*. This was John Hughes, miner and ex-serviceman who had been shot with a musket in his hand and had died the same day. Eight witnesses gave evidence in a report which in fact constitutes one of the first full accounts of the action at the Castle Inn. The jury was drawn from householders who had not been at the Inn; its chairman was Christopher James himself; he took notes and Evan Thomas warned Melbourne that a report would soon appear in the press. Sure enough, it shortly appeared in the *Cambrian* (and seems in fact to be more accurate than the official transcript sent to the Home Office). Evan Thomas's accompanying letters were among the first, and the best, of the analyses and explanations Melbourne was constantly demanding. The Marquess of Bute, his mineral agent Robert Beaumont, Anthony Hill, J.B. Bruce, Colonel Brotherton, Major Digby Mackworth who was sent down on special mission by the War Office, and others, sent in their descriptions and explanations of the rising to a Home Office which seemed insatiable in its hunger for sheer information.

Evan Thomas's hurried and doubtfully legal inquest was hardly enough to ward off the press and parliament. The Swansea coroner Thomas Thomas, whom constable William Rowland had been hunting, was finally reached on 18 June and spent two days in Merthyr over 20 to 21 June. He was markedly more regimental.[13] He briskly proposed to dig up two or three of the bodies. There was evidently a collective shudder. He reported that all the gentlemen 'including the medical gentleman', presumably William Thomas the Court, earnestly begged him not to. The corpses would have so decomposed that there would be a danger of a malignant fever, they said; besides a crowd would surely gather, including kinsfolk of the dead. There might be another outbreak at any affront to what Evan Thomas had delicately called 'the strongest of their prejudices'. Unabashed, Thomas Thomas ordered the disinterring of poor old John Hughes, who had gone through the war and fought in six battles and, in his dying words, had asked his friends not to blame the soldiers who were only doing their duty. A respectable jury duly stared at his rotting corpse laid out in a yard before retiring to the Castle Inn to return a verdict of 'Excusable Homicide'. In the course of these impeccably lawful proceedings, 300 to 400 'miners and workmen' turned up and told Thomas Thomas to leave their friends' bodies alone. It was a tense moment but it passed. The indefatigable coroner, who was evidently a veritable Napoleon of the charnel house, then proposed to dig up a woman, presumably in the interest of a proper balance. The horrified gentlemen were saved by news that Rowland Thomas, one of the last men to be shot, had only just died. He had been hit in the thigh, but he had diseased lungs and a hernia, said Job James. He could not sleep without opiates and had seemed convinced he would die. He did so, timing it well enough perhaps to prevent a resumption of the riots which had killed him. The same verdict was returned and the coroner, dispatching an excellent report to Melbourne, left as briskly as he had come. No doubt Melbourne was as glad to see him leave as Merthyr surely was: he had just made it for the parliamentary session.

Two days later, Melbourne had to get out of Anthony Hill the depositions taken on 8 June in justification of the decision to open fire. Magistrates' reports and that of Colonel Morgan at the time had said *magistrates* had given the order to fire; one even suggested that the order to fire had been given before, but had been forestalled by, the crowd's rush on the troops. None of the witnesses at the inquests or the Assizes mentioned the point; the officer at Crawshay's window clearly did not wait for any magistrate and one suspects none of them did. The depositions, glowing in their praise of the Highlanders (and justifiably so) would come in useful.[14]

The Merthyr, which had to face another panic before the end of June, was then a harassed, haunted and tense place. The new colliers' union was sensed rising all around in hidden, secret menace; sheer hatred stalked the streets.[15] William Crawshay was being belaboured on all sides. He was blamed for stirring his men into radicalism and then provoking them from the Castle Inn window, for driving them mad by his wage cut and then proving them right by withdrawing it. The *Observer* in London pilloried him; so did several local magistrates; he knew what 'his men' now thought of him — he was to contribute money to the defence fund of those soon to stand in the dock. He had written one of the *Cambrian*'s accounts of the troubles; before the end of June he published *The Late Riots at Merthyr Tydfil* in tough but tortuous self-defence.[16]

He and Anthony Hill were trying to sort out the hideous mess of bills and accounts which the troops at Penydarren had left behind, which totalled something over £1,000.[17] Some of the smaller accounts they managed to clear quickly, but the War Office took three months to examine the Merthyr documents. Not until November did they cheerlessly inform the town that they would pay normal billeting rates but no more, which left a deficit of over £450. This extraordinarily frustrating business was to drag on until April 1833 and was only settled then by what had become a traditional remedy, a levy on the ironworks, by number of furnaces. Alderman Thompson, gloomily contemplating the shambles at Penydarren House — 'If he saw a nail on the ground or a lump of coal . . . he would pathetically lament at his approaching ruin' — started sending in demands for hundreds at a time. The Court of King's Bench awarded Joseph Coffin and Mary Rees over £590 as compensation for the destruction of their houses; it was to be levied on Caerphilly Hundred which in practice meant the town. The slump was getting worse; there was no sign of the Whigs letting Merthyr into the Reform Bill and William Crawshay was not on speaking terms with his father, though that at least was normal, since Crawshay family relationships tended to the Hanoverian.

It was as the full misery of their situation was dawning on the established and the respectable in Merthyr that Melbourne learned that the troops there had to sleep in their clothes without blankets. The War Office had already complained that there was no proper accommodation for soldiers in Merthyr and Melbourne had written to Bute as early as 14 June saying he proposed to withdraw them and set up garrisons of infantry at Brecon and Cardiff, of cavalry at Abergavenny. Now on 19 June he addressed a peremptory letter to Merthyr. Unless provision was made for the troops, he would withdraw them 'forthwith'. He actually ordered Evan Thomas to requisition bedding, buildings and furniture from the inhabitants and to raise money from the ironmasters.[18]

Evan Thomas sent in a dignified refusal, at the second time of asking. If the troops were withdrawn before the Assizes and their aftermath, lives would be in danger . . . 'the connections and relatives of the parties whose blood was so unfortunately and infamously spilt all centre in and about this place'. If he tried to requisition houses, bedding and furniture . . . 'no doubt the Inhabitants will contribute them, but from the same cause and with the same feelings as the neighbouring Inhabitants of Aberdare furnished arms and ammunition to the insurgents on the 4th and 5th, viz., fear for their property and persons'. (Evan Thomas was clearly no slouch at the cut-and-thrust!) As for the ironmasters, it was unfair to impose on them, when they had already advanced large sums (presumably he meant the Peny-darren bills), had made no wage cut for a twelve-month and had been asked for no rise and whose property was exposed to attack in 'Tumults arising decidedly out of a state of high political excitement' (which is an interesting indicator of attitudes).[19]

Eighty-seven of the leading citizens assembled at the Castle Inn under Anthony Hill and sent a formal reply on 21 June. If the troops were withdrawn, the mob, infuriated by calamity, would at once break into riot. They felt this so strongly, that they had already begun to supply bedding, blankets and furniture; all the soldiers would be provided by the following day. They begged, however, to be excused the expense of this exercise and asked Melbourne to send down a barrack-master and quarter-master. Melbourne agreed to let the troops stay, but while he wrote a conciliatory, indeed slightly shame-faced, letter to Evan Thomas, he told the Merthyr people that he had no intention of sending any officer down, but would consider claims for compensation after the troops had gone, if those who supplied bedding 'think it right to require compensation . . .'[20]

It was in this state of tension that the Assizes opened.[21] At much the same time, letter after letter was coming into the Home Office on the activities of *The Union* and of the colliers' union in particular. Monmouthshire was reported disturbed, the Ruabon report came in, and there were indications that the union was striking root over the whole coalfield from Swansea in a great arc round to Newport.[22]

The Glamorgan Summer Assizes opened on 9 July at Cardiff. Justice Bosanquet of the south Wales circuit was assisted by Baron Bolland of the north Wales circuit which was postponed, so heavy was the burden of trying the Merthyr rioters. It cost over £258 to bring 99 witnesses from Merthyr and the county paid out over £780 to the Merthyr

solicitor William Meyrick (who had actually been one of the
Tory victims of the political riot of 9 May and was to stand as Tory
candidate for Merthyr in 1835 as sworn enemy of the Jameses and
William Perkins). It was Meyrick who organised the prosecution.[23]
Mr Maule appeared for that prosecution and Mr Sockett for the
defence. Unfortunately the official record of the trial has disappeared;
all we have are the reports of the local press,[24] a transcript of the trial
of John Phelps, sent to London because he was a Pensioner[25] and
Meyrick's transcript of the prosecution's evidence in the case of
Lewis and Richard Lewis, sent to Melbourne as the result of a petition
for clemency.[26] The *Sentence List*, published later, groups individuals
and does not strictly correspond to the list of indictments which may
be inferred, however, from trial reports.[27] There appear to have been
14 separate indictments.[28] A total of 28 people were charged, 14 of
them in connection with *Reform* raids on houses, 11 of them for
seizing arms, mostly outside the Castle Inn and 5 for violent actions at
Aberdare and Hirwaun; several people of course appeared under more
than one charge.

The twenty-eight sacrificial scapegoats included two women, one of
them aged 62. They seem broadly to represent the changing composition of the crowds.

Puddlers	5	Miners	8	Shoemakers	2
Finers	1	Colliers	4	Smiths	1
Corkers	1	Labourers	4	Women	2

Ironstone miners were most numerous, followed by puddlers. Broadly
speaking, skilled men and artisans were a third of the accused, colliers
and labourers a third, miners nearly a third in themselves. Their average
age was nearly thirty.[29]

The Merthyr hearings began on 13 July.[30] The first case heard was
that of John Phelps and the attack on Thomas Williams's house. He
was found not guilty of breaking into the house, but guilty of robbery
and putting Jane Williams in fear. Next came David Thomas, *Dai Llaw
Haearn*, who was tried for the attack on the Williams houses and
found guilty. The third case covered the attack on Thomas Lewis's
house, when Lewis Lewis, David Hughes, Thomas Llewellyn, David
Williams, David Thomas again, David Jones and Thomas Vaughan were
all charged. It was a long trial. Henry Kirkhouse, Crawshay's under-
manager, appeared to speak for Thomas Llewellyn and David Jones,
Dai Solomon. The judge charged the jury in a 'very elaborate manner';

he dropped the charge against David Williams who had been forced to appear at the house and pointed out that most of the evidence was against Lewis Lewis, David Thomas and Thomas Vaughan. The jury's verdict was that Thomas Llewellyn, David Williams and David Jones were not guilty, Lewis Lewis, David Thomas, Thomas Vaughan and David Hughes guilty. They were, however, 'strongly recommended to mercy, in consequence of its being a riot'.

It was the fourth case, heard on 14 July, which attracted most comment. Lewis Lewis, whose name everyone knew, and Richard Lewis, whose name had appeared in the local newspaper only on 18 June, were jointly tried on the charge of wounding Donald Black, a private of the 93rd, outside the Castle Inn on 3 June. On this charge, the jury found Richard Lewis guilty and Lewis Lewis not guilty. They added that they thought Lewis Lewis guilty of encouraging the mob to *disarm* the soldiers (*disarm* underlined in all reports of the verdict).[31]

At this point, Justice Bosanquet stopped the trials. Four were enough, he said; the remaining ten indictments were abandoned. Several of the prisoners awaiting their turn pleaded guilty and were given 'slight punishment'; others were acquitted or discharged. In the event, John Morgan, *John the Racer*, got one year's hard labour, as did Joan Jenkins the woman of 62. Women had been very active in the riots, said the judge, and should not be spared because of their sex. Joan's sons, however, got only six months'. David Richards and David Jones, together with Margaret Davies who had also been at Coffin's house, were sentenced to a year's hard labour. The rest, outside the first four indictments, were acquitted or discharged. John Phelps was sentenced to 14 years' transportation. Sentences of death were recorded against David Hughes, Thomas Vaughan and David Thomas, but the judge made it clear that they would actually suffer transportation for life.

The sentences of death passed on Lewis Lewis and Richard Lewis, however, were to stand.[32]

These proceedings are curious. They resulted in one very striking anomaly. As is clear from the judge's summing up and other evidence, there were wholly separate indictments covering the general attack on the Castle Inn, the firing at the Inn from Morlais Tip, the onslaught on Coffin's house and other incidents in which Lewis Lewis had been prominent, which were abandoned. This notorious man, singled out as the 'leader' of the Merthyr Rising by everyone in authority, was tried in court only as an accessory to the attack on Lewis's house and the stabbing of Donald Black, though these were capital charges enough. Yet, in his summing up, Bosanquet referred frequently to the offences which had not been heard in court and was marginally more severe on Lewis Lewis than on Richard Lewis.[33]

A little over two weeks later, however, Lewis Lewis was reprieved; his sentence commuted to transportation for life. Richard Lewis was hanged at Cardiff on 13 August. As *Dic Penderyn*, this man was to live on in the minds of his countrymen as a martyr. He has so lived for nearly 150 years; today, he lives more vividly than ever.

Although a veritable cult has grown around his name, we know very little about him. At his trial, he was described as a miner. He is said to have lived in Ynysgau. The family tradition is that he was very strong (at his trial he was called 'a very powerful man'), handsome, a good worker, but fond of his drink. That tradition remembers that he fought and beat a constable notorious for bullying and blackmail. He was involved in street argument and fist fights during the *Reform* Illumination of 3 May and was said to have been a strong debater on the rights of working men. He was one of the deputation which went into the Castle Inn on 3 June.[34]

After his execution, his body was taken to what was called his birthplace in Aberavon. Local historians identify him as the son of a Lewis Lewis and his wife Mary.[35] The parish registers of Pyle-Kenfig list a Lewis Lewis with a wife Mary who was a cordwainer (shoe-maker) of Cornelly near Pyle; Richard Lewis certainly had kinsfolk in that area.[36] This Lewis Lewis is said to have been a Methodist. Dic's sister married Morgan Howells, a minister with the Calvinistic Methodists;[37] Dic himself was attended by four Wesleyan Methodist ministers on the scaffold.[38]

Lewis Lewis of Pyle is said to have moved to Aberavon and then Merthyr, where he worked as a miner. One narrative places the move in 1819, though a child was born to Lewis Lewis the Cornelly cord-wainer in Pyle in 1821.[39] The family had some experience of those mobile and marginal trades in which *Lewis* Lewis worked; Dic's brother, *John y Calchwr*, burned lime at Cefn Cribbwr for a year. As a youth, Dic himself is said to have hauled timber at Llanelly ironworks (Brecon), to have broken a law over the handling of horses and to have run away to Penderyn parish, where he is reported to have been 'acquainted with' or 'attached to' *Lewsyn yr Heliwr*. This was in 1828, when he would have been 20.[40] He was married and a child is said to have been born to him just before his execution. One dramatic but unverified account says his wife walked to Cardiff on the eve of the execution with the child in her arms, to find the child dead when she got there.[41] Merthyr parish registers have two Richard Lewises marrying in 1830, one in July, the other in October. The latter would fit the tradition; he married a Mary Thomas.[42]

The persistent parallels to, and even suggestions of a direct connection with, *Lewis* Lewis breed confusion and frustration. One prime source of confusion is the *Newgate Calendar*, which joyfully seized on the trials and embellished its account with a Phiz drawing of the Hirwaun flag ceremony in French Revolution style. Returning from Dic's execution, the Wesleyan ministers reported that they heard Lewis Lewis in his cell crying that Dic was innocent. In the *Calendar*, this becomes a statement of *Lewsyn* that he could have saved Dic, 'because he was his brother'.[43] They were certainly not biological brothers. If Lewis Lewis said this at all (which may seem unlikely since there is no local report) he might have meant it in a metaphorical sense, which would suggest trade union membership, but there is no evidence of this either.

Apart from the surname and some parallels in career, there is the joint patronymic *Penderyn*. Lewis Lewis was sometimes called Lewis Penderyn and the two men have occasionally been confused. Dic's name is said to derive from the name of the Lewis family cottage in Pyle. Why should a Lewis cottage in Pyle carry the name *Penderyn*, anyway? Richard Lewis seems actually to have worked in Penderyn parish in 1828; he is said to have been close to Lewis Lewis; like him, he moved between hauling and ironstone mining. The trial which hanged him was actually a joint trial.

In striking contrast to *Lewsyn*, however, nobody in contemporary accounts of the rising singled him out by name at all. He does not figure in any of the inquests and depositions which have survived. He surfaces only in that brief mention in the *Cambrian* of 18 June and then at his trial. This makes such accounts as we have of his trial all the more perplexing.

The transcript which Bosanquet sent to Melbourne read: 'The Prisoners were indicted that they on 3 June 1831 at the parish of Merthyr Tydfil, with a bayonet affixed to a certain gun which the said Richard Lewis held in both his hands, one Donald Black in and upon the right hip did stab, cut, wound with intent in so doing and malice aforethought to kill and murder the said Donald Black . . .'[44]

Mr Maule presented a joint case against both men. He described the scene at the Castle Inn and Lewis Lewis's role, attributed the 'gooseberry' remark to *Lewsyn* and said that Richard Lewis stabbed Black. The struggle lasted for over a quarter of an hour during which time Lewis and Richard Lewis, and *especially Richard Lewis* 'fought with desperation and did not quit the place until nearly the whole of the rioters had fled'.

Seven witnesses gave evidence for the prosecution. The magistrate J.B. Bruce mentioned nobody by name, while William Williams and William Rowland, two of the Specials inside the Inn, spoke only of Lewis Lewis. The bulk of the evidence was in fact directed against *Lewis* Lewis. The critical testimony in the case of Richard Lewis was that of James Abbott a barber who had served as a Special at the Castle Inn. He was more confused, less coherent than any other witness either at the Assizes or the earlier inquests; he talked of gunshots before the volley from the Castle windows, which nobody else heard, muddled up incidents and repeatedly stressed that he did not understand Welsh and so could not follow the exchanges between the crowd and the magistrates.

Most of his evidence in fact concerned Lewis Lewis, whose role he described at length. A striking feature of his testimony was his evident determination to avoid incriminating either *Lewsyn* or the crowd, if he could. While admitting to Maule that Lewis Lewis made speeches 'considerably higher than the rest of the people', he stressed, in his replies to the defence counsel Sockett, that the crowd for much of the time had paid no attention to the *Huntsman* and on Lewis Lewis himself added – 'He might for ought I know have been giving the same advice as Mr. Crawshay and Mr. Guest'! He thought the front ranks of the crowd might have been pushed against the soldiers by those behind who might, in turn, simply have been anxious to hear what was being said. He even added, on their seizing the muskets of the Highlanders – 'They might for all I know have laid hold of them to prevent an involuntary mischief'!

His statements on Richard Lewis, while brief, were very different. To Maule's junior, Evans, he said that when the attack on the soldiers began, he saw a Highlander coming up the steps of the Inn and struggling with two or three men to keep his musket, which he lost. Richard Lewis was one of the attackers . . . 'as he was on the top step or thereabouts Richard Lewis charged him with a bayonet and made an incision in the thick part of the thigh, somewhere above the knee considerably . . .' Abbott took the soldier, who was Donald Black, into the brew-house (which served as clearing station) bleeding like a pig. He said (he) 'had not the slightest doubt as to his stab having been given by Richard Lewis'.

Mr Sockett, in his cross-examination of Abbott, was concerned almost entirely with *Lewis* Lewis, though in the course of statements, the barber repeated that he had seen Black struggle with Richard Lewis. Re-examined by Evans, he said that several people had fought with Black and that Richard Lewis had struck the soldier . . . 'I saw Richard Lewis struggling with Donald Black and two or three others. Certainly two. Richard Lewis got possession of the musket and stuck the bayonet in him. I was indignant and that made me notice him . . .'

This, without doubt, was the evidence which hanged Dic Penderyn. Only one other witness claimed actually to have seen Richard Lewis stab the soldier. This was James Drew, intriguingly enough another barber and possibly Abbott's assistant.[45] He had seen both Lewises in the crowd. He had seen Richard Lewis, with one or two others, wrestle with Donald Black. He had seen Richard Lewis push the bayonet into the fleshy part of Black's thigh.

Only two other people mentioned Richard Lewis at all; the mass of evidence was obsessively concerned with Lewis Lewis. Thomas Darker, a radical draper, had been in the passage of the Inn and had seen the deputation to the masters come out . . .' I saw Richard Lewis first in the passage coming out with the deputation. The first time I saw him after he came out was about five to ten minutes. I saw him at the front of the Castle with his hat off, he waved his hat and shouted . . .' Under cross-examination, Darker said . . . 'Richard Lewis was standing by the door with his hat up . . .' He did not know what had been said from the Castle window just before he waved his hat.

Donald Black himself (now promoted to Lance-Corporal) was categorical . . . 'I cannot say I saw him stab me', he said of Richard Lewis . . . 'He stood near the place where I was stabbed . . .' He saw both prisoners in the crowd, but did not see them laying hands on anyone . . . 'Only saw Richard Lewis taking his hat off and cheering but not laying his hands on anyone in the crowd . . .' It was before the rush that he had seen him. Black's cross-examination was concerned wholly with *Lewis* Lewis. The soldier had obviously been riveted by *Lewsyn*. He had been stationed at the door of the Inn, right by Lewis Lewis and the red banner. He had been alarmed to see *Lewsyn* working his way behind him. Captain Sparks had pushed one man back into the crowd and *Lewsyn* had said belligerently in English — 'You would not do so to me.' Captain Sparks, said Black, 'shook his head at him and gave a sort of laugh', adding obscurely but in the kind of soldier's lateral thinking which can be understood — 'Recruits do not like to be laughed at . . .'!

In a trial, then, dominated by the actions and speeches of *Lewis* Lewis, in which Richard Lewis's alleged stabbing of Black figured virtually as a consequence of the former, Darker and Black were evidently used to establish Richard Lewis's presence in the deputation and among the crowd near the front door of the Inn. James Drew was a rather taciturn confirmation of James Abbott, who was the fulcrum of the prosecution's case.

What is totally frustrating is that, apart from the sidelong light thrown by the prosecution transcript, we have no record whatever of what was said by or for the prisoners in their own defence. The only words put in the prisoners' mouths appear in the summary of evidence sent to Melbourne . . . 'Richard Lewis said on Friday morning this riot began to get up. Leaves it to his Counsel. Lewis Lewis said nothing.'

Justice Bosanquet pronounced sentence 'at great length' and manages to deepen the perplexity. The *Cambrian* singled out as his main argument the point that if the jury believed that Lewis Lewis exhorted people to attack the soldiers, then he was as guilty, 'if not more so', than the hand which actually inflicted the wound.[46] This is something of a gloss on Bosanquet's actual statement, but it could be argued that it simply made explicit what was implicit in the judge's summing up.

For he spent most of his time on *Lewis* Lewis.[47] He concentrated on his role in the attack on Thomas Lewis's house — which was the only charge on which the *Huntsman had actually been found guilty*. He then, however, broadened out to take in Lewis Lewis's other offences, including those which had not been heard in court. The judge wished heartily that he had seen evidence that *Lewsyn* had repented of his offence at Thomas Lewis's, that the latter had been something done 'under sudden excitement for which you was afterwards sorry . . .' Instead, the judge found that *Lewsyn* had taken an 'active and leading part . . . in almost every part of the proceedings . . .' On the following day, he had instigated the crowd to attack the soldiers, had tried to get behind them; he had demanded powder from Thomas Lewis with a musket in his hand and had been involved in the sniping from Morlais Tip. Later on, he had been seen armed and in the company of other armed men at 'some little distance' from Merthyr . . . 'Seeing the part you have taken in the early parts and the leading part that you have taken throughout . . .' there was no hope of a reprieve.

On Richard Lewis, the judge was equally immovable but marginally less severe . . . 'The offence committed by you, Richard Lewis, was committed on that day on which the Mob was so numerously assembled and whether at your immediate suggestion or whether in consequence of that which was uttered by the other Prisoner, I find you either the first or one of the first to make an attack upon the military . . . it is upon your head and upon the heads of those who immediately instigated to that attack that the responsibility must rest of the Blood which has fallen . . .'

Lewis Lewis, then, was actually condemned to death for the attack on Thomas Lewis's house, for which offence the jury had 'strongly recommended' mercy, though his leading role throughout was stressed and his responsibility for the stabbing of Donald Black suggested. Richard Lewis, taken as 'the first' actually to attack the soldiers, was condemned on what seemed an even more serious charge, even though throughout his trial he had been treated as a secondary offender, almost as a weapon ultimately directed by Lewis Lewis.

It was the less rather than the more guilty, however, who was to take two minutes to die at the end of a rope.

Notes

1. Melbourne, annotation of Bute to Melbourne, 9 June, with second annotation probably by Denman, the Attorney-General; Melbourne to Bute, 11 June: HO 52/16 and HO 41/10; Home Office (quoting Melbourne) to Bute, 20 June: HO 41/10.

2. Crawshay London House to W. Crawshay II, 15 June: Crawshay Papers (NLW), Box 2 (575d).

3. All correspondence to 9 June was read by the King and most was circulated around the government: HO 52/16.

4. Melbourne to Normanby, 5 November 1839: Marquess of Normanby archives, Mulgrave Papers, Mulgrave MM/242.

5. Watkin Williams Wynn to Melbourne, 8 June: HO 52/16.

6. Evan Thomas to Melbourne, 18 June; Bute to Melbourne, 3 July; Notes relative to the Colliers Union Society in the parish of Ruabon, 29 June: HO 52/16.

7. Letters went out on 10 June to Sir Henry Bouverie, military commander in the north, to the Earl of Derby and to Foster the Manchester magistrate: HO 41/10. Correspondence of Melbourne with Bute, late June and July: HO 52/16.

8. The *Prompter* (Carlile), *Poor Man's Guardian* (Hetherington), June-August 1831; *Hansard*, 3rd series, iv, pp. 204-6 (21 June), p. 274 (23 June), pp. 397-400 (27 June), pp. 660-9 (4 July), pp. 828-8, 840-72 (5 August); *Annual Register* (1831), p. 60.

9. Captain Bloomfield of 11th to Brotherton, 12 June; Bute to Melbourne, 12 June; Horse Guards to Home Office, 24 June; Bute to Brotherton, 12 June: HO 52/16 and HO 52/14.

10. Melbourne to Bute and to Merthyr magistrates, June to July, passim: HO 41/10 and HO 52/16.

11. Melbourne, as well as repeatedly demanding explanations of the Rising, began pressing for information on an inquest from 12 June, evidently spurred on by complaints in the 'London prints' (*Cambrian*, 25 June);

he repeated requests for both a general explanation and a coroner's report on 13 and 14 June; Bute passed the letters on to the Merthyr magistrates who, on 14 June, sent William Rowland to Swansea to look for the West Glamorgan coroner, Thomas Thomas, since the East Glamorgan coroner had left the country. Bute himself went to Merthyr on 14 June and consulted Evan Thomas the Chairman of the Quarter Sessions who was still there. On that day, Melbourne wrote to Bute to say the Commander-in-Chief had reported that Merthyr was a very inconvenient station for troops and that he proposed to withdraw them. This letter seems to have galvanised the Merthyr men into action. Evan Thomas, Bruce and Hill wrote to Bute on 16 June, strongly protesting against the removal of the troops; on the same day, Evan Thomas wrote his long report on the rising for Bute to transmit to Melbourne, and decided to hold some kind of inquest the next day, sending in a second report on 18 June. It was then that Melbourne learned that the East Glamorgan coroner had left the country – 'a gross dereliction of duty': Melbourne to Bute, 13, 14, 15, 16 and 19 June: HO 41/10; Hill and Bruce to Bute, 14 June; Bruce, Hill and Thomas to Bute, 16 June; Evan Thomas to Bute, 16 June, and to Melbourne, 18 June; Bute to Melbourne, 15 June: HO 52/16; *Cambrian*, 25 June.

12. This inquest is reported, with the transcript of testimony, in Evan Thomas to Melbourne, 18 June (HO 52/16) and reported (more accurately) in *Cambrian*, 25 June.

13. William Rowland found that the Swansea coroner had gone to London and Thomas Thomas did not receive his orders until his return on 18 June; he went to Merthyr at once and started the inquests on the Monday: letter with transcript of testimony in T. Thomas to Melbourne, 26 June; reported in part in *Cambrian*, 25 June.

14. The depositions, all sworn to before J.B. Bruce on 8 June, were sent up by Anthony Hill to Melbourne on 26 June: HO 52/16; Colonel Morgan in his dispatch from Penydarren House on the evening of 3 June, stated specifically that four magistrates, Bruce, Hill, Guest and Morgan, gave the order to fire and that the crowd rushed the soldiers before the latter could do so (Morgan to Bute, 3 June). Though this was read by the King, it appears to be a 'terminological inexactitude', to quote another states-man, Winston Churchill, who was also involved in mythology over soldiers and south Wales miners.

15. There were many anonymous personal threats to J.B. Bruce, accused of being 'precipitate' in calling for soldiers; London newspapers like the *Observer* pilloried Crawshay and the *Sun* denounced the yeomanry; *Cambrian*, 18 and 25 June; W. Crawshay II, *The Late Riots* . . .

16. The copy I have used is in Cyfarthfa Castle Museum, Merthyr Tydfil; it reveals his authorship of the account by a Gentleman of Merthyr in the *Cambrian* of 11 June.

17. I have examined this process in detail in 'The Merthyr Riots: settling the account'.

18. He had given warning on 14 June, in a letter which spurred the Merthyr magistrates into the activity of 16-18 June. The news of the misery of the troops at Merthyr reached him at the same time as that of the absentee East Glamorgan coroner; the consequences were two fierce letters, to Bute and to Evan Thomas, Bruce and Hill at Merthyr on 19 June (HO 41/10 with copy in Merthyr petition of 21 June, HO 52/16). On 20 June, Major Digby Mackworth wrote to the Horse Guards to report the end of his mission and his belief that the troops could be safely withdrawn

because the miners were 'ashamed and cowed'; he added, however, that the magistrates were 'of a decidedly opposite opinion'; Mackworth to Lord Fitzroy Somerset, 20 June: HO 52/16.

19. Evan Thomas to Home Office, 21 June: HO 52/16.

20. Petition of Masters and Principal Inhabitants of Merthyr, 21 June: HO 52/16. Melbourne to Evan Thomas and to Merthyr magistrates, 23 June: HO 41/10.

21. The *Cambrian* added its mite by reporting that Owen Davies, a 58 year old Merthyr workman from Cardiganshire had witnessed the shooting on 3 June and 'has been raving mad ever since': *Cambrian*, 25 June.

22. On 3 July, Bute reported on the unions and linked them with Thomas Llewellyn (about to be tried at Cardiff) to 'prove' the existence of a wide-ranging conspiracy. On 6 July, the magistrates of Mold in Flintshire reported an attack by union miners on blacklegs from Anglesey as soon as soldiers had withdrawn after a six weeks' stay; the power of the union oath was such that the mass of the colliers, unaware of the planned onslaught, were at a moment's notice, 'summoned out of their beds by the orders of a few chosen leaders': HO 52/16. It was on 2 July that the *Cambrian* confidently predicted a trial for High Treason at Cardiff.

23. W. Meyrick to Melbourne, 7 July: HO 52/16. Glamorgan Quarter Sessions (GRO), Minute Book 17, Michaelmas 1831, Epiphany and Easter 1832; Treasurer's Accounts, 28, 29 June, 14 July, 19 October, 15 November 1831; 27 January, 17 March 1932; Clerk of the Peace, Letters and Returns: Summer Assizes, 1831.

24. *Cambrian*, 16 and 23 July.

25. Trial of John Phelps, Circuit Letters, HO 6/16 and in *Cambrian*, 16 July.

26. Transcript of trial with judge's sentencing: HO 17/128, part 2, bundle Zp37, printed in part in Alexander Cordell, *The Fire People*, pp. 363-8.

27. Sentence List, Glamorgan Summer Assizes, July 1831; the copy I consulted is in National Museum of Wales, Welsh Folk Museum, St Fagans, Cardiff.

28. Judge's sentencing statement, *Cambrian*, 23 July, correlated with Sentence List.

29. This information comes from the Sentence List.

30. The Grand Jury sat on the Merthyr accused all day on 12 and 13 July and found all save three of 'near fifty Bills' to be true; Diaries of Lewis Weston Dillwyn, ii, 133 (foreman of Grand Jury); transcripts of Phelps's trial (the first) and of the two Lewises, date them 13 and 14 July respectively.

31. *Cambrian*, 16 and 23 July.

32. *Cambrian*, 23 July.

33. Judge's statement, HO 17/128, part 2, bundle Zp37.

34. Isaac Evans, letter in *Tarian y Gweithiwr*, 14 August 1884 (by the nephew of John Evans who married Dic's widow); Petitions on behalf of Dic in HO 17/128, part 2, bundle Zp37; transcript of trial there and account in *Cambrian*, 23 July.

35. Anon., 'Hen Lythyr Diddorol', *Y Drysorfa*, lxxxix (1919), pp. 418-19, recounts conversation with a man over 80 who witnessed the execution and the burial and knew Dic's family history; Dewi Cynon, 'Dic Penderyn', *Darian*, 16 March 1922; D. Emrys Lewis, 'A forgotten martyr', *Aberafan and Margam District Historical Society*, 1928.

36. Pyle and Kenfig parish registers, bishops' transcripts (NLW): entries for births of children to Lewis and Mary Lewis, 1807-21; there is nothing in the Aberavon registers. I owe these references to Professor David Williams;

Morgan Howells, who married Dic's sister, wrote to his daughter in October 1851 from Pyle and gave news of the people 'at home' (Howells himself was born in St Nicholas, Glamorgan, and preached in Newport); E. Morgan, *Boanerges* (below): a Miss Lewis, kin to Dic, was living in Kenfig Hill in 1874: James Evans, *Western Mail*, 30 March 1933.

37. Morgan Howells, Calvinistic Methodist minister, married Miss Lewis, a member at Newport in September 1827; they had five children and she died 16 September 1841, aged 41 (*Welshman*, 1 October 1841). Morgan Howells was minister of a celebrated chapel, Ebenezer, which is today described as his memorial chapel (off Commercial Street, Newport). James Evans, general inspector for Wales, Ministry of Health to Professor David Williams, 11 May 1949 and in *Western Mail*, 19 May 1947 (James Evans's mother was the daughter of Morgan Howells and niece to Dic Penderyn). I owe this letter to Professor David Williams. For Howells, E. Morgan, *Boanerges, neu hanes bywyd y Parch Morgan Howells* (Cardiff, 1853).

38. Rev. Edmund Evans (Wesleyan); diary for 12-13 August 1831, *Eurgrawn Wesleyaidd* (1870), p. 356; letter in *Eurgrawn Wesleyaidd* (1831), p. 318; confirmed by *cofiant* Rev. David Williams in the same journal (1865); see also *Cambrian*, 20 August 1831.

39. James Evans, statement, 11 May 1949, where he says Dic started work in the mine with his father; D. Emrys Lewis, 'A forgotten martyr'; Pyle-Kenfig parish registers, baptism of daughter Mary to Lewis and Mary Lewis of Cornelly, shoemaker, 11 February 1821.

40. Anon., 'Hen Lythyr Diddorol', *Y Drysorfa*, op. cit.; D. Emrys Lewis, op. cit.; Dewi Cynon, *Dic Penderyn*, op. cit.

41. James Evans, letter to *Western Mail*, 30 March 1933, reports birth of child; the same man (grandson to Dic's sister) reports story of child's death at the execution in statement of 11 May 1949.

42. Merthyr parish registers, bishops' transcripts (NLW), 2 October 1830. See also entries in *Bywgraffiadur* and *DWB* by Professor David Williams, to whom I am grateful for key references to local material.

43. *Cambrian*, 20 August 1831; *New Newgate Calendar*, Lord Birkett (ed.), (Folio Society).

44. Transcript (by Meyrick) in HO 17/128, part 2, bundle Zp37, published in part in Alexander Cordell, *The Fire People*, pp. 363-8.

45. Unlike Abbott's, I have not been able to find his name in any directory.

46. *Cambrian*, 23 July 1831.

47. Judge's statement, HO 17/128, part 2, bundle Zp37.

8 MARTYR

Bosanquet pronounced sentence at eight in the morning of Saturday, 16 July. Within hours, a crowd broke into James Abbott's barber shop in Merthyr. They dragged two men from the chairs in which they were being shaved. They chased out the customers. 'Murderer! Hangman!' they shouted at Abbott.[1]

The *Cambrian*, relieved at Bosanquet's leniency, hoped that the working men of Merthyr would note that the lives 'of only two of their fellow-workmen' had been deemed sufficient retribution. The two dozen and more who had died without benefit of Bosanquet were presumably cancelled out by the act of rebellion, even if their participation in it had taken the form of knitting in an upstairs room. People in Merthyr, with those two dozen corpses on their minds and consciences, found the very idea of two further deaths by the state's ritual noose utterly intolerable. In a town whose magistrates were becoming more and more frightened at the shadowy menace of *The Union* rising in secret all around them, people who had given evidence at the Assizes went in fear of their lives. J.B. Bruce was personally threatened.

There was a widespread feeling, shared by many of the 'respectable', that those most guilty had already met their deaths at the hands of the Highlanders. Taliesin Williams began to get up a petition for the condemned, with the help of Henry and William Morgan. A reprieve was expected. On the 16th, the day of the sentencing, the Marquess of Bute wrote to Melbourne . . . 'Mr. Justice Bosanquet will of course make known to your Lordship in the usual manner that as in other cases of capital conviction arising out of these unhappy riots, he desires to commute the punishment to transportation for life . . .'[2]

In fact, Bosanquet's manner was anything but usual. He reached Carmarthen on his circuit and sent in his formal report on 17 July. On Richard Lewis, he was brief and formal, but he evidently felt some need to justify his decision to overrule the jury's recommendation to mercy in the only case on which Lewis Lewis had actually been found guilty. 'He was not convicted of any other offence than that of the robbery' at Thomas Lewis's, the judge said, but because of his many other violent actions and because he had been 'one of the most active and leading persons', Bosanquet felt unable to recommend mercy. To which the Home Office simply added a note: 'It appears that the law should take its course in both these cases.'[3]

Within four days, however, Bosanquet had changed his mind. He made the perhaps understandable but what must be counted in the circumstances the startling decision to reprieve *Lewsyn yr Heliwr*.

Morgan Morgan of Bodwigiad had gone into action on behalf of a Penderyn man, had broadcast the fact that *Lewsyn* had saved the life of a constable outside Coffin's house and had even called the *Huntsman* 'the devoted victim'. When Bosanquet wrote to Melbourne from Carmarthen on 21 July, no petition on behalf of Lewis Lewis had reached him, though he had been told in Merthyr before he left that one would be presented, begging mercy on the ground that the *Huntsman* had saved the life of a Merthyr constable, John Thomas. The judge referred Melbourne to the original depositions taken at Merthyr in the immediate aftermath of the rising for information on the incident.[4]

His letter of 21 July makes remarkable reading.[5] 'I have again and again considered the case of the two prisoners who were left for execution,' he wrote. 'With regard to Richard Lewis ... I have seen no reason to alter my original opinion', but with regard to Lewis Lewis, he was now 'disposed to recommend that he may be spared upon condition of being transported for life'.

The central argument was rooted in the actual processes of condemnation . . . 'However active and prominent his conduct may have been, I think that I should not have left him for execution on account of the particular offence of which he was convicted, had it not been for the subsequent occurrences in which he appeared to have been involved and when I consider that he is not convicted of any offence arising out of them and that the jury recommend him to mercy . . . I doubt the propriety of carrying that sentence into execution . . .' Certainly a telling point, though one on which he had come to precisely the opposite conclusion a few days earlier and it reads rather oddly in view of the fact that Lewis Lewis was not convicted on any other indictment precisely because the judge himself had stopped the trials after the fourth.

He supported his decision with some external considerations. 'It appears upon the statement of John Thomas himself that after he had been knocked down and beaten by several men and beaten on the ground with bludgeons, he called the prisoner to assist him, who jumped down from a wall to do so and that when he had escaped and hidden himself and was followed by 200 or 300 men and beaten, the prisoner came and interceded for him, saying — "Honor, honor, he has had enough!" ' *Lewsyn* had probably saved the constable's life.

Moreover, the people had been vastly excited; there was great discontent over the Court of Requests, wages, the politics of Reform — 'more than usual violence' could have been expected. Matters had certainly got worse, but this was 'after the fighting had begun' and besides, 'the prisoner is not convicted of any of them' (Bosanquet having consciously or unconsciously ensured that he could not have been!). So, after long and careful consideration, the judge had decided to grant a respite to Lewis Lewis's execution for a week; he was going to send the order on the 23rd or 24th . . .' and to follow it with a reprieve in a few days, unless I hear to the contrary from your Lordship . . .'

Bosanquet made one further reference to *Richard* Lewis, which was ominous . . . 'It is clear that the persons most actively engaged suffered severely by the firing which their attack upon the military brought upon them; and I am induced to think that one example in the person of an individual who actually commenced this attack may satisfy the exigency of public Justice.'

While this letter was being drafted and in apparent ignorance of it, the Merthyr people were busy with their petition. Ultimately, over 11,000 people signed it, which must have meant most of the adult population.[6] The disappearance of this petition has proved singularly frustrating, for its form was fateful. Commenting on a later effort to save the life of Dic Penderyn, Bosanquet was to say that the arguments then advanced had nowhere appeared in this first petition.[7] The submission on behalf of Lewis Lewis presumably followed the lines indicated by Bosanquet's decision to reprieve him. It may be inferred that the petition on behalf of Richard Lewis was non-specific, couched in the vocabulary of a generic humanitarianism. Otherwise, it is difficult to account for a procedure which proved catastrophic.

The drafters of the Merthyr petition prepared a statement in which both prisoners admitted their guilt. They presumably acted on the assumption that a show of contrition might help. That statement, however, was *never presented* to the prisoners for their signature; both of them, and Richard Lewis in particular, vehemently *denied* their guilt. When news reached Merthyr that the 'confession' had nevertheless gone up to London, there was massive anger.[8]

The 'confession' had a disastrous effect on both Bosanquet and the Home Office. Henry and William Morgan took the petition to Windsor, where Melbourne granted them an interview on 25 July. At that interview, Henry Morgan told the Home Secretary that Richard Lewis 'uniformly denied the act of stabbing and declares that he would do so with his dying breath'. He claimed that Josiah John Guest, no less, had told him 'that it was the *received opinion* that the man who actually stabbed the soldier was *not Richard Lewis*'.[9]

Melbourne had received Bosanquet's letter reporting his decision on Lewis Lewis and on 26 July he ordered a stay of execution for the *Huntsman* so that the judge could 'reconsider' his case. That same day, Henry and William Morgan wrote a painful and formal letter in their best Sunday handwriting asking for a reply to their petition. The 'confession' and Bosanquet's letter evidently weighed more heavily in Melbourne's mind. On 27 July, he blankly rejected the Merthyr petition. Richard Lewis's grave had already been dug and a coffin supplied, though they were having some trouble finding a hangman. The execution was fixed for 30 July, three days later.[10]

Hardly had Melbourne sent off his letter to the Morgans' London hotel, however, than he was called out of the House of Lords by the Lord Chancellor, Henry Brougham himself, to confront the constable John Thomas in person, accompanied by the Quaker ironmaster of Neath Abbey, Joseph Tregelles Price, carrying two further petitions on behalf of the condemned men.[11]

Joseph Price, a well-known humanitarian, had visited the prisoners in Cardiff jail on Sunday, 24 July.[12] Lewis Lewis evidently retold the story of John Thomas, but it was by Richard Lewis that the Quaker was transfixed. Dic repeatedly asserted his innocence but said that he forgave his accusers. In this state of mind, to quote the ironmaster, Richard Lewis admitted that he had been one of the deputation which went into the Castle Inn, but he said that he had left by a back door with a man called Johns. At no time, he claimed, had he ever been at the front of the Inn. He had remained at the side of the Inn for 15 or 20 minutes until the first shots were fired. He then ran away, he said, down the Glebeland, through the Archway and over the Iron Bridge. He named two people who had seen him. Price must have asked whether James Abbott had any reason to lie, for 'on being asked if he had ever had any quarrel or scuffle with Abbott', Richard Lewis replied that he had clashed with the barber on the night of the *Reform* Illumination in Merthyr and that Abbott had threatened to be 'up with him the first chance he had'. He cited a Will John David in support.

These 'simple declarations' so impressed Joseph Price that he at once rushed to Merthyr, where John Thomas the constable enthusiastically rallied in support. Without telling them what Richard Lewis had said, Price got statements from seven people. Nancy, wife of

Evan Evans, said she had been standing with Richard Lewis by the Tap Room at the side of the Castle Inn for twenty minutes before the shooting, asserted that he had not been at the front of the Inn when the soldiers opened fire and that she saw him run away at the first shot. Her son Evan ran with him; Dic had outstripped him in the race through the Arches. Elizabeth Lewis also saw Dic there and William Philip, a Cyfarthfa puddler, claimed to have run away with him. Moreover, Benjamin Davies, a Penydarren navvy who was also with Richard Lewis, said that he wore a blue suit, whereas Thomas Cottrell, a waiter at the Castle who was at an upstairs window, claimed to have seen the soldier stabbed by a man in a 'coat of a sort of *drab* colour', certainly not blue. Ann Morgan, who lived opposite the Castle, also saw the stabbing — 'she cried murder!' The aggressor wore a drab coloured frock coat and duck trousers and was certainly not Richard Lewis whom she knew well. David Abraham, a Special at the Castle, had been standing near James Abbott. He knew Richard Lewis and had not seen him at the front of the Inn. On the contrary, he had seen him at the side and 'cautioned him against going forward'. Price was unable to trace Johns, the fellow-member of the deputation, but reported that several others had been ready to testify on Richard Lewis's behalf.

With this 'counter-evidence' which had not been presented at the trial and with the constable John Thomas in ardent lieutenancy, the Quaker went on his desperate last-minute mission to London. In a Piccadilly hotel on 27 July, he drafted two, clearly hurried, petitions. That on behalf of Lewis Lewis is the only clear statement of his case which exists.[13]

> Lewis Lewis acknowledges that he was on the Lamp Post opposite the Castle Inn, that he there and then spoke of his poverty, having a wife and four children and his earnings only 8 shillings a week at Penydarren. That he cried for bread. That he did not say a word to encourage the men in the mob to seize the soldiers' arms. He declares this solemnly. That another man called out 'We must have cheese too'. That this other man took his place at the Lamp Post. That there are a score of men who can testify to the truth of what he says.
>
> Says he saw a man fall by a shot from a soldier and shortly after the soldier ran at him with a bayonet and pinned him by his clothes to the wall and that then he struggled with the soldier to get from him.

He states that he was among the mob on the evening that Coffin's house was attacked. That John Thomas the constable was there. That the mob attacked him with intent to kill him and prevent his bringing evidence against them. That he took the man's part at the risk of his own life and referred to John Thomas to confirm his statement, in proof that he had no desire to take life.

John Thomas the Constable declares that Lewis Lewis at the time of the Riot at Coffin's house, saved his life. That the Rioters hurt him dreadfully and that Lewis Lewis threw himself over him to protect him and declared he would lose his life rather than John Thomas should be killed and begged the men to desist from beating him. That Lewis Lewis received a severe blow in endeavouring to shelter him.

John Thomas the constable aforesaid, under a feeling of anxiety and duty to save the life of Lewis Lewis, has accompanied the writer Joseph Price to London and unites with him in proffering their earnest petitions to the King to mitigate the sentence of death for such other punishment as in mercy may be seen meet.

Both men signed this dramatic document (in which *Lewsyn*'s behaviour is wholly consonant with his performance outside Thomas Lewis's house) which was hammering at a door which was already opening. The petition for Dic Penderyn, however, which reported at length on the seven new witnesses and was signed by Price alone, was startling. Price got some help from Lord James Stuart, a county MP, and submitted copies to the Home Office and the Lord Chancellor. The former did not respond. Brougham, however, 'expressed a serious doubt whether the credibility of Abbott the principal Witness, was not affected'. He took Price and Thomas to argue their case face to face with Melbourne outside the House of Lords.[14]

On 28 July, Melbourne wrote two letters which threw Merthyr, and south Wales with it, into crisis. He ordered a stay of execution for Richard Lewis until 13 August. On the same day, by sheer coincidence, he informed the magistrates at Merthyr that he proposed to withdraw the troops from the town and set up alternative garrisons at Brecon, Cardiff or Abergavenny. Two days later, Bosanquet wrote from Cardigan to confirm the reprieve for Lewis Lewis and to urge that the *Huntsman* be removed as quickly as possible, because of the general excitement. The removal of the others condemned to transportation had been ordered on 21 July; the order transferring Lewis Lewis to the Hulks after them went out on 3 August.[15]

When the news reached Merthyr, there was a panic. Digby Mackworth saw two of the town's leading citizens at Caerleon and reported to the War Office on 30 July. 'The Political Unions', he wrote, were multiplying at an alarming rate and the respites granted the two Lewises 'will have a very injurious effect and induce the people to imagine that Government will not, and dare not visit them capitally for political disturbances . . .' In Merthyr, there was 'great alarm'.[16]

On 1 August, the chief constable and ninety of the Inhabitants, including the radicals, signed a dramatic appeal to Melbourne to keep the military in Merthyr, to protect them from 'a lawless and almost countless mob of thousands aggravated by vindictive feelings of vengeance for the past . . . and all the concomitants of a licentious and senseless rabble . . .' They went on:

> We further beg to state that the workmen have formed secret associa-
> ations and clubs amongst themselves and from their conduct and
> behaviour towards witnesses and others reluctantly engaged in the
> late prosecutions at the late Cardiff Assizes, from insinuations
> thrown out by many, and from the insiduous [sic] and poisonous
> nature of communications made by Strangers calling themselves
> delegates from some parts of England, we firmly believe they would
> seize the first favourable moment for assembling in large bodies
> and would commit excesses hitherto unknown in the district if
> military aid were not on the spot.[17]

The direct connection between the popular response to the Cardiff trials and the growth of the new colliers' union was stressed by both Anthony Hill and J.B. Bruce. 'Lewis Lewis's reprieve, to whom all the bloodshed of the 3 June and subsequent calamities may be solely attributed,' wrote the latter, 'will, I too much fear, give encouragement to further excesses.'[18] Hill reported that his workmen were forming union lodges, 'do not settle to their work . . . nor do they exert themselves to earn so much money as they are capable of . . . they are listless and unsettled . . . they are only waiting some demonstration elsewhere and the removal of the military . . .' The people who gave evidence at the Assizes 'are continually molested and reviled. Much excitement has prevailed in consequence of the conduct of some gentlemen who seem to prefer their own view of the case to that of the legal tribunal . . . Crowds were collecting around the Castle Inn during the whole day these gentlemen were collecting *information* unauthorised and not upon oath, all of which might have been readily produced upon the trial had the Counsel for the Defence deemed it prudent . . .'[19]

Public attention had been greatly excited over the case of the two Lewises, reported the *Cambrian* on 5 August, 'but particularly Richard Lewis, alias Dick Penderrin, whose case appears to be one of peculiar interest, having given rise to the most extraordinary exertions on his behalf that were, perhaps, ever made by an individual on a similar occasion'.[20]

The struggle for the life of Dic Penderyn was becoming indistinguishable from the struggle for trade unions, for workers' control, from that rebellion of the working class which was driving the inhabitants of Merthyr into two hostile, spiritual ghettoes. If some people were determined to 'make an example', after the reprieve for Lewis Lewis, 'ringleader and author of all the mischief', only Dic could serve.

Joseph Price first tried to undo the effect of the deadly 'confession'. He got an affidavit, dated 1 August, from Daniel Jones, chaplain of Cardiff prison and two ministers: 'We hereby humbly certify that we have respectively attended Richard Lewis now under sentence of death in the Gaol of this place since his conviction, and that he had uniformly and solemnly denied any participation in or knowledge of the act of wounding or endeavouring to wound the Soldier, for which offence, he, the said Richard Lewis, is condemned to die.'[21]

Price saw Lewis Dillwyn, the Swansea magistrate who had been foreman of the Grand Jury at the Assizes and reported to Lord James Stuart that Dillwyn believed Dic Penderyn to be innocent, though the Swansea man had written to Stuart the previous day in 'a quite contrary' sense. Three respectable persons in Merthyr told Price that the belief in Richard Lewis's innocence was so universal that 'very unpleasant impressions will long remain if after *all* the sentence of death be not remitted'.[22]

When Price encountered Justice Bosanquet in Brecon on 4 August, however, he found that his first submission had failed. From Cardigan, on 1 August, Bosanquet had sent up to Melbourne a transcript of the evidence for the prosecution and his own sentence speech, together with his reasoning on Price's first petition. The judge found it 'singular' that this material had not been presented at the trial, though the prisoner had been 'very ably defended' and he noted that the earlier petition had not relied on these arguments. Richard Lewis's statement was inconsistent with the evidence of Black and Darker (who had seen the miner cheering outside the front door of the Inn) and of Drew as well as Abbott. Dic's account of a previous quarrel with Abbott had come in response to a leading question. Bosanquet thought that Richard Lewis could well have been at the back or side of the Inn twenty minutes before the firing (a subtle distortion of what had actually been said) and that some person in a drab coat might have been seen stabbing a soldier, without these facts in any way invalidating the truth of the prosecution's charge.[23]

Price had a long talk with Bosanquet at Brecon, however, and learned that it would be proper to seek further information. This time, the Castle Inn was besieged by people anxious to testify on Dic's behalf. In a new petition, Price cited thirteen further witnesses. A Marsden, who was either the chief constable at the time of the shooting or his brother, testified that he had seen Richard Lewis go out through the *back* door of the Inn, while the wife of James Rice said she had seen him before but not after the deputation, dressed in a blue jacket and trousers. Henry Jones, gentleman, had seen no-one so dressed in front of the Castle, while Thomas Burnell, chandler and Thomas James, miner, saw a soldier stabbed by someone in 'a flannel smock' or 'smock frock and trousers'. One or two of the men killed had been so dressed, Price said.

His most effective new evidence, however, was directed against Abbott's credibility. William Jones, a Cyfarthfa fitter, had been in Meyrick's office when Abbott went over his evidence before the trials. To a statement that he had been standing on the steps of the Inn, Abbott had replied in correction that he had been in the passage. Jones considered that if he had been in the passage, thronged as it was with soldiers, it would have been impossible for him to have distinguished a person stabbing a soldier outside. William Edwards, master collier and miner and undertaker of job work at Penydarren, had been in the passage of the Inn, several yards from the front door, alongside James Drew, the only other person who had positively identified Richard Lewis as the man who stabbed Black. Edwards had found it impossible to see 'who in particular inflicted any wound on a soldier' and Drew was further down the passage than he was. Moreover Drew had been with him most of the day afterwards and had never mentioned Richard Lewis.

Price further cited Will John David and Edward Mathews a puddler who on the night of the *Reform* Illumination in Merthyr, had seen James Abbott strike Richard Lewis near the Bush Inn. So had David Rees a miner who was a Baptist preacher; both Rees and David heard Abbott say . . . 'Come thee, I will be up with thee again the first opportunity I can get . . .' or words to that effect. Price confronted

Abbott himself, who denied that he had known Richard Lewis previously and who produced three tradesmen who had been present at the row at Merthyr over the Illumination and who said they had not seen the barber there, though Adam Newell a grocer (who later, as a bankrupt, tried to organise the sale of votes during the 1835 election) admitted that Abbott *could* have been in the street.

Arguing at length around this evidence and pointing out that 'many lives have already been taken legally', Joseph Price begged mercy for Dic Penderyn, 'fully believing also that its extension in this case will contribute to allay a feeling of irritation, to restore order and maintain tranquility'.[24]

On 5 August, Price went to Brecon to show the petition to Bosanquet. At this point, Bosanquet himself began to weaken. In an important letter to Melbourne, written at Hay on 6 August, he maintained:

I cannot say that the statements which he has communicated lead me to doubt the correctness of the evidence upon which the Prisoner has been found guilty. But I believe that the enquiries which Mr. Price has made have induced him to entertain a sincere opinion that there has been either misrepresentation or mistake in the evidence given upon the trial and that it was not by the Prisoner's hand that Donald Black the soldier was wounded and from what he states to me, I am led to apprehend that other persons of respectability at Merthyr partake of that opinion.

Under the circumstances, it may be a matter for your Lordship's consideration whether it is advisable that the sentence of Death should be carried into execution, there being reason to think that the justice of it will be considered doubtful among the inhabitants of the place where the effect of the example is most intended to operate. I do not suppose that the fact of the prisoner's guilt is capable of much further elucidation. It certainly took place amidst great confusion and could be distinctly seen only by a few. The firing of the soldiers from the windows of the Castle Inn took place immediately after the attack upon those who were in front and there can be little doubt that several of the foremost persons concerned in the attack and consequently the most guilty, were killed upon that occasion. There appears to be a strong impression, however erroneous, that the individual who wounded Donald Black was among the slain.

Bosanquet went on to report the refutation of the earlier 'confession' and added in a postscript . . . 'There is an appearance of firmness and candour in Mr. Price's communications and in the manner in which he has obtained his information.' The next day, Bosanquet reached Presteigne to find Melbourne's letter of 4 August, written in response to the judge's first report on Price. This ordered the execution to proceed. Bosanquet at once sent an urgent letter, drawing Melbourne's attention to his most recent assessment of the case and added: 'If upon further consideration your Lordship should be induced to recommend a commutation of the sentence of Death, I need hardly repeat the suggestion which I made in respect to the other Prisoner, that the early removal from Cardiff of Richard Lewis will be highly desirable . . .' However hedged about these letters, it seems fairly clear that Justice Bosanquet had come around to the opinion that Richard Lewis ought to be reprieved.[25]

Price, on finding Melbourne's first answer waiting him at Neath Abbey, also wrote at once about the new petition, and Lord James Stuart sent on all his material to the Home Office.[26] In the last resort, then, the decision was Lord Melbourne's. Among the papers on the case is an undated note: 'My dear L, I have looked at the paper and have no doubt the Law should take its course. Bank check. It cannot any where be found. I am sure it never came. H.B.' It is not clear which paper this refers to, but the signatory was presumably Henry Brougham the Lord Chancellor.[27]

On 9 August Melbourne rejected the second petition.[28] On 13 August, still protesting his innocence, Dic Penderyn went to the scaffold at Cardiff amid widespread horror and dismay. He was hanged from a platform with fancy iron work set back thirty yards from St Mary Street. Most of the respectable inhabitants had quit the town in protest; all the shops closed. Hundreds of farmers came in on their *gambos* (sled-carts). At the Drop, one foot hitched on the platform. The hangman pulled on his legs and he was dead in two minutes. As schoolchildren on their breakfast break came to stare at the body, onlookers (estimated at anything from 500 to several thousands) said a thunderstorm broke. At nine the body was taken down to lie overnight in the *Prince Regent*, Crockherbtown and on the following day, crowds followed the coffin across the Vale to Aberavon. Dic's brother-in-law, Morgan Howells, preached from the churchyard wall of St Mary's. The body, denied the churchyard, was buried at the gate. Some said a white bird settled on the coffin.[29]

The *Cambrian* observed that his execution proved the case for 'an early and complete revision of our Criminal Code'. Daniel Jones resigned the chaplaincy of Cardiff prison. 'There go the devils!' shouted a woman after the Crawshays on their way to church. Three days after the execution, James Abbott sent a desperate appeal to the Home Office. Ever since the trial he had been frequently insulted in the street; people crowded abusively into his shop. People shouted 'Murderer!' as he passed. On a Saturday evening, he had normally taken 18 to 20 shillings; since the trial, scarcely two shillings. His customers feared for their lives. On the night of Dic's execution, a crowd of 200 gathered in front of his house, shouting that he would be hanged before that day week, kicking his door, throwing two-pound stones and breaking three of his windows. He took his children out of their beds and sent them with his wife to a neighbour's house, climbing out through a back window. He himself hid for an hour among the kidney beans in a neighbour's garden. At two in the morning, his wife and children returned. He went to the back window and begged them to come out, but they would not, so in the end he went in himself. The crowd dispersed about three in the morning, but he was afraid that his life was in great danger.[30]

After the execution, there was a remarkable exchange in the columns of the *Cambrian*. On 20 August, the paper printed two accounts of the hanging. The first, translating his words, said that Dic had cried on the scaffold, 'I am going to suffer unjustly. God who knows all things, knows this is so.' On the Drop, he repeated that he was innocent and begged mercy for those who had borne false witness. The four Wesleyan ministers returning from the gallows then heard Lewis Lewis crying bitterly in his cell, 'Richard is innocent! for I know him not to have been there. I was by the soldier. If I had been sharing the same fate, I would have disclosed it on the scaffold.' The day before, Richard Lewis had admitted he had been a rioter but said many others had been also.

The second account quoted him more fully. 'He conceived himself to be in a just cause and that, being neither a robber nor a murderer, he did the same that many others were doing and that nothing capital could be proved against him.' After his sentence, however, 'he became at intervals harsh and morose, the great impression on his mind was that he had been unfairly put forward and sacrificed or sold, as he expressed it, to screen others who were more guilty than himself. He repeatedly said he was to die for thousands, which he seemed to feel as the peculiar hardship of his case'. His courage did not forsake him and his last words were given in English translation as 'Here is wrong' or 'Here is hard measure'. His actual words were *'O Arglwydd, dyma gamwedd'*; one translation would be 'O Lord, this is injustice'.

This account added, however, that a fellow prisoner had pointed out to Governor Wood of Cardiff prison that Dic had a scar on the outside of his right leg near the knee, which would have been made by a bayonet. Why was it there, if he were innocent of stabbing Donald Black?[31]

The elegaic tone of these reports and the shattering quotation from Lewis Lewis provoked an anonymous correspondent into an important letter, which was published the following week. He said there were plenty of witnesses to Dic's presence in front of the Inn, none of whom had been examined at the trial. Richard Lewis had been one of that deputation whose spirit was conveyed by the alleged statement of one of them — 'Damn them, I wish my knife was three or four inches in their bellies!' After the shooting, Dic was seen at a place called the Wern; as he was talking to a farmer, a bayonet fell out of his sleeve. On the 4th, day of the guerrilla actions, he was on the hill between Merthyr and Aberdare, when many saw him with a bayonet. He showed the wound on his knee to a respectable freeholder and said, 'I had it from the soldiers at the Castle Inn'. He told a farm servant that he had been wounded twice in the hand, which was in fact tied up in a bloody handkerchief.

More remarkably, this correspondent went on to attack the constable John Thomas. Thomas, before the execution, had threatened Abbott and had been compelled to swear to keep the peace with him. Even in the presence of magistrates, Thomas had sworn to be 'up with' Abbott. He had been going around pubs saying, 'Abbott has sworn a damned lie!' This John Thomas, said the correspondent, was 'very well known' at Merthyr (an expression implying he was notorious). During the examinations of Richard and Lewis Lewis, he had in fact been very active in collecting evidence *against* them — 'If you haven't enough evidence, my brother Tom saw the soldiers stabbed out of a window . . .' The magistrates had to call him to order.

The writer said he had withheld these details in order not to prejudice Richard Lewis's petition, but he was outraged by the attack on Abbott's house and called for severe punishment of the offenders.[32]

This called forth two responses. *Man of Glamorgan*, published on 10 September, was fully prepared to concede that Dic 'was, beyond all question, *somewhere* in the fray near the Castle Inn'; he seemed to accept the evidence on the bayonet and the wounds to hand and knee. But was Dic guilty of the crime of stabbing Donald Black? All the evidence suggested not. The prisoner had denied it to his death. 'His companion in condemnation but not in death, avowedly a more active leader of the riots than himself', had resolutely exculpated him. Lewis Lewis's statement that Dic had not been *there* might well have meant the exact spot where Donald Black was, where Lewis Lewis himself was. The writer cited Price's efforts − 'Mr. Price is as well known for a clear head as for a kind heart'. He confessed to as much doubt over Dic's guilt as Lord Brougham had felt.[33]

The second letter, published on 17 September by *A Subscriber* was bitterly hostile to Dic. He challenged the translation of Richard Lewis's last words. There had been no positive assertion of innocence, 'only an equivocal denial of his guilt'. What he had meant was that he was being made to suffer when there were many who deserved it more than himself. The writer cited the 'decided proofs' at the trial and the 'strong corroborative evidence' discovered after the execution . . . 'Donald Black swore that the person who stabbed him had a fresh wound in the knee. On examination of the body, a newly cicatrised wound was discovered in the knee.' As for Lewis Lewis, Governor Wood would certify that he had actually said that Richard Lewis *was* in the scuffle in the Castle passage-way. Joseph Price had been given time to prove Dic innocent and had failed to do so. It was certain that he had been at the Castle. Without the soldiers' action, there would have been a massacre. What was needed was not any white-washing of Dic Penderyn but an effort to make people realise how lenient the government had been . . . 'the guilt of Richard Lewis is fully established in the minds of every one, except those who wish to make a party question of this melancholy business . . .'[34]

This writer must have been privy to proceedings at the trial and within the jail; there is no reference anywhere else to Black having sworn to a wounded knee. He also injected a harshly partisan note, which provoked a reply from *Man of Glamorgan* written on 20 September and published on 24 September, just as the massive anti-union lockout was beginning at Dowlais and Plymouth works. He denounced *A Subscriber*, 'whose ingenuity at evasion is equalled only by the acerbity of his insinuations'. Proofs of Dic's last words were available on oath. He did not deny that Dic had been present at the riot, but he re-asserted the grave doubts as to his guilt in the actual stabbing of Black.

His most significant comment, however, was that Joseph Price had abundant proofs of Dic's innocence which he was ready to publish, *but at a more opportune moment*. *Man of Glamorgan* had no wish to pursue the subject further either . . . 'because in the present state of local excitement, it appears to occasion great misconception among more than one class . . . I desire no further discussion . . . of a subject, which, under present circumstances, may lead to great and mischievous perversions of the one honest and legitimate object I have in view . . .'[35]

The struggle over the unions which was just beginning, as dour and unrelenting as the Rising itself and as ferocious as anything in the history of the south Wales coalfield, created a climate in the desperately divided community which was that of civil war. It ended only when thousands were literally starved into submission. In these comments, the exigencies of naked class conflict cut clean through the hearts and minds of decent, troubled men. In those comments, it is actually possible *to see* Dic Penderyn becoming *a specifically working-class martyr*.

After this, there was silence. Silence that is, in the official and respectable world. In the minds and hearts of ordinary people in Merthyr and south Wales, of their children and their children's children, Dic's last words echoed longer and louder than all the muskets of the soldiers. And, over forty years later, on 14 October 1874, the *Western Mail* announced that the Rev Evan Evans, Nant-y-Glo, on a visit to Pennsylvania, had heard a deathbed confession from a Welshman, Ieuan or Ianto Parker, who said that it was he, not Dic Penderyn, who had stabbed Donald Black outside the Castle Inn.[36]

The figure of Richard Lewis, of course, has become encrusted with legend, but I believe it possible to make some statements.

In face of the evidence now available, I find it utterly impossible to believe that Richard Lewis stabbed Donald Black. He was hanged for a crime he did not commit. In this sense, which is central and decisive, the popular tradition was and is perfectly correct.

On the question of his presence at the front of the Inn and of his participation in the attack on the soldiers, the evidence seems too brutally contradictory to be reconciled. The two men who claimed to have seen him stab Black, Abbott and Drew, seem to me discredited, on practical physical grounds alone, without taking into consideration any possible prejudice. Both Black himself, however, and Thomas Darker said they saw Dic waving his hat and cheering near the front door, before the rush on the soldiers. Darker explicitly states that he saw this five or ten minutes *after* the deputation came out.

Those statements have an air of authenticity; it is the kind of incident which might well stick in people's minds. They were not necessarily correct in their *chronology*, however; close study of the evidence presented by witnesses at the inquests held in June makes it clear that they were often, and understandably, confused over precise timing (on the order of Lewis Lewis's speeches, for example, and those of other men lifted on shoulders). The evidence of Darker and Black might be thought outweighed by that of no fewer than *ten* people who asserted that Dic never left the side of the Inn; three of these were inside the Castle and 'on the other side'; one of them might have been a chief constable. Both friends and enemies of Dic claimed that many more people could have been mobilised to give evidence, which would clearly have been no less contradictory.

It is possible to take a leaf out of Bosanquet's book and argue that Dic could have moved between side and front. I agree with the *Cambrian* correspondent who called Dic's assertion of innocence 'equivocal'; he quite clearly considered himself to have been a 'rioter', though not a 'murderer' or a 'robber'. But in what precise sense did he mean it? It is difficult to know what credence to place in the 'evidence' on his alleged appearance with a bayonet on Aberdare mountain and the wound in his knee. This posthumous testimony, like that in his favour showered on Price, was brought forward in a time of bitter social and political conflict and in an atmosphere of civil-war tension. Dic's life *had* become a 'party question'.

Bosanquet was evidently influenced by such considerations. He found the failure to produce this evidence either at the trial or in the Taliesin Williams petition 'singular'. Dic was said to have been 'very ably defended' but we know nothing about that defence . . . 'Richard Lewis said on Friday morning this riot began to get up. Leaves it to his Counsel. Lewis Lewis said nothing . . .' One reason, no doubt, was the familiar predicament of Welsh-speakers in a monoglot English court and the inhibitions this induced, which were sometimes the cause of injustice. More important, I think, is the fact that Merthyr was under military occupation, had been swept by police raids and man-hunts. The outstanding characteristic of the new trade unions was their impenetrable *secrecy* and occult oaths. Many of those who died after the shooting were buried in total secrecy; many of the wounded nursed themselves in hiding. It was a *Luddite* situation in this respect, a culture as secret and shut off from a hostile world as that of the Scotch Cattle in Monmouthshire. People would certainly be reluctant to come forward and expose themselves. Not until somebody as impeccably respectable as Joseph Price acted, with some support from the gentry of the town, would they come forward. Nevertheless it also seems true that the fight for Dic Penderyn had become indistinguishable from the general workers' struggle now focused on the trade unions, which were themselves, at least in their spirit, simply the insurrection of June carried on by different methods.

Some very important evidence is provided by a letter which Isaac Evans wrote much later to the workers' paper *Tarian y Gweithiwr*, published on 14 August 1884. Isaac's uncle married Dic Penderyn's widow and the writer reported what was evidently a family tradition. This asserted that Dic had fought and beaten a constable *Shoni y Crydd* (John the Shoemaker/Cobbler). As a result, the police were out for revenge. Dic, in consequence, kept clear of the riots; he and Evans's uncle took refuge on Aberdare mountain, the latter returning before Dic. Police, hunting him after the riots as a marked man, found him away from home. Their suspicions confirmed, they lay in ambush for him and took him in his bed, whereupon Abbott ('unprincipled', according to Evans) swore his life away.

This tradition strikes echoes. For the moment, one may simply note that it is perfectly possible to reconcile it with Dic's own account given to Price (the tradition's denial of his presence in the crowd set aside). On the other hand, it is not impossible to reconcile it with an actual participation in the attack and a subsequent flight after the shooting. It seems to be some confirmation of his presence on Aberdare mountain, whether he had a bayonet or not.

Inescapable here, of course, is the devastating statement attributed by the Wesleyan ministers to Lewis Lewis immediately after Dic's execution: 'Richard is innocent! for I know him not to have been there. I was by the soldier. *If I had been sharing the same fate, I would have disclosed it on the gallows*.' (My italics.) Here, it is necessary to move with the utmost caution. One obvious implication of that last sentence, of course, is that Lewis Lewis's silence on the innocence of Dic Penderyn was a *condition* of his *not* sharing the same fate. If thinking of this order is driven through to its logical extreme, it opens a veritable abyss of horror, because it points to judicial murder by conspiracy. I have come to suspect that there *was* an element of 'conspiracy' in the death of Dic Penderyn, but I do not at all believe that it operated at such a high level in such simplicity with such appalling implications.

At his trial, part of Lewis Lewis's evidence was given in secret.[37] The natural assumption is that, in some respects, he turned King's Evidence. This is not necessarily true, however; Lewis Lewis seems to have been remarkably open during the first investigations after the rising was over. As early as 9 June, Evan Thomas wrote from the Talbot Inn, Penydarren to Bute, in an evidently perturbed state of mind: 'The depositions already made in Lewis Lewis's case have disclosed facts of so serious a nature that I think it would be very desirable to have the advice of some Legal Man on behalf of Government as to the Commitments . . .'[38]

The rebels could certainly have been tried for treason. The natural-justice action of 2 June had obviously been well planned. It was an insurrection from the beginning. The rebels seized muskets from soldiers in a direct onslaught, they laid hands on 'the property of our Sovereign Lord the King', they laid hands on the sovereignty. They waged war against the King. One of the delegations to Penydarren House lived in hourly expectation of a general insurrection, which the rebels certainly tried to incite throughout the coalfield. There was wild talk of revolt throughout the kingdom. As early as 8 June, Sir Watkin Williams Wynn reported from north Wales mining circles that a date had been mentioned in Merthyr for a general strike of all the colliers of Britain. After it was all over, men remembered that wandering pedlar who had said three weeks earlier that something extraordinary was going to happen in Merthyr. Not to mince words, the Merthyr Rising was a local attempt at revolution. In these circumstances, it is quite conceivable that evidence from the most obvious 'leader' would be heard in secret. No doubt, Lewis Lewis would have felt compromised by his action; no doubt, he must have implicated other people. There is a natural tendency to link this evidence in camera with Abbott's curious defensiveness in court about *Lewsyn* and with Bosanquet's decision to stop the trials after the fourth (which in fact landed the judge in his painful dilemma). On the other hand, when Bosanquet wrote his report to Melbourne on 17 July, he clearly had no intention of reprieving either of the condemned. There does not seem to be any evidence of any deal *there*.

It may well be, however, that services helpful to the prosecution which Lewis Lewis might have rendered (consciously or unconsciously) were an unspoken factor in Bosanquet's change of mind over the next few days. Legend tended to attribute Lewis Lewis's reprieve to his connections among the gentry. Certainly Morgan Morgan of Bodwigiad, his 'squire' (whose 'huntsman' legend says *Lewsyn* was) was active in his cause — but so he was on behalf of the two constables who had to fight so hard to capture *Lewsyn* in Hendrebolon woods. Morgan evidently took his responsibilities towards Penderyn people seriously! William Thomas the Court, on the other hand, Merthyr's 'squire', was positively hostile to Lewis Lewis. On the one hand, the man was widely feared among the local Establishment; on the other, people *did* remember his generosity. There was a particular honour about the man. He was *chware teg* itself towards David Williams's mother; he had rescued not only John Thomas but J.B. Bruce and Anthony Hill; even his forcing of Thomas Lewis to hold the can of powder at the Morlais Tip would have seemed to working people, who knew Thomas Lewis as a crook and an exploiter (and whose evidence the prosecution dared not use) as natural justice. This is not to say that pressure was not brought to bear on Bosanquet; it clearly was. The reprieve for Lewis Lewis, however, can be quite adequately explained in terms of Bosanquet's own statements, with perhaps some allowance for that evidence in secret.

What is extremely difficult is to connect any proceedings of such a character with *Richard* Lewis *himself. A Subscriber*, so hostile to Dic, told the *Cambrian* that Governor Wood of Cardiff prison could testify that Lewis Lewis had said that Richard *had* been present in the struggle at the doorway of the Castle Inn. Dic's feeling that he was 'dying for thousands' and that he had been 'sold' – *camwedd* – perfectly understandable – may have had some personal reference to Lewis Lewis. One seems to sense a certain strain between the two men, who knew one another. The order to remove Lewis Lewis to the Hulks was first issued on 3 August; it had to be repeated on 16 August, after the execution.[39] We do not know why.

It seems to me that any strain between Lewis and Richard Lewis must date *from* the former's reprieve, not before. To assume otherwise is to assume that the prosecution went to infinite trouble from the very beginning simply to make sure that this one man, Richard Lewis, was hanged. This is impossible to believe. What *is* far more plausible is that some people, after the shock of *Lewsyn's* reprieve, were determined that *somebody* should hang.

There certainly are sinister overtones to the case of Dic Penderyn. There is his family's assertion that he was a marked man because of his feud with *Shoni Crydd*. There is the obvious doubt about Abbott, who had also fought with Dic – over politics. One of the victims of the political riot of 9 May was William Meyrick himself, parish solicitor and solicitor to the Crawshays, who actually briefed the prosecution. Meyrick was a grey eminence in Glamorgan Toryism; he was feared and disliked, particularly by the radical leaders, the Jameses and William Perkins. *A Subscriber* and another *Cambrian* correspondent hostile to Dic (and to John Thomas the constable) certainly knew what had been going on behind the scenes at the trial and in Cardiff jail. Governor Wood turns up, with his allegation that Lewis Lewis pointed the finger at Richard Lewis, with information on the wound in Dic's knee. The reprieve of *Lewsyn* certainly caused alarm among magistrates. There was the looming threat of the colliers' union; the reprieve would 'induce the people to imagine that Government will not and dare not visit them capitally for political disturbances'.

I think Melbourne himself was influenced by such considerations. He was obsessed with *The Union*. He and Peel before him had been angered and nonplussed by the new techniques of mass picketing which the NAPL employed. This was associated in their minds with intimidation.[40] Melbourne was anxious to learn more about the ropes the Merthyr rebels carried. The reports about the colliers' union from Watkin Williams Wynn and Ruabon came in during the investigations and the trials. Melbourne was left in no doubt about the Merthyr shopocracy's fears and the magistrates' anger over the reprieve for Lewis Lewis. Indirectly, through the oblique prism of Melbourne's mind, Dic Penderyn probably *did* die a martyr to the National Association for the Protection of Labour.

In these circumstances, the visible determination to *stop* any further reprieve for Richard Lewis is explicable and the personal predicament of such as James Abbott and William Meyrick would hardly have weakened it. If Lewis Lewis *did* say that Richard *had* been active in the struggle outside the Castle, when did he say it? We do not know. One possible time, of course, would have been that of the mysterious 'confession' which both men were said to have made for the Taliesin Williams petition, but which both men repudiated. Henry Morgan made it clear to Joseph Price that the motives of the Merthyr drafters were benevolent. But the 'confession' was never presented to the prisoners. Why not? Cardiff prison again? It was out of that prison that there came the stories of *Lewsyn*'s alleged incrimination of Dic, of Black's alleged oath on the wounded knee; *A Subscriber* seems to have been at home within the jail. Why was not Lewis Lewis removed to the Hulks when the order of 3 August arrived, despite the urgency with which Bosanquet pressed for it? The decision or omission can be located within the prison. When the Home Office received Bosanquet's last letter of 7 August and drafted its fatal answer on 9 August, it minuted the text – 'Is Lewis Lewis removed? Do you know?'[41] Three days after Dic's execution, the Home Office had to repeat the removal order. Who knows what pressures were exerted within the closed world of that haunted jail? Lewis Lewis might well have been induced to believe that his reprieve *was* conditional. Certainly in the resistance to a reprieve for Dic Penderyn, it is from Cardiff prison that there comes a whiff of the cabal.

We shall probably never know the full truth about Lewis Lewis. Legend has run free around him. He sailed for New South Wales, in the company of Thomas Vaughan, David Hughes and *Dai Llaw Haearn* on the convict ship *John* on 26 January 1832. Rumour says he returned, was seen ghost-like at the opening of the Taff Vale Railway, but he was certainly working on a farm in New South Wales in 1837.[42]

Even more hypnotic (from the necessarily callous standpoint of the professional historian) is the family tradition of Dic's fight with *Shoni Crydd*. For *Shoni Crydd* was none other than John Thomas himself, the constable who spoke up for Lewis Lewis and so hated James Abbott!

On 9 December 1830, a special meeting of the parish vestry was called in Merthyr to hear complaints against illegal practices by four of the parish constables, Peter Charters, William Charters, John Thomas and Richard Thomas. The chief constable was instructed to prosecute them at the parish's expense. Many of the leading radicals were present and the man who brought the complaints forward was Thomas Burnell the chandler, who actually gave evidence in support of Dic Penderyn to Joseph Price (though he said in that August of 1831 that he did not know Richard Lewis).

The case was heard before Glamorgan Quarter Sessions in the spring of 1831 and Peter Charters was punished. He had exploited people's ignorance of the new Beer Act to extort blackmail money from those who ran beershops under the illusory threat of prosecuting them for trading without licences (which they no longer needed). His close colleague in this enterprise was John Thomas, whom the *Cambrian* called 'John the Cobbler [*Shoni Crydd*] – the terror of Merthyr'. The anonymous correspondent of the same newspaper, after Dic's execution, called him 'well-known'.[43]

This would be something more than a squalid racket. The beershops were central to working-class life, particularly in an ill-endowed town like Merthyr and among a working population not far removed from rural roots, in which the *cwrw bach* (bid-ale) was an important social institution. Furthermore, in this period, the beershops or 'kiddlewinks', or indeed *cwrw bachs* as they were called, were often a radical political force. During this ferocious 1835 election in Merthyr, the beershop keepers linked by the Tory *Merthyr Guardian* with 'readers of The Workman newspaper' tried to organise themselves into a political pressure group, hostile above all to the Tory candidate who was William

Meyrick himself and who was defeated by a mass mobilisation of the working class behind the radicals; they threatened to practise 'exclusive dealing' against Tory shopkeeper voters.[44]

We do not know whether Dic's fight with *Shoni Crydd* was over the beershop issue (Dic was fond of his drink). But if Richard Lewis stood up to a 'well-known' character like John Thomas, he would have made himself 'well-known', not least to the constables.

The family tradition asserts that, in consequence, those constables were out to nail Dic Penderyn after the rising. The *Cambrian* correspondent says that in the immediate aftermath of that rising, John Thomas was very active in collecting evidence against the rebels. The letter-writer's remark that *Shoni Crydd* pressed his brother Tom on the magistrates — he had seen soldiers stabbed from a window of the Castle — finds an echo and riveting one, in a report by Evan Thomas, who said that a *shoemaker* at a downstairs window of the Inn, who had to dodge shots fired at the Castle, saw 'Lewis' thrust at the soldiers with a bayonet twice. In this context, however, this Lewis is unmistakably *Lewis* Lewis.[45]

The next we hear of John Thomas, however, is that he was desperately anxious to save Lewis Lewis's life, because the *Huntsman* had saved his own, that he was consumed with a passionate hatred of Abbott, that he was going around pubs saying that Abbott had 'sworn a damned lie' and had to be restrained by legal injunction from physical violence against the barber and that he was working in a kind of frenzy for Joseph Price, arguing with Lord Melbourne face to face.

This John Thomas was dead by 1834. He left a widow and four children destitute. The Tory *Merthyr Guardian* at that date reported that he had been 'charitable and benevolent' and that Merthyr people were raising a fund for his widow and children. The 'terror of Merthyr' apparently died poverty-stricken but popular.[46]

It is possible that these bare, brute facts mask a personal tragedy of peculiar intensity. John Thomas was clearly a brave man; it took courage of unusual order to stand up outside Coffin's house on the night of 2 June in what must have been terrifying circumstances. He presumably suffered from a sense of duty. (Was he the officer who wanted to prosecute the 36 cases after the 'justice' raids of 2 June?) He had clearly also been a bully and a blackmailer. He was familiar with that Tyburn Fair world of Merthyr which became *China* (whose *Emperor* was known to issue challenges to constables) in which a good proportion of Merthyr's working people, including Dic Penderyn (who was said to have lived in the heart of it) were from time to time

involved. It was a world which lived (like the majority of the population) outside the law; it had its own law, its own peculiar sense of
'honour'; rough and squalid though it often was, it could and did
respond to a certain kind of hero, as it did to that horse-breaker from
a marginal mountain parish, *Lewsyn yr Heliwr*.

Psychological speculation, of course, is dangerous, but it is surely
not impossible to visualise a situation in which this constable John
Thomas, as rough and open to corruption as his fellows generally were,
locked into a feud with Dic Penderyn, perhaps over the beershop issue
(where Dic might have acted as a 'champion') pressed forward eagerly
against him after the rising and then found, after all the killing, that
two men were to be put to death with all the awful panoply of the law
(which the the world which became *China* was infinitely more repulsive
than most murders) one of whom, the *Huntsman*, had actually thrown
himself across Shoni's battered and prostrate body to save his life.
He would find, further, that Abbott the barber was falsely swearing Dic
Penderyn's very life away, while *Lewsyn* was being spared, largely
(as John Thomas would surely have imagined) as the result of the
constable's own testimony. It is not difficult to imagine such a man
suffering a crisis of conscience — which would surely disconcert such
men as William Meyrick and anonymous correspondents to the
Cambrian, as it *did* disconcert Anthony Hill. If something of this order
did happen (as I believe it did) then in my opinion, John Thomas is as
fit a subject for legend and the novelist as Dic Penderyn himself. In all
the bloody and dramatic history of the Merthyr Rising, the story of
Shoni Crydd may be, in some ways, the most poignant personal tragedy
of them all.

This was not how Merthyr people saw it, even if they did warm to
the constable in his last years. It was Dic they made into their martyr.
It was Dic, not *Lewsyn*, whom they chose to remember. Surely, whatever the ambiguity of *Lewsyn*'s behaviour in prison, this is significant?

What makes a man a martyr? Death, of course — but *unjust* death.
It is his innocence, his representative character; it is the sense of
injustice. Working people in Merthyr needed a symbol of injustice and
they made a Dic Penderyn out of Richard Lewis.

Clearly he was fairly well known. He seems to have moved between
the tavern world of Shoni Crydd and the respectable world of Morgan
Howells his Methodist minister of a brother-in-law. He was known to
be a strong debater on the rights of working men. He may have stood
up to the constable as some kind of champion. He was politically active
during the Illumination troubles, at least in the ranks, if no Thomas

Llewellyn, and he was picked out as a delegate from the crowd outside the Castle Inn.

This hardly makes him a 'leader', certainly not in the sense that *Lewsyn yr Heliwr* was or that Thomas Llewellyn briefly was. What sort of 'delegates' could have been chosen in such circumstances? In any case, it was not any 'leadership' which made him a *martyr*; it was his very innocence, his innocuousness, his sense that he 'was only doing what thousands of others did'. He did literally 'die for thousands'.

Though he was known, it was through this kind of 'anonymity' that he achieved his immortality. He stood on no box in the High Street to make speeches. His was not a face *above* the crowd. The face of Dic Penderyn was the face *in* the crowd, the face the Merthyr working man chose as his own. The voice crying innocence from the scaffold was the voice the Merthyr working man chose as his own. For south Wales, the voice of Dic Penderyn on that black Saturday in August was the Voice of the People.

Notes

1.   *Cambrian*, 23 July.
2.   Bute to Melbourne, 16 July: HO 52/16.
3.   Bosanquet to Melbourne, 17 July: HO 17/128, part 2, bundle Zp. not printed by Alexander Cordell (henceforth simply HO 17/128).
4.   Bosanquet to Melbourne, 21 July: HO 17/128; *Cambrian*, 6 August; David Jones, *Before Rebecca*, p. 152.
5.   Bosanquet to Melbourne, 21 July : HO 17/128.
6.   *Cambrian*, 6 August.
7.   Bosanquet to Melbourne, 1 August: HO 17/128; Alexander Cordell, *The Fire People*, pp. 373-4.
8.   Joseph T. Price to Lord James Stuart, 4 August 1831, quoting Henry Morgan who presented the first petitions: HO 17/128; *Cambrian*, 5 August 1831.
9.   Henry and William Morgan (Windsor) to Melbourne, 26 July: HO 17/128; J.T. Price to Lord James Stuart, 4 August, quoting Henry Morgan: HO 17/128.
10.   Henry and William Morgan to Melbourne, 26 July: HO 17/128; Home Office to Henry Morgan, 27 July: Criminal Book: HO 13/58, p. 154; *Cambrian*, 30 July and 6 August.
11.   *Cambrian*, 6 August; petitions of 27 July by J.T. Price and John Thomas: HO 17/128.
12.   He tells the story in his Petition for Richard Lewis of 27 July: HO 17/128.
13.   Petition on behalf of Lewis Lewis, by J.T. Price and J. Thomas, 27 July: HO 17/128. Both petitions were drafted in Hatchett's Hotel, Piccadilly,
14.   Brougham quoted in Melbourne to Bosanquet, 29 July: HO 13/58, pp. 162-3; *Cambrian*, 6 August.

15. Melbourne to High Sheriff of Glamorgan, 28 July: HO 13/58, p. 159;
     Melbourne to Bosanquet, 29 July, sending on Price's petition and asking
     for comment and transcript of evidence, ibid., pp. 162-3; Home Office
     to Merthyr, 28 July: HO 41/10, and Merthyr response, 1 August: HO
     52/16; Bosanquet to Melbourne, 30 July, reprieving Lewis Lewis and
     urging removal of prisoner: HO 17/128; removal of first prisoners
     condemned to transportation, Circuit Letters: HO 6/16; Bosanquet
     to Melbourne, 18 July; order to remove, 21 July, to High Sheriff of
     Glamorgan: HO 13/58, pp. 146, 147; orders to remove Lewis Lewis, 3
     August: HO 13/58, pp. 186-7.

16. Digby Mackworth to Colonel Egerton, extract sent to Melbourne, 30 July:
     HO 52/16.

17. Petition of the Inhabitant Householders of Merthyr Tydfil, 1 August;
     William Perkins entered a dissident note: enough had been done to deter
     the workmen although their spirit was bad; the new unions were
     'doubtless injurious upon principle' but their articles called for good
     behaviour. He thought there was no call for alarm, but was falling in with
     the 'general sentiments' of the Trade: Perkins to Bute, 1 August. Anthony
     Hill sent all the documents up to Melbourne on 1 August: HO 52/16.

18. Bruce to Hill, 1 August, enclosed in Hill to Melbourne, 1 August: HO
     52/16.

19. A. Hill to Melbourne, with enclosures, 1 August: HO 52/16: Hill reported
     that the Bute works would receive troops and interviewed Melbourne on
     it.

20. Editorial of 5 August in *Cambrian*, 6 August.

21. Affidavit, 1 August: HO 17/128, quoted in Alexander Cordell, op. cit., p. 375.

22. J.T. Price to Lord James Stuart, 4 August: HO 17/128.

23. Bosanquet to Melbourne, 1 August: HO 17/128; Alexander Cordell,
     op. cit., pp. 373-4.

24. Second Petition, J.T. Price, 5 August: HO 17/128; Alexander Cordell,
     op. cit., pp. 376-80. Andrew Marsden, brother to the chief constable
     William, and also a draper, was in the house of William Perkins on the
     morning of the shooting, 3 June, when Rowland Thomas staggered in,
     'walking lame': testimony of Marsden, inquest of 22 June in T. Thomas
     to Melbourne, 26 June: HO 52/16. Newell's bankruptcy and performance
     in the 1835 election: *Cambrian*, 3 April 1830 and Wilkins, *History of
     Merthyr Tydfil*; he had been present at the Waun Fair meeting but
     apparently saw little and heard less: second inquest on John Hughes, 21
     June, in T. Thomas to Melbourne, 26 June: HO 52/16.

25. On Price's trip to Brecon on 5 August, J.T. Price to Home Office, 6
     August (HO 17/128) and *Cambrian*, 12 August (the newspaper was
     evidently being briefed by Price); Bosanquet's significant letter to
     Melbourne of 6 August from Hay is in HO 17/128; Melbourne's reply
     to the judge's report of 1 August is in HO to Bosanquet, 4 August:
     HO 13/58, p. 183; Bosanquet replied from Presteigne on 7 August:
     HO 17/128.

26. Melbourne's reply to first petition in HO to Price, 4 August: HO 13/58,
     p. 182; J.T. Price to HO, 6 August; Lord James Stuart, annotation on
     Price to Stuart, 4 August: HO 17/128.

27. HO 17/128.

28. Melbourne to Bosanquet and Price in Home Office to the same, 9 August:
     HO 13/58, p. 198.

29. *Cambrian*, 20 August; William Luke Evans (eleven years old in 1831)
     reminisces, *Cardiff Records*, v, p. 322; Anon., 'Hen lythyr diddorol',

Y Drysorfa, lxxxix (1919). The second *Cambrian* account put the onlookers at 500; Edmund Evans the Wesleyan minister said there were thousand of onlookers: diary 13 August, *Eurgrawn Wesleyaidd* (1870), 356; the white bird, oral testimony Mary Catherine Williams, Dowlais, 1943 (my grandmother).

30. *Cambrian,* 13 August; Glamorgan Quarter Sessions (GRO), Minute Book, Michaelmas, 1835, pp. 64, 85; W. Crawshay II to W. Crawshay I, 20 August, Crawshay Papers (NLW), Letter-book, 3 (132); Affidavit of James Abbott, sworn before J.B. Bruce, 16 August: HO 52/16.

31. *Cambrian,* 20 August.

32. *Cambrian,* 27 August.

33. *Cambrian,* 10 September.

34. *Cambrian,* 17 September

35. *Cambrian,* 24 September.

36. James Evans, statement of 11 May 1949, remembered going as a child with his mother to visit her aunt, Mrs Sarah Morgan of Tredegar, a sister of Dic Penderyn; the old lady was 'weeping tears of joy' because she had just read the news in the *Western Mail.*

37. HO 41/28, fo. 138.

38. HO 52/16.

39. HO 13/58, 3 and 16 August, pp. 186-7.

40. Masses of material in HO 40/30, 52/13 and the LSE papers behind the Webbs' history of trade unionism, particularly A/1/199, 200, 120 and A/26/5, 6; S. and B. Webb, *History of Trade Unionism,* pp. 120, 138 ff.

41. Bosanquet to Melbourne, 7 August: HO 17/128.

42. Transportation register: HO 11/8, p. 255; General Muster of Convicts, New South Wales: in HO 10/34, p. 10.

43. MT Minutes, 9 December 1830; *Cambrian,* March 1831, 27 August.

44. *Merthyr Guardian,* December 1834 to January 1835, especially 13 and 20 December 1834.

45. Evan Thomas to Bute, 16 June: HO 52/16.

46. *Merthyr Guardian,* 14 June 1834: obituary.

9 MOVEMENT

Yr wyf yn deisyf arnat i ddyfod yn ddiatreg i nôl fy nghorff, oher-
wydd nid oes dim tebygolrwydd am ddim arall yn bresennol. Dos at
Philip Lewis a gwna iddo ef ddyfod a chertyn i lawr heno, a chymaint
o ddynion a allo, mewn rhyw wedd, i ddyfod gydag ef. Yr wyf yn
credu fod yr Argywydd wedi maddau i fi fy amrywiol bechodau a'm
troseddiadau, ond am yr wyf yn cael nghyhuddo nid yr wyf yn euog
ac am hynny gennyf achos i fod yn ddiolchgar.

The only document Dic Penderyn left to history was the letter he wrote
or dictated, in literate Welsh with the stamp of the chapel on it, to his
sister, on the eve of his execution.

I ask you to come at once to fetch my body, since there is no
likelihood of anything else at present. Come to Philip Lewis and get
him to bring down a cart tonight and as many men as he can manage
to bring with him. I believe the Lord has forgiven me my divers sins
and transgressions, but since I am accused, I am not guilty and for
that I have reason to be grateful.

The letter was printed and sold to raise money for his widow.[1]
'Prepare, prepare, for dust thou art and unto dust thou shalt return.
So, therefore, fall down on your knees and lay your right hand on this
Holy Book and your left hand on your heart and say after me this
solemn obligation:
   'Question: What is your name?
   'Is it of your own free will that you come here to join this Friendly
Society of Coal Mining? . . .'
Even as one ritual was being enacted at Cardiff, another (also bearing
the stamp of the chapel) was taking place in lodge after lodge across the
coalfield as Dic Penderyn's friends and fellows knelt while the Clerk of
the Lodge read from his Secret Paper, in the formidable and occult
initiation ceremonies of the early unions.

I never will instruct any person in the art of coal mining, tunnelling
or boring, or engineering, or any other department of my work,
except to an obligated brother or brothers or an apprentice. So help

me God.

I will never work any work where an obliged brother has been unjustly enforced off for standing up for his price . . .

I will never make known any signs, tokens, passwords, or guess or write them on stones, sand, wood, tin, lead or anything visible or invisible to the eye . . .

I will never make these obligations known to either master, manager, or underkeeper, overlooker, book-keeper or any person, except to a legal obligated brother . . .

'When thou shalt vow a vow unto the Lord thy God, thou shalt not slack to pay it; for the Lord thy God will surely require it of thee; and it would be sin in thee. But if thou shalt forbear to vow, it shall be no sin in thee. That which is gone out of thy lips thou shalt keep and perform, *even* a free-will offering, according as thou has vowed unto the Lord thy God, which thou hast promised with thy mouth' . . . (Deuteronomy, xxiii, 21-23 and Numbers, xxx, 2 . . .).

During August, the colliers' union, with its secret oath and its ceremonies, marched across the coalfield from Swansea to Newport like a ghost army and masters felt the ground slide from under their feet.[2]

Its public articles were resolutely respectable.[3] Any who abused masters or foremen, who rioted or were disorderly, were expelled, 'as this Society is intended for the encouragement of honesty, sobriety, industry and peacable behaviour'. Fines of 2s 6d were imposed for speaking disrespectfully of the king, the state and the laws, parliament and magistrates. Similar fines were inflicted for drunkenness, swearing, gambling, fighting; 6d for any discussion of religion or politics. All meetings began and ended with a prayer.

The secret articles were tougher. They were directed essentially at *control*. There was protection against blacklegs, restriction on free entry into the trade. The central planks of the union's platform were resistance to wage reductions, the equalisation of wages between workplaces, control over many aspects of hiring, firing and work practice which made serious inroads into managerial authority. In the service of this programme, the union, directed from Bolton, was prepared to use selective strikes, manipulation of the poor law, boycott and various forms of persuasion and intimidation. Cemented by the solemn oath and a profound secrecy, its discipline was ferociously effective.

Every lodge was run by an elected committee of seven, which chose a president and vice-president who served for six months and a secretary and treasurer who served for a year and were salaried. Three lodge delegates went to quarterly meetings. The key officials were four *inspectors*, who were to look into any dispute. Action was based on their report and their objective was to establish control over the workplace. The entrance fee was stiff, 10s 6d; in north Wales, young men stole their parents' savings to join; subscriptions seem to have varied. Affiliated to the National Association for the Protection of Labour, the union, which enrolled furnace-men, engineers and miners as well as colliers, was perhaps the most sophisticated form of labour organisation yet to emerge. It was able to raise funds in Newcastle and deploy them in Staffordshire and was informed by a political drive and vision. The loyalty it could command, its underground power, terrified masters and magistrates. Wherever it penetrated, letters from panicky masters sound like the despairing cries of a crumbling order, like messages from a country under enemy occupation.

In Merthyr, while a William Perkins could point to the respectability of the union's public articles, most could talk only of oaths and secret articles and servants controlling masters.[4] The union grew in south Wales in the shadow of Dic Penderyn, in an atmosphere of sedition and revolt and as a direct outgrowth from the insurrection of June. Digby Mackworth, in his letters, persistently confounded trade and political unions and he had good reason.[5] There was a dreadful polarisation in Merthyr as an already imperfectly integrated society ground apart like some clumsy cast-iron mechanism.

After the initial scare over Dic Penderyn's execution had passed, Alderman Thompson asked for the withdrawal of the troops from Penydarren and at a meeting of magistrates on 23 August, it was decided that, if a sufficient reserve were kept at Brecon, Abergavenny and Cardiff, the cavalry could be withdrawn from Merthyr, a garrison of 100 infantry would be enough. Captain Wharton of the 43rd was sent down from London to set up quarters at Penywern in Dowlais for the 11th Foot, who had relieved the 98th, coming in by steamboat from Portsmouth.[6]

Within two days, however, Digby Mackworth was sending an alarmist letter from Monmouthshire — 'The political Union clubs are doing infinite and if not soon checked, irreparable mischief. I am told by the magistrates of Merthyr that every individual miner there is a member of a Secret Society and has taken Oaths of Secrecy.' Merthyr, in particular, turned in on itself in an obsessive struggle. The renewed campaigns over the Reform Bill, the celebrations of the Coronation, seem to have passed the town by.[7]

It was at this point that Josiah John Guest of Dowlais resolved on action. On 27 August letters went out from Dowlais House to other regions which had been affected by the union, to Monmouthshire and north Wales, Newcastle-upon-Tyne and Cumberland for certain, probably to other coal regions. It was a circular of enquiry. Every answer conveyed the same message: nip the movement in the bud, crush it before it could grow. Unity among masters was essential.[8]

The most active response came from W.H. Bevan of Beaufort in Monmouthshire. He devised a dismissal form to service united action:

> I hereby certify the Bearer *William Jones Collier*, 'not being a member of any Union or other Society combined for the purpose of regulating Wages' is this day discharged from the employ of *Messrs Kendalls and Bevan*, in pursuance of notice to that effect given by (or to) the said *William Jones* on the *2nd of August last. W.H. Bevan.*
>
> Would not the above form answer all purposes? Should the man be a Member of the Union, the words between the Commas being drawn through with the pen would be a sufficient hint. The Notices should be printed in duplicate so that a Register would be kept of each man's discharge. The Words scored under to be left blank. Will Mr. Guest give it his Consideration?[9]

Mr Guest would and tried to concert joint action. Once again, Dowlais and Cyfarthfa diverged. 'The men have in my opinion as much Right to have unions as the Masters', William Crawshay I wrote to his son at Cyfarthfa, 'the Old Laws are quite sufficient if acted upon between Masters and Men'. In the depressed state of the iron trade, Cyfarthfa, confident in its capital, thought that unions, by raising costs and reducing the make, would be helpful. 'The union of the men', repeated the senior Crawshay early in September, '. . . cannot injure us. I wish them success and should be happy to pay them better as soon as others do so. They will not be so unconscionable as to expect it before.' The son at Cyfarthfa was perhaps less bland, but there was little co-operation between Dowlais and the Crawshays; in fact William Crawshay II maintained some contact with union men, and with their preacher William Twiss, throughout.[10]

By 10 September, however, the *Cambrian* reported that six proprietors had agreed to dismiss all union men by a certain date, despite the excitement which was gripping the town. The Swansea newspaper itself promptly launched a sustained campaign against the unions. It began, in the same issue, with two horror stories. John Williams a roller at Dowlais had been intimidated by union men because he had not joined . . . 'I think I shall be killed tonight.' He caught his leg in a Level wheel (it had to be amputated) and the paper asserted that union men had stood by in callous indifference. At the Plymouth works, they had shown the same cruelty towards John George, a collier buried in a fall. These stories were lies. A month later, the *Cambrian* had to print a retraction, naming the union men who had at once rendered assistance (George being himself a member). It twice refused however to publish an evidently angry letter from one Merthyr man; his letter was 'waste paper . . . the tone and temper of which betrays a defect in self-government not perfectly consistent with the undertaking of teaching the working classes how to govern themselves . . .'[11]

Only two works in the end took action. Dowlais seems to have gone over to the offensive early in September. It was followed by Plymouth works whose notice was to expire on 24 September. Perhaps the fact that both ironmasters were also magistrates is significant. Men were required to give up the union on pain of dismissal. There were massive refusals. Two furnaces were blown out at each works. 'A spirited and honourable manufacturer had better shut up his establishment than be controlled and dictated to by his own workmen' exhorted the *Cambrian*.[12] By the end of September, thousands of men were out of work and production was almost stopped. Gangs of them moved down the Neath and Swansea valleys. At Neath Abbey works, 40 to 50 miners joined the union and there was a 'subterranean schism'. Joseph Price called his men to a meeting in the pattern-maker's shop on the day the Plymouth notices expired. Over 150 turned up. Price made a reasoned but intransigent attack on the union. 'A Welshman made a remarkably good speech in the Welsh language' against it. The meeting, to the *Cambrian*'s satisfaction, voted against the union and the fifty men were dismissed; collieries in the Rhondda followed suit. But at Merthyr, the resistance was virtually total, the men living in 'false hopes of large remittances expected from The North'.[13]

So began one of the most bitter struggles in the history of the coalfield, a harsh, unrelenting dour battle which in its tenacity sharply recalls the armed struggle of June. The men responded in classic NAPL style. At the other works they stayed in, to support the Dowlais and Plymouth men. They sent flour and other supplies as lay-off allowances rapidly ran out. Support came from Monmouthshire and from as far afield as Maesteg. Presumably the funds raised by their brothers in north

Wales helped. None could come from England where Bolton itself was engaged in what proved to be its death struggle.[14]

The masters were able to turn the whole force of what organised society existed against the men. One minister at Dowlais had to apologise to Guest for simply attending a union meeting.[15] Calvinistic Methodists meeting in Tredegar declared union membership incompatible with chapel membership. Some chapels split. In this struggle, working men could expect no help from the great majority of the political radicals; E.L. Richards pressed the claims of master miners who wanted to be enrolled as Specials to defend property.[16]

The men, though often reduced to begging, were peaceable and utterly indomitable. The chief propaganda weapon against them was the secret oath, which was used to conjure up visions of horrors unimaginable. A special pamphlet was brought out against it — *On the Oaths Taken in the Union Club* by *Looker-On*. It denounced the oath as a violation of the Third Commandment. Josiah John Guest's brother, Thomas, was very active in the distribution of this booklet, sending copies in Welsh to north Wales and others all over the country.[17] He may well have had a hand in it. Its style was his. A Wesleyan whom some thought 'too rigid', his presence at Dowlais was sufficient to stifle any and every frivolity. He had been present at the Acrefair riots in north Wales during the union campaign there.[18] In November, he wrote a *Plain Address* to union men who were also church and chapel members:

With respect to the oath of initiation into the lodge and as to which I am rejoiced to hear the consciences of many have been troubled, let me ask are there any oaths imposed on individuals seeking membership with a Christian Church or any other religious Society? I answer decidedly No, our Bibles teach us, Swear not at all, thou shalt not take the name of the Lord thy God in vain, let your communication by yea, yea, nay, nay, whatsoever is more than this cometh of evil, so that this very oath as a profanation of God's Holy Name cometh of evil and we cannot have fellowship with evil without grieving the spirit of God . . .

. . . is it not written 'provide things honest in the sight of all men' and again, 'take heed and beware of covetousness' so that in providing for your own house you are not to infringe on the providential order of God by invading the rights of others, by attempting to force upon those whom God has set over you, the adoption of such regulations and the payment of such wages as would be beneficial to yourselves while they would be ruinous to your masters . . .

. . . Is not this 'Union' a confederacy that brings you into those places where as men fearing God you should not be found, the Public House is not the usual place of resort for the Disciples of Christ . . .

. . . God requires of you, Isaiah 1.16.17, 'Cease to do evil, learn to do well', come out from among them and be ye separate . . .[19]

Few seem to have come out, at least from among the evil, and in early October there was a sudden increase in tension. The re-appearance of the Union Preacher, William Twiss, or a man bearing his name, was not officially reported until 17 October,[20] but he may have come sooner, for in the early days of that month the men adopted new tactics which disconcerted the magistrates. They began to turn up in great gangs at the Police Office to demand poor relief; failing this, to demand legal action against parish officers who refused them such relief. They sent their wives along. From mid-October, Twiss began to billet the men and their families out in groups of from 80 to 100 in the neighbouring parishes, where they made similar demands. These were tactics which had actually been advocated at the political meeting on the Waun on 30 May.[21]

A dramatic account of the interrogation of two tough-minded unionists by the parish vestry appeared in the *Cambrian*.[22] The toughest was William Howell, a filler at Dowlais who used to earn £4 to £4 10s a month. With a wife and two children, he had contributed five shillings to the union, which he had joined three months earlier and was then getting 4 to 5 shillings a week from it, 'not half enough to support his family'. He took an oath when he joined the union and 'considers that oath as binding as the one he has taken today'. He would not bend under tough questioning on the secret articles:

Will not say whether there is a statement that the masters, before the world will come to its place, must be brought more on a level with the workmen, but thinks they ought to be . . . Declines answering whether there is a rule which states that the masters are not to be instructed (the workmen having already taught them too much) . . .

In a revealing echo of June, the magistrates asked whether union men were forbidden to buy the goods of other union men taken by process of law. When the magistrates asked whether union men were forbidden to share trade skills and secrets with non-unionists, William Howell exploded – 'Knows what all this means from the beginning; it is some of the *bloody* turncoats who say that'. He ended on a defiant note: 'The Union is so important and necessary to him that he would rather live on 6d a week than give it up.'

Morgan Thomas of Plymouth, a collier, was at great pains to stress the discipline and regularity of the union. The men themselves were not to judge whether masters could afford a certain price or not; Twiss, delegate from the Northern Lodges, had told them that Authority Lodge would decide. He knew nothing about Authority Lodge but had heard of No. 1 Lodge, Bolton. 'He cannot say how a Stranger from the North should know whether the Masters' Trade will afford an advance of wages', but he asserted that only an Inspector of the union, and there was one such at his No. 2 Level, was to judge the value of work. He would take the opinion of the Inspector before that of Mr Steele, the Plymouth manager: 'he knows, he thinks, the value of work . . .'

J.B. Bruce, the stipendiary, harassed by these crowds, wrote a worried letter to the Home Office on 5 October. Parish officers had proved that there was an abundance of work available if the men gave up the unions, but this they refused to do. Four thousand men were now out, supported mainly by the men at Cyfarthfa and Penydarren who had not been dismissed for union membership. 'The workmen say,' reported Bruce, 'they do not wish to control their masters and they they do not exceed the powers given them by 6 George IV cap. 129 and that therefore the Masters have no right to annex any conditions to their returning to work.'

Bruce was clearly nonplussed by this pugnacious erudition. Had he the right to order poor relief? He had sent post-haste for magistrates from the surrounding districts and for E.P. Richards, a distinguished Cardiff solicitor. He feared 'the excitement naturally attendant on questions where want of food may occur'.[23]

The Home Office got the letter on 7 October. They were clearly equally nonplussed. On the 10th Melbourne referred the matter to the Law Officers.[24] The Attorney-General replied the same day; he had been unable to contact the Solicitor-General and merely gave his personal opinion: 'I think that a workman willing to hire himself but refused employment because he belongs to a Union is entitled to parochial relief unless the union be illegal or unless the members of it are bound by stipulations inconsistent with the performance of the servant's duty to his master.'[25]

On the next day, 11 October, the Law Officers delivered their formal Opinion from Lincoln's Inn:

> If the present had been an abstract question as stated in the letter submitted to us . . . we should have stated it as our opinion that the Magistrates were justified in withholding such relief. But if the Employment can only be had upon the terms of the labourer submitting to a condition imposed upon him by his employer as to political or other public matters which the law does not impose upon the labourer, we are of opinion that although the master has a right not to give employment except to those who may submit to his condition, yet that the labourer is not on his part bound to submit to the condition and that in such case he is entitled to relief, if the employment to which such condition is attached is the only employment he can get. The question submitted to us therefore taken in connexion with the Magistrate's letter seems to resolve itself into this: whether the union societies of which the workmen are members are illegal societies. If not, we think that the workmen are entitled to parochial relief and we see no grounds stated for thinking that they are illegal.[26]

Not a word of this Opinion was permitted to get back to Merthyr. For on the 7th, the Home Office had already replied to Bruce. Apparently with the assistance of Denman the Attorney-General, it took Melbourne three drafts to get the letter right:

> with regard to the question of the right to parish relief in the circumstances which you have stated, it appears to me that from . . . [deleted].
>
> The question of the right of the men to parish relief appears to be one of some doubt and difficulty and which it is impossible to determine without exact knowledge of all the actual circumstances . . . [deleted].
>
> You have therefore [deleted]. It appears to me that you have exercised a sound discretion in calling for the assistance of as many of the Magistrates acting for the Hundred as can be procured and in submitting the case to a Solicitor of high character and great experience. The opinion which you and the other Magistrates in assistance will be able to form will I (do not doubt) [deleted] feel no doubt be conformable to the law and I have as little doubt that

when you have formed it you will act upon it with (that) [deleted] the firmness as well as (that) [deleted] the discretion which is required by the difficult nature of the circumstances in which you are placed.[27]

This masterly exercise in ambiguity induced the Merthyr magistrates (one is tempted to say, of course) to refuse poor relief, a decision the *Cambrian* thought 'reasonable'.[28] With the connivance of Melbourne the Home Secretary, they appear to have been acting in direct contravention of the law.

By late October, 4,000 men and their families were half-starved. Crowds hung around the club-houses; beggars infested the streets, mass meetings were threatened. Shop-keepers were once again frightened. Into this tense situation exploded the political crisis of the autumn, the Lords' rejection of the Reform Bill, the massive public resistance campaigns, the struggle between middle-class and working-class radicals, the outbreak of widespread violence and, just across the water, the catastrophic Bristol Riots.

Merthyr was caught up in the national campaign of the radicals. A meeting 'on the hills' was projected for 17 October. By this time, 100 men of the 98th Foot under Captain Stephens had returned to the town, the 11th moving to Cardiff to be sucked into the Bristol Riots. As soon as news of the projected *Reform* meeting reached the magistrates, there was a spasm of alarm. The men were 'tolerably quiet', but they were starving, restless and excited. Twiss was active from the Miners Arms in the Georgetown area; the *Great Agitator*, Colonel Love of the 11th called him. There was a scurrying of magistrates and officers. Love alerted the cavalry at Abergavenny and arranged for rapid transport of the Reserve of the 11th from Cardiff if necessary. The meeting, however, did not take place.[29] By this time, five of Dowlais's twelve furnaces were stopped and thirty-four of fifty forges. The works had a good stock of ironstone raised by fifty miners who had gone back to work and the patches could supply enough coal for six months. A few men had gone back to work and more had been recruited from the ever-growing number of unemployed, but the great mass of the men were still out and more determined than ever. The military and Bute's mineral agent thought there was no serious danger of riot, but men were crowding the club-houses and patrolling the streets. In the Swansea valley, miners were on a go-slow. Twiss was preaching sermons and billeting the men out. 'How long they will be peaceable with stomachs only half-filled,' Bruce reported, is problematical.'[30]

The final crisis exploded with the Bristol Riots. By the end of October, excitement was reaching a climax from 'privations and distress'. Threatening letters went to the men who were trickling back to work and one *Unionist* menaced the magistrates with 'destruction'. News of the terrifying riots at Bristol threw the whole of the south Wales coalfield into crisis. Anthony Hill reported in alarm that the men knew the Reserve of the 11th Foot had moved to Bristol; he begged Melbourne not to move any troops from Brecon or Abergavenny. At Newport, Colonel Love, on his way to Bristol, ran into a hostile crowd who threatened to cut the steamboat adrift. Melbourne promised not to move any more soldiers and to return the 11th as soon as possible; he called upon magistrates for maximum effort.[31]

In response, the 'respectable' were enrolled as special constables throughout south Wales. This was in fact part of that national mass mobilisation of the middle class as Specials during November, which together with the propaganda war and the cholera, helped secure the defeat of self-consciously 'working-class' radicals and left the field clear for those populist and semi-respectable radicals represented by the Birmingham Union and Francis Place, who had a clear monopoly when they organised their civil disobedience campaigns of the final phase of the *Days of May* in the following year. At Swansea, 304 Specials were mobilised together with 50 Pensioners and organised into sections of ten and divisions of fifty. Several hundred pikes were stored in the new Town Hall; at the same time charitable collections were made to relieve the massive distress and misery in the town. Newport was afraid of the vast, under-employed and ill-fed mining population in the valleys who were enrolled in their unions and determined to become masters instead of servants. There were thousands of Irish, too, prepared to work for a pittance and a growing hatred between them and the Welsh. Public meetings were mobilising and arming the 'respectables' and the town asked for a military man or officer of the metropolitan police.[32]

In Merthyr, where the people had been vastly excited by the news from Bristol, and where 'we are in momentary expectation of a riot', and also in Monmouthshire, trouble was expected on Guy Fawkes Night. The indefatigable magistrate William Powell, at Abergavenny, mobilised and armed a force of 350 men and together with Anthony Hill, helped post the military in readiness for a 'visit from the mountains'. Nothing happened, but authority was warned that the union men of Merthyr and Monmouthshire planned to combine at a vast meeting on 7 November as part of a nation-wide campaign of simultaneous meetings organised by the London radicals. Merthyr delegates got to Carmarthen, seething in one of its periodic bouts of turbulence.[33]

At this very moment, the lock-out was reaching its paroxysm. The men's funds were nearly exhausted. A crisis was expected within days. 'We expect the close of this week to see the climax of our efforts' wrote a Merthyr man. The situation, however, was desperate . . . 'This place is in a dreadful state. The moment the news arrived of the disturbance at Bristol, the Union Clubs all met, what happened I know not. All is quiet but everyone is apprehensive. Thousands are out of employment and starving. The men know all that passes and are evidently plotting. They talk of revolution . . .'

William Twiss the Union Preacher, preached that week from Isaiah, xxiv.21: 'And it shall come to pass in that day that the Lord shall punish the host of the high ones that are on high and the kings of the earth upon the earth. And they shall be gathered together as prisoners are gathered in the pit and shall be shut up in the prison . . .'[34]

To counter the threat of 7 November, the Merthyr magistrates called a special meeting of 15 of the leading Inhabitants, including the James family and the most prominent radicals. They decided to mobilise and arm 200 Specials on 5 November; as many Pensioners as possible would also be armed. Anthony Hill was to leave for Bristol at once to fetch Colonel Love to Merthyr while Captain Howells was to supply weapons from Cardiff. Troops were essential, for Specials were very 'unequal to the sort of mob they have to deal with, so much more ferocious and more dangerous armed than an agricultural mob'. The meeting asked Melbourne to send down 'forthwith' two sergeants and five or six privates of the metropolitan police to organise a defence and constabulary force.[35]

The Home Office replied that the police officers could not be spared (similar requests were flooding in from all over the country), but throughout the 5th there was a nerve-racking search at the Home and War Office. 'My dear Lamb, I shall bore you to death with these fellows', Lord Fitzroy Somerset wrote. The Home Office finally found Thomas Jamieson, a retired Inspector, the War Office, after failing with two other men, one Cliff, former sergeant with the 7th; they seem to have set off for Merthyr on the 8th.[36]

From Friday, 5 November, the mobilisation at Merthyr and in Monmouthshire was set in train. With the maximum possible publicity, the 200 Specials and the Pensioners paraded the streets. Colonel Love brought the Reserve of the 11th Foot into the town. As they passed through Newport on their return from Bristol, they were hissed and jeered by the crowd. The 98th were also very visible and cavalry were set on the move from Abergavenny. This, the news of the crushing of the Bristol Riots, the weather and the generally desperate predicament of the union had their effect. On the eve of the projected meeting, notices were sent out postponing it. On the 7th itself, the 14th Dragoons rode from Abergavenny to Tredegar 'to secure the Clydach pass' and prevent any junction of Blaina, Beaufort and Ebbw Vale men with Merthyr. Colonel Love and a force reconnoitred the hills. They found groups gathering, but no organised meeting. The Specials patrolled the streets which were full of hungry and footloose men. The Almighty lent a hand. The weather was tempestuous, thunder, lightning, torrential rain.[37]

While riots broke out in Brecon, Worcester and the Forest of Dean and there was arson at Cowbridge and Newport, an enormous relief swept Merthyr, and it was this point that the starving and hopeless men of the union, with Bolton itself going under, broke. Masses of Dowlais men began to renounce the union, though a hard core still held out. The Plymouth men met on the 12th and resolved to go back to work on the 14th, but there was what the *Cambrian* called a 'mischievous intervention' by a large body of Cyfarthfa men and a considerable force from Nant-y-Glo who dissuaded them, for a day or so. Twiss threw in his hand on the 15th, 'made his escape' said the *Cambrian*, which jeered at his consumption of gin and tobacco. Over the next few days, the men of both works went back and 'utterly renounced' the union. The *Cambrian* was simultaneously magnanimous and superior. The great majority of the workers were 'well conducted men'; they had been 'deluded by emissaries'; they were now 'delighted' that their employers were charitable enough to re-employ them. By this time, puddlers and other skilled men who used to get 18 to 25 shillings a week 'before the union' were earning ten shillings on the roads. Unemployment however and distress were still severe. Large numbers of families were being shipped back to Carmarthenshire, Cardiganshire and Pembrokeshire. The expense of removals had reached the staggering total of £500 'since the Union Clubs'.[38] Not all was gloom, however. On the day the men went back, the Wesleyan Missionary Society met at Merthyr and, under the chairmanship of Thomas Revel Guest, raised £30 towards 'the claims of the Heathen'.[39]

So this dramatic and terrible year closed. In the course of six months, nearly 5,000 people, a fifth of its population, left the town.

When a vestry meeting on the town reform plan was called in November, the irrepressible Joseph Coffin was the only man who turned up.[40] Ironically, the Truck Act had passed, Blackwood market had re-opened; some church bells rang in celebration.[41] They rang hollow. True, Taliesin Williams emerged just after Boxing Day to announce a *History of Merthyr Tydfil* and to describe at inordinate length, with copious quotations in both languages, the ancient Glamorgan practice of wassailing, and if Mrs Siddons had recently died in Brecon, young Miss Haughton of the Theatre Royal Haymarket scored a stunning success in *Rob Roy* in the newly opened Merthyr theatre, which had moved from Aberystwyth. She and it did not stay long.[42] More characteristic was that other drama when the whole town was thrown into alarm by the report of an attack by 'four ruffians' armed with pistols and bludgeons on two officers of the 98th returning to their barracks in Dowlais. It was even more enraged when this turned out to be a hoax staged by the officers; the *Cambrian* preached a testy sermon on the folly of provoking a working population suffering poverty and unemployment which was at the moment peaceful. And the new year opened with a disturbing half-memory of June; William Jones the watchmaker was robbed and no fewer than 98 watches under repair were taken.[43]

It was a grim, silent, shuttered town under military occupation which closed the most eventful year in its history by appointing a Board of Health to face the oncoming cholera.[44]

Notes

1. Isaac Evans, letter, *Tarian y Gweithiwr*, 14 August 1884; Martin Phillips, letter, *Western Mail*, 23 February 1933; Islwyn ap Nicholas, *Dic Penderyn* (1944); Alexander Cordell, *The Fire People*, p. 344.
2. On the initiation ceremony of the colliers' union, see *Cambrian*, 12 November 1831.
3. On the nature of the union: 'Character, Objects and Effects of Trade Unions' (1834) reprinted in *Trades Unionism a Hundred Years Ago* (Manchester, 1933); Looker-On, *On the oaths taken in the union clubs* (1831); for the affiliation to the NAPL, *Voice of the People*, 30 April 1831 and *United Trades Co-operative Journal* (1830) passim; Notes relative to the Colliers Union Society in the parish of Ruabon, 29 June 1831: HO 52/16; for a general discussion, G.D.H. Cole, *Attempts at General Union* (1953) and more specifically, my 'Merthyr 1831: Lord Melbourne and the trade unions', *Llafur*, i (1972), pp. 3-15.
4. W. Perkins to Bute, 1 August 1831, in A. Hill to Melbourne, 1 August: HO 52/16.
5. Digby Mackworth to Colonel Egerton, 30 July in HO 52/16; John Betts

of the NAPL in November 1830, would have agreed with him; trade and political unions 'must be looked upon as one', he said in Ashton: HO 40/27.

6. Thompson to Home Office, 16 August: HO 52/16; Home Office to Merthyr magistrates and to Board of Ordnance (for barrack furniture), 25 August: HO 41/10. Melbourne had yielded to the panic of 1 August, but now he relied on Merthyr supplying the temporary barracks at a cost of no more than £80 over six months. By September, barracks had been provided at Dowlais. Captain Wharton of the 43rd, Barrack-Master, came down to install barrack furniture; as soon as it had come, the troops were to leave Penydarren for Dowlais. The barracks at Penywern were to be there for over a generation. By that September, too, the two companies of the 11th had been relieved by a similar number of the 98th (who had taken over in Brecon): *Cambrian*, 8 October.

7. Digby Mackworth, extract from letter, 25 August: HO 52/16. The *Cambrian*, late in 1831, is full of Reform meetings, just as it had been full of illuminations to celebrate the coronation in September; Merthyr is not mentioned; the one exception is the report in the paper for 22 October that the *Carmarthen Journal*, for its opposition to Reform, had been burned in the public bar of the Bush; even this the *Cambrian* lifted from the *Monmouthshire Merlin*.

8. Letters to these regions all dated 27 August indicated by the replies, in *Iron in the Making*, pp. 58-61; in November, masters in Mostyn, Flintshire were seeking information on how to combat the union, ibid., pp. 62-3.

9. W.H. Bevan to J.J. Guest, 2 September 1831: *Iron in the Making*, p. 60.

10. W. Crawshay I to W. Crawshay II, 27 August, 7 September; W. Routh to W. Crawshay II, 24 September 1831 and correspondence during October and November: Crawshay Papers (NLW), Box 2 (585a, 587a and b, 588 and passim). By 1834, however, the Crawshays had joined in the attack on trade unions.

11. *Cambrian*, 10 September, for the first news of a proposed lockout and the horror stories; retraction in issue for 8 October; the sneer at the Merthyr man, *AB* in issues for 24 September and 1 October.

12. *Cambrian*, 24 September.

13. *Cambrian*, 1 October.

14. J.B. Bruce to Melbourne, 5 October: HO 52/16 and copy in Law Reports: HO 48/28; Bruce to Bute, 19 October: HO 52/16; *Cambrian*, 8, 15 and 22 October.

15. L. Evans Evan to J.J. Guest, 27 September 1831: *Iron in the Making*, p. 61.

16. *Cambrian*, 26 November, reporting the Methodist Session of 19 October; E.L. Richards to J.J. Guest, 12 November 1831: *Iron in the Making*, p. 218; the *Monmouthshire Merlin* joined the *Cambrian* in its onslaught on the unions, atrocity stories and all.

17. Welsh copies are in the library of the University College of North Wales, Bangor, a reference I owe to my friend and colleague, Jenkin Beverly Smith.

18. Charles Wilkins, *History of Merthyr Tydfil*, pp. 177-8; Description of Acrefair riots, 30 December 1830: HO 52/16.

19. Plain Address . . . Cardiff, 7 November 1831: *Iron in the Making*, pp. 61-2.

20. Colonel Love to Melbourne, 17 October: HO 52/16.

21. Bruce to Melbourne, 5 October; Hill to Bute, 31 October: HO 52/16.

22. *Cambrian*, 15 October.

23. Bruce to Melbourne, 5 October: HO 52/16; E.P. Richards was Bute's

manager.

24. G. Lamb, Home Office to Law Officers, 10 October: HO 49/7, p. 429.

25. Thomas Denman, Attorney-General to G. Lamb, Home Office, 10 October: HO 48/28.

26. Attorney-General and Solicitor-General, Lincoln's Inn; Opinion, 11 October: HO 48/28.

27. Draft, Melbourne and Denman: HO 52/16; final letter, 7 October: HO 41/10.

28. *Cambrian*, 15 October.

29. Colonel Love to Melbourne, 15 and 17 October: HO 52/16; Home Office to Love, 17 and 19 October: HO 41/10; *Cambrian*, 8 October.

30. Robert Beaumont to Bute, 19 October; Bruce to Bute, 19 October; Bute to Melbourne, 23 October: HO 52/16. In reply Melbourne sent a very fierce letter against trade unionism; Melbourne to Bute, 24 October: HO 41/10. By this time, Bruce had acquired the secret articles of the union (which appeared in the *Cambrian* by November) and magistrates were quick to send in *Cambrian* reports on the interrogation of unionists by the vestry.

31. A. Hill, with Guest to Melbourne, 31 October and Bruce to Melbourne, 1 November; Colonel Love to Melbourne, 7 November: HO 52/16; G. Lamb, Home Office to A. Hill, 1 and 2 November: HO 41/10.

32. For example, Swansea magistrates to Home Office, 8 November, 10 November; Colonel Love to Swansea magistrates, 3 December; the latter to the former, 6 December; Love to Melbourne 7 December and Swansea magistrates to Melbourne 14 December: HO 52/16. Prothero and Phillips, Town Clerks of Newport to Melbourne, 5, 16 and 23 November: HO 52/14; Home Office to Newport, 7 and 19 November: HO 41/10; Mayor of Monmouth to Melbourne, 7 November: HO 52/14.

33. Hill to Melbourne, 31 October: HO 52/16; W. Powell to Melbourne, 7 November: HO 52/14. *Cambrian*, 22 October, 12 November; David Jones, *Before Rebecca*, p. 129.

34. *Monmouthshire Merlin*, 12 November.

35. Hill to Melbourne, 3 November, enclosing report of the meeting and his own covering letter of 2 November: HO 52/16; the Home Office replied on 3 and 5 November, promising the immediate return of the 11th Foot: HO 41/10.

36. G. Lamb, Home Office to Hill, 4 November; Lord Fitzroy Somerset to Lamb, three times on 5 November; Lamb to Bruce, 5 November: HO 52/14 and 41/10.

37. Report of special constables, 7 November, Colonel Love and A. Hill to Melbourne, 7 November: HO 52/16; gratified replies from Home Office, 9 November: HO 41/10; *Cambrian*, 12 November, which printed the union oath and commented on the secret articles. The NUWC called off the central London meeting planned for 7 November.

38. Home Office to Hugh Bold, Brecon, 14 November: HO 41/10; *Cambrian*, 12 November; the collapse of the union is reported at length in *Cambrian*, 19 and 26 November 1831; removals expenses in issue of 7 January 1832.

39. *Cambrian*, 26 November.

40. MT Minutes, 7 December.

41. *Cambrian*, 24 September, 22 October.

42. *Cambrian*, 31 December 1831, 11, 25 February 1832.

43. *Cambrian*, 18, 25 February, 3 March 1832.

44. MT Minutes, 23, 30 November 1831.

10 1831 IN MERTHYR

'Had it been for the trifling reduction which I proposed and quietly obtained without remonstrance,' wrote William Crawshay in self-defence after the Rising, 'surely it would have broken out sooner and been unconnected with the other circumstances in which the turbulent spirit did first manifest itself . . . Had it been for Reform only there was no need of the animosity shown to the Iron Masters for I, for one, was with them in this cause and had as they knew drawn up and headed their petition . . .' Had it been over the Court of Requests only, the affair should have stopped with its destruction. He singled out the immunity with which the men had attacked James Stephens's house, the weakness of the military force, 'the dissemination of inflammatory and political tracts so common now in this district'. The outbreak was not caused by 'any of these circumstances alone in particular', but specifically by their concatenation.[1]

Quite so: the crisis of 1831 was *global*. It was quite literally a crisis of *working-class identity*.

The impact of *Reform* upon the local contradictions of national crisis *forced* awareness of themselves as *a working class*, defined *against* the rest of society, upon large numbers of working people, who exercised a moral hegemony over the remainder. True, the ground must have been preparing. Monmouthshire had clearly reached the point where sustained and organised trade unionism had crossed the horizons of possibility and men's minds. In Merthyr preliminaries are invisible, but there was certainly some qualitative change during the 1820s. True, they needed an initial 'warrant' from a radical ironmaster. Their ideologies were only in part autonomous. The distinction between Dowlais and Cyfarthfa persisted during the Rising and to some extent throughout.

Nevertheless, *from the beginning*, the better-off acted *on behalf* of their less fortunate fellows; from the beginning, it was an *insurrection* designed to effect *Reform* and overthrow a social order. Thousands had rallied around the vanguard minority even before the troops arrived. They attacked those troops, they waged war against the forces of the Crown, with massive support from all sectors of working people, even the normally alien Irish. Their rising for *Reform*, justice, control, 'honour' to quote *Lewsyn yr Heliwr*, was followed by a martyrdom which circumstances transformed into an inescapably *working-class* martyrdom and by a desperate struggle for trade union rights in which they could look for no allies outside their own ranks and in which, once more, the men of Dowlais and Plymouth fought as a vanguard *for* their fellows, and *for their fellows over the whole coalfield from Monmouthshire to Maesteg.*

In a single year, indeed in six months, working people in Merthyr moved from one of the most archaic forms of protest and struggle to one of the most sophisticated, through the harrowing experience of an exemplary martyrdom which is remembered to this day. If there is such a thing as a 'mutation of consciousness', this must have been one.

Independent action was defeated. By the end of 1831, there were military garrisons in Merthyr, Brecon, Cardiff, Abergavenny and Newport. The middle class were armed against them. They had to find other means to express and if possible enforce their will, under other people's hegemony. The achievement of a *working-class identity*, however momentary, had been dramatic, indeed traumatic; its power persisted, in a very real sense it alone made *possible* the many shifts, devices, indirect forms of pressure which the continuing crisis made *necessary*.

After their local defeat, which was followed by the defeat of 'working-class' political radicalism in the nation, there was a revival of the ironmaster and democratic campaign in Merthyr.[2] An attempt to 'introduce the Scotch Cattle system' in the spring of 1832 failed; Guest was able to rally thousands of workers behind a petition for free trade even as he gave up his truck shop when Merthyr was, after all, suddenly and inexplicably offered an MP by the Reform Bill. (Itself a by-product of the drama of 1831.) His election in the December was simply a festival of newfound civic pride, but it rested on an unspoken compact between himself and the much more radical Political Union of D.W. James which felt it could control the tiny new ten-pound shopkeeper-publican electorate of some 500.

Within two years this probationary relationship had been forged into an alliance. For the Tories were disconcerted by Guest, whom they denounced as a turncoat. There had been mutterings against his unopposed return in 1832, an abortive scheme to run Meyrick against him. In November, with the occult support of the Marquess of Bute, J.B. Bruce and the Tories launched the *Merthyr Guardian*, the town's first newspaper. In 1833, its editor William Mallalieu opened a press war against the vaguely liberal *Cambrian* and spat venom at Guest.

THE POLYTECHNIC OF WALES
LIBRARY
TREFOREST

'It appears that Merthyr is neither more nor less than a rotten borough,' it thundered in 1834, 'the patronage of which is vested in the Jameses.' Unitarianism was a conspicuous omission from its periodic listing of the creeds worthy of respect. *Destructives* were creeping to power in the shadow of Dowlais, which had itself sold out to subversion.

The one theme which was constant in the *Guardian* throughout 1833 and 1834 was fear of the municipal corporation. Scheme after scheme was mooted to equip the town with institutions proper to its new status – gas light, a direct railway to London, factories, a new branch mail – and after the municipal corporations bill was published, a town meeting in November 1833 loudly endorsed Guest's promise to work for incorporation. *Lord Mayor James* and Taliesin ab Iolo his *Poet Laureate* became the *Guardian*'s bogeymen.

Within the parish, contradictions exploded. The reform launched with such éclat in 1831 ran into a morass. In the killing misery of 1832, when Anthony Hill reduced his workforce by another 20 per cent, when seven weeks' removals of pauper families cost over £500, when Crawshay faced a persistent underground guerrilla from his workers, the parish slumped £1,675 into debt. The police officer was abruptly dismissed, a middle-class attempt to increase the rate assessment of the ironworks brought head-on collision with the masters, parish officers were sacked wholesale and finally both parties submitted to an outside valuation.

Bayledon and Fosbrook presented their new valuation in November 1833. It quadrupled the yield of the rates. It proposed to rate the coal, limestone and equipment of the ironworks, which sent Crawshay into a temper and a threat to bring a case before the King's Bench. It also proposed to bring the £6 cottages under the rates; without them the ironmasters would be paying two-thirds of the rate levy. Their solution was the old one, a bill to rate the owners, rather than the occupiers. The middle-class response was equally familiar, a blank negative.

Throughout 1834 there were furious struggles in vestry; people at times had to retire to separate rooms to avoid physical conflict. The townsmen rated the Canal Company; the ironmasters took their case before the King's Bench. Crawshay broke with the Jameses and their friends and shifted towards their enemies, who were already affronted by Guest's performance in the Commons, particularly his vote against the Corn Laws and in favour of the reform of the Church in Ireland. Penydarren and Plymouth were ready to join Cyfarthfa in jacking Dowlais out of power.

Looming, often sensed rather than seen, behind these manoeuvres was the *presence* of 'a working class'. It is a presence which can be *felt* behind the print of the *Guardian*, the cadences of orators. 'Readers of the *Workman* newspaper . . . Frequenters of the kiddlewinks . . .' are repeated points of reference. That presence from time to time became visible and tangible. A rash of troubles through 1833 mushroomed into the brief but potent upsurge of the Owenite Grand National Consolidated Trades Union, broken by the ironmasters' concerted action in 1834. In Monmouthshire, this syndicalist drive was accompanied by a renewal of the Scotch Cattle. This time, authority flooded troops and spies in and broke them, hanging Edward Morgan as another Dic Penderyn. Equally characteristically, the year of the unions in Merthyr saw the birth of the first working-class newspaper in Wales, the bilingual *Y Gweithiwr/The Workman*, edited by Morgan Williams and John Thomas.

At the end of that year of 1834, parliament was dissolved, William Meyrick came forward as a defender of the Church; Crawshay, with the backing of Hill and Thompson, committed 'Cyfarthfa' to his support. The election which followed was the most ferocious Guest ever had to fight. It was a bitter, vituperative, savage business, a head-on clash between industrial giants. For the key weapon was *the working class*, which had no vote. Under the threat of exclusive dealing from Cyfarthfa workers, the electorate, much of it already committed to Guest, splintered. Adam Newell, a bankrupt grocer, tried to organise a group to sell votes. By mid-campaign, Guest's caucus calculated that his estimated majority had shrunk to ten. Their campaign became more stridently radical and Nonconformist. Thomas Revel Guest was pressed into service.

More significantly, so was Morgan Williams. For the key to the election was precisely *the working class*. The decisive moment was a mass meeting on Aberdare mountain, organised by Morgan Williams and harangued by relays of Dissenting ministers, notably John Jones the Unitarian social democrat of Aberdare. Once more a familiar barrier was broken. There was a massive defection of Cyfarthfa men to Guest of Dowlais. Exclusive dealing in the Tory cause lost all credibility and Meyrick withdrew.

From this moment, Nonconformist radicalism in its most intransigent form gripped Merthyr Tydfil. Twelve attempts to levy a church rate in three years were voted down; the parishioners refused to pay for church gaslight or an organist. The radicals sacked Meyrick and replaced him with William Perkins. They tried to eject J.B. Bruce. They started a newspaper in opposition to the *Guardian* which, shouting defiance as from a besieged garrison, withdrew in a shower of broken windows to Cardiff. When the parish was virtually replaced by a Board of Guardians under the new Poor Law in 1836, Guest's men and the radicals swept the board, in an atmosphere of partisan ferocity. E.J. Hutchins served as a chairman in Merthyr, D.W. James was his deputy, Job James the surgeon. The largest town in Wales fell to radical Dissent.

No less significantly, in the immediate aftermath of the 1835 election, the radicals publicly recognised their debt to the non-voters and pledged themselves to work for manhood suffrage. Guest in the course of the campaign shifted along the 'liberal' spectrum towards radicalism; he became an advocate of the ballot which he had previously opposed; populism infused his public discourse. In the election of 1837, when J.B. Bruce came out against him, Crawshay this time performing a reverse somersault in face of the weathercocks flourished by workmen, there was another mobilisation of the working class extending well beyond Guest's stronghold in Dowlais; the candidate of the radicals became a sharp critic of the Poor Law, for which he had voted.

This kind of indirect pressure which mobilised working men could exert was limited in its effect, particularly during the mass immigration and ecological disaster of the 1830s and 1840s. But it was real. For all the fragmentation and sporadic character of working-class initiatives, the kind of identity established in 1831 could and did persist and periodically re-assert itself. Chartism grew directly out of it.

The kind of triangular symbiosis between workers, radicals and Guest which characterised the years from 1831 to 1836 was also limited, in its life-span. It did not outlive the 1830s. *Unitarianism* as a political ideology began to dissolve into the new 'liberal' consensus in the massive re-stabilisation and re-alignment which followed the storms of the frontier years. One central factor in that very re-alignment, however, was precisely the rise of working-class Chartism as a mass movement, which forced it.

Merthyr was one of the strongest centres of Chartism in Wales. In Merthyr, Chartism could embrace *both China* and the eisteddfod intelligentsia and it proved remarkably persistent. Characteristically, the first generation of Chartist leadership was a direct descendant of the *Jacobinism* of the eighteenth century; its first spokesmen were the John brothers and Morgan Williams. The bilingual Chartist press was produced in Merthyr. Equally characteristically, Merthyr, in contrast to Monmouthshire and its Scotch Cattle strongholds, did not take part in the march on Newport in 1839; its men were largely moral-force men. Even when the nature of the leadership changed after the climacteric year of 1841 and became more visibly plebeian, its respectability did not.

In the years of mid-century, of course, the predicament of working people, the social location of 'the working classes', their perception of themselves and others' perception of them, changed radically. In Merthyr, as elsewhere, there was re-alignment, re-stabilisation: the impact of Temperance, the creation of the Glamorgan constabulary and the sustained battle for *China*, the Anglican revival, the obsession with education, the elaboration of a new and subtly but decisively different consensus around that Josiah John Guest who seemed to hold the Merthyr seat on a life-lease from the Almighty, the melting of old Unitarians and new Chartists into that form of absorptive and, in some respects, emasculating 'liberalism'. Even during those years, it is possible to catch echoes from the frontier experience, which grew louder in the renewed activism of the 1860s. In 1868, in a Merthyr whose 'working classes' had been enfranchised at a stroke, Henry Richard won a striking success, and at the expense of Josiah John Guest's natural political heir, to become the first Welsh Nonconformist radical to be elected on the votes of working men and on a specifically working-class thrust of grievance and aspiration.[3] At that point the historian can once again feel, elusive through his fingers, a few thin threads running back to the conjuncture of 1829-34; he can sense the presence of a half-formed 'tradition' which is hardening into 'memory'. Sarah Herbert of Dowlais, a dedicated worker for Henry Richard, was the sister of a Chartist and devoted to the cult of Dic Penderyn; she was neither singular nor unrepresentative. It may well be significant that the virtual fusion of working-class aspiration and Nonconformist democracy which was ultimately to turn workers' movements into the marching wing of Liberalism seems first to have occurred in the Aberdare region which, at that time, was displacing Merthyr itself as a focus for initiative and growth, but which, after all, had been a bastion of revolt in 1831.

The actions and attitudes of these later generations were characterised by ideological adaptation and subordination; the interest lies in the degree of effectiveness and militancy which they were able to achieve within a subaltern existence. In this, of course, they differ markedly from 1831 and the years which immediately followed.

Nevertheless, from 1831 for a generation and more, it becomes possible to talk in terms of 'movements', however sporadic, and to trace connections, however tenuous, in a way which is simply not possible before that date. Not only in Merthyr but, given differences in structure, cimate and the alternatives available, in industrial south Wales generally, there is a *qualitative* change after that *Reform* crisis of which Merthyr's Rising, Martyr and Movement were the climax. The very scale and tenacity of those actions, their impact, the geographical spread of their effect, their martyrology, define them as one of those structural, almost geological shifts which accompany a profound change in opinion and attitude. With all the qualifications and modifications made necessary as knowledge broadens and deepens, it seems to me that the initial response which this remarkable year provokes can stand.

In Merthyr Tydfil in 1831, the prehistory of the Welsh working class comes to an end. Its history begins.

Notes

1.   W. Crawshay II, *The Late Riots at Merthyr Tydfil* (Merthyr, 23 June 1831).
2.   For what follows, my 'The Making of Radical Merthyr', *Welsh History Review,* i (1960).
3.   The master of this later period is Professor Ieuan Gwynedd Jones of Aberystwyth. Of his many studies, particularly relevant are his 'Dr. Thomas Price and the election of 1868', *Welsh History Review*, ii (1964), iii (1965), and the more general essay, 'The Merthyr of Henry Richard', in Glanmor Williams (ed.), *Merthyr Politics: the making of a working-class tradition* (University of Wales, Cardiff, 1966).

Index

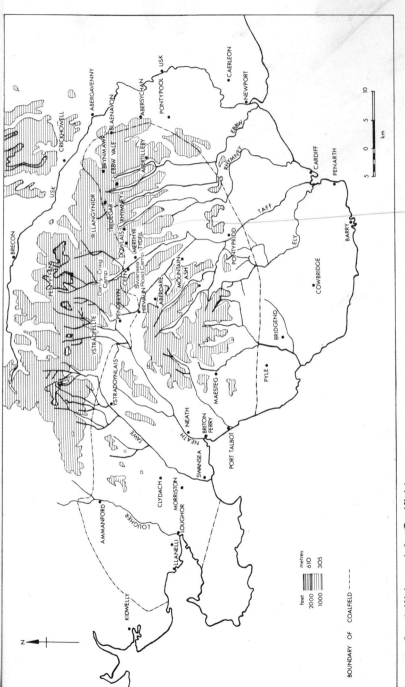

Figure 1: South Wales and the Coalfield

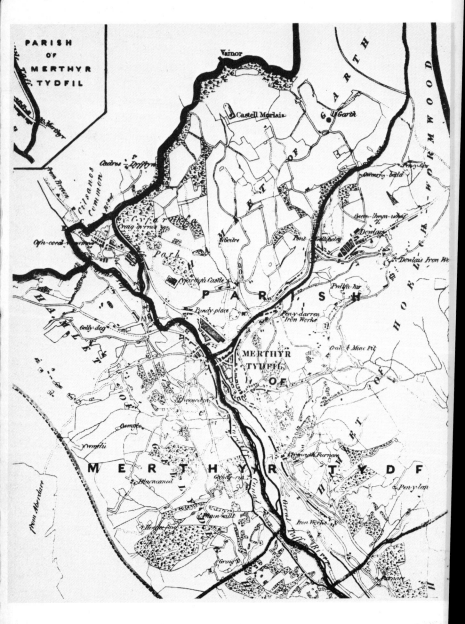

Figure 2: Merthyr Tydfil 1832
Source: From the northern (town) section of the map by R.K. Dawson,
1832 for the Boundaries Commission under the Reform Act of 1832.

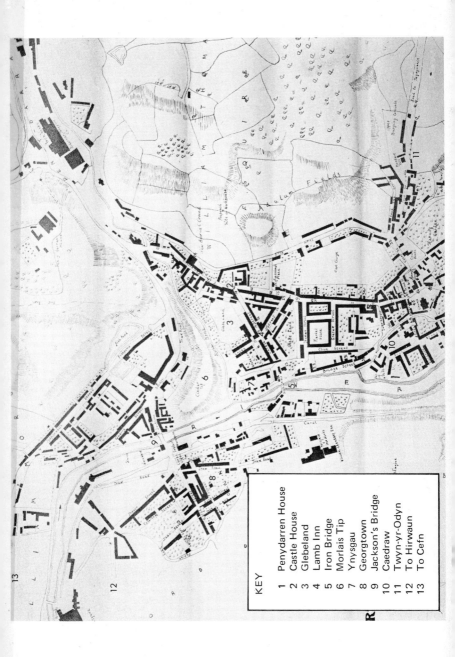

KEY

1 Penydarren House
2 Castle House
3 Glebeland
4 Lamb Inn
5 Iron Bridge
6 Morlais Tip
7 Ynysgau
8 Georgtown
9 Jackson's Bridge
10 Caedraw
11 Twyn-yr-Odyn
12 To Hirwaun
13 To Cefn

Figure 3: Merthyr Tydfil 1836 (John Wood Plan)

Figure 4: Castle Inn and High Street, Merthyr Tydfil (Drawing by local artist ten years later)